ILLITERACY IN THE UNITED STATES

SEE LAST PAGES IN THIS BOOK FOR A COMPLETE LIST OF
THE UNIVERSITY OF NORTH CAROLINA SOCIAL STUDY SERIES

The University of North Carolina Press, Chapel Hill, N. C.; The Baker and Taylor Company, New York; Oxford University Press, London; Maruzen-Kabushiki-Kaisha, Tokyo; Edward Evans & Sons, Ltd., Shanghai.

ILLITERACY IN THE UNITED STATES

BY

SANFORD WINSTON

Associate Professor of Sociology North Carolina State College

CHAPEL HILL
THE UNIVERSITY OF NORTH CAROLINA PRESS
1930

COPYRIGHT, 1930, BY
THE UNIVERSITY OF NORTH CAROLINA PRESS

TO ELLEN

PREFACE

The rôle of education in equipping the individual for adjustment to the complexities of modern life grows increasingly significant. The recent efforts in the United States to eliminate illiteracy are largely in recognition of this fact. Because of these factors, it is believed that the timeliness of the subject warrants the publication of this book instead of holding up publication until additional data are forthcoming. The trends discussed, as well as the relationships analyzed, are believed to be true in so far as results based upon present data may be considered true.

The first objective, therefore, was to analyze the trend of illiteracy in the United States and its present relation to sex, age, urban and rural environment, race and nationality, and school systems. The second purpose was to emphasize the fact that illiteracy, as a measure of educational status, achieves importance as it affects other social phenomena. Its relationship with the selected factors of birthrate, infant mortality, early age of marriage, size of family, mobility, suicide, and urbanization has been quantitatively determined.

All the results of the statistical techniques utilized have been presented with a definite knowledge of their limitations. Social data are exceedingly complex and the most careful methods of refining them still leave many factors uncontrolled. Each factor studied was selected because its relationship to illiteracy could be definitely posited on an empirical basis. In no case are the results to be regarded as exact measurements but rather as probabilities on the basis of which concrete inferences are possible.

All data and the computations based upon them have been computed with the greatest care and thoroughly checked. In a study involving such a number of complicated calculations, however, errors can scarcely be excluded. If any such are found, the author is responsible, although every effort has been made to reduce them to a minimum. The methodology followed is included in Appendix A.

The author wishes to acknowledge his indebtedness for unvarying stimulation and keen criticism to Professor Pitirim Sorokin; for various suggestions and criticisms to Professors R. W. Murchie, E. H. Sutherland, W. F. Ogburn, and Dean Carl C. Taylor; for advice on certain technical questions to Professors Henry Schultz, F. C. Mills, G. W. Foerster, and Bruce D. Mudgett, Dr. Mordecai Ezekiel, and especially to Professor Marc Leager; for constant stimulation and assistance in many details to Ellen Winston. Finally a word of appreciation is due Professor Howard W. Odum for his coöperation in the furtherance of the study's publication.

S. W.

CONTENTS

PART I

THE GENERAL PROBLEM OF ILLITERACY IN THE UNITED STATES

Chapter	Page
I. SCOPE AND METHOD OF THE STUDY	3
II. ILLITERACY IN THE UNITED STATES, 1870 TO 1920	7
III. ILLITERACY AND SEX	28
IV. ILLITERACY AND AGE	41
V. ILLITERACY AND URBAN AND RURAL ENVIRONMENT	48
VI. ILLITERACY AND RACE AND NATIONALITY	57
VII. ILLITERACY AND SCHOOL SYSTEMS	68
VIII. ADJUSTED ILLITERACY RATES	73
IX. CONCLUSIONS TO PART I	79

PART II

ILLITERACY IN RELATION TO CERTAIN SOCIAL PHENOMENA

X. THE RELATION OF ILLITERACY TO BIRTH-RATE | 85
XI. THE RELATION OF ILLITERACY TO INFANT MORTALITY | 94
XII. THE RELATION OF ILLITERACY TO EARLY AGE OF MARRIAGE | 101

Chapter		Page
XIII.	THE RELATION OF ILLITERACY TO SIZE OF FAMILY	109
XIV.	THE RELATION OF ILLITERACY TO MOBILITY TO OTHER STATES	117
XV.	THE RELATION OF ILLITERACY TO SUICIDE	125
XVI.	THE RELATION OF ILLITERACY TO URBANIZATION AND TO SCHOOL SYSTEMS	132
XVII.	CONCLUSIONS TO PART II	140

APPENDIXES

APPENDIX A, METHODOLOGY ... 149
APPENDIX B, SUPPLEMENTARY TABLES ... 157
BIBLIOGRAPHY ... 163

PART I

THE GENERAL PROBLEM OF ILLITERACY IN THE UNITED STATES

CHAPTER I

SCOPE AND METHOD OF THE STUDY

In presenting this investigation of illiteracy in the United States and its relation to other social factors the study has been divided into two parts. Part I deals with the general problem of illiteracy as it exists in the United States at the present time, together with the trend of illiteracy for the past fifty years, and a brief summary of the data on illiteracy prior to 1870. The connotations in regard to sex, age, urban and rural environment, race and nationality, and school systems are also investigated in some detail. Finally, the method of standard population is utilized to present a corrected alignment of the forty-eight states when the native whites of native parentage alone are considered. Part II studies illiteracy in its relation to certain selected social phenomena. These latter include birth-rate, early marriage, infant mortality, size of family, urbanization, mobility to other states, and suicide. Simple, partial, and multiple correlations have been utilized to study the various relations while the regression equations offer a basis for prediction.

There are five earlier studies on illiteracy in the United States of significance. The first of these, by Edwin Leigh, was published in the Report of the Commissioner of Education for 1870[1] and consisted of a thorough revision of the data of the 1840, 1850, and 1860 censuses. This was followed by Charles Warren's study, "Illiteracy in the United States in 1870 and 1880."[2] In this he has made a distinct

---
[1] *Annual Report of the Commissioner of Education, 1870*, pp. 467-502.
[2] U. S. Bureau of Education, *Circular of Information No. 3*, 1884.

contribution in adequately presenting in greater detail and depth of analysis the results of the 1870 and 1880 census reports. In 1905, a bulletin of the Bureau of the Census, "Illiteracy in the United States, 1905,"[3] was prepared under the supervision of W. F. Willcox. In it comparisons of the results of the 1900 Census with those of the two preceding Censuses were made. For the first time, the data were sufficiently accurate to permit reliable detailed comparison with recent data. The fourth study is a bulletin published by the United States Bureau of Education in 1913, "Illiteracy in the United States and an Experiment for its Elimination."[4] It is chiefly a summary of the 1910 Census data on illiteracy, the second part containing a study of the Rowan County, Kentucky, experiment for the elimination of illiteracy. The fifth study, "Adult Illiteracy," by W. Talbot, was published in 1916.[5] It deals chiefly with the data on the illiteracy of immigrants from 1900 to 1914, showing that the most illiterate immigrants came from Mexico and from southern and eastern Europe, and the least illiterate immigrants from northwestern Europe.

There are various reasons for studying illiteracy. First, illiteracy is important because it is a form of isolation. The illiterate is unable to communicate with his fellows in written symbols and hence is largely restricted to his immediate social groups for many forms of social stimuli. Illiteracy is a definite form of individual isolation. Second, modern culture is dependent upon written symbols to an important extent. Third, the illiterate person is handicapped in his reactions to stimuli and situations, to the extent that these phenomena utilize the written word. More fundamental than this, however, is the fact that

---

[3]Bureau of the Census, *Bulletin No. 26*, 1905.   [4]*Bulletin No. 20*.
[5]U. S. Bureau of Education, *Bulletin No. 35*, 1916.

Scope and Method of the Study 5

his range of stimuli is limited to those stimuli which are not conveyed by means of written symbols. Fourth, illiteracy is one of the factors in societal phenomena. Up to the present time the importance of its relations to other phenomena has not been adequately studied.

The definition of illiteracy which is basic to this investigation is that adopted by the Department of the Census of the United States and by most foreign countries. "Illiteracy, as defined by the Census Bureau, signifies inability to write in any language, not necessarily English, regardless of ability to read. . . . In general, the illiterate population as shown by the census figures should be understood as comprising only those persons who have had no education whatever. Thus the statistics do not show directly or definitely the proportion of the population which may be termed illiterate when the word is used to imply lack of ability to read and write with a reasonable degree of facility; but they do afford a fairly reliable measure of the effect of the improvement in educational opportunities from decade to decade."[6]

This definition introduces the important point that the illiterates are at one end of a frequency distribution set up on a basis of education. There is a high percentage of individuals in the population who, while not classified as illiterates, lack facility in reading and writing. Beyond these are the various gradations in education. The illiteracy data are presented in such form that they can be quantitatively studied.

The reliability of the data utilized is adequately discussed in the census report.

There is undoubtedly a margin of error in the statistics of illiteracy, resulting from a variety of causes. In some cases there may be unwillingness to admit illiteracy on the

[6] *Fourteenth Census of the United States*, vol. II, p. 1145.

part of persons enumerated. Furthermore, in parts of the country where practically all native white persons are literate the enumerators are likely to acquire the habit of returning them as such without the formality of an inquiry, and in this way a few isolated cases of illiteracy may be overlooked. On the other hand, in the case of Negroes the opposite assumption may sometimes be made by white enumerators, while, in the case of the foreign born, inability to write in English may sometimes be taken as constituting illiteracy, although the instructions make it clear that a person able to write in any language is to be returned as literate. For the United States as a whole and for the states and large cities the figures are probably nearly enough accurate to supply a sound basis for judgment as to the relative illiteracy of different classes of the population, of persons in different age groups, and of males as compared with females. Beyond question comparisons between different censuses show the general tendencies with substantial accuracy. The returns for small areas, however, may be open to question in some cases.[7]

The adequacy of the supplementary data will be discussed as the data are presented. For the purposes of this study, the census data have been taken only for the past fifty years. Before that time the validity of the returns is questionable. A brief summary of the earlier years is included for historical purposes. Data from 1870 to 1920 are used to present general tendencies while detailed analysis is largely limited to the census of 1920 in which the illiteracy data are more adequately presented than in any preceding census. Hence the limitations of the analysis of the data are largely dependent upon the census organization of the material, although reorganizations of the data have been made in many instances.[8]

---

[7] *Loc. cit.*

[8] The data are presented for "all classes," ten years of age and over, unless otherwise specified.

CHAPTER II

ILLITERACY IN THE UNITED STATES, 1870 TO 1920

Before beginning an analysis of the data on illiteracy in the United States from 1870 to 1920, a brief summary of the earlier census reports on illiteracy may well be included for purposes of completeness. The first census data with reference to illiteracy in the United States were gathered in the 1840 census. At that time, an enumeration was made of the number of white persons over twenty years of age who could neither read nor write. The data were published by states and territories, and by counties, and subdivisions of counties.[1]

In 1850 classification was first made. The census for that year gave the ratio of white illiterate to total white, the ratio of illiterate native white over ten years of age to total native white, the ratio of free colored (Negro?) illiterate to total free colored, and the ratio of foreign illiterate to total foreign over twenty years of age, "supposing the (foreign) illiterate to be all white." This information was given for the geographical divisions, the thirty-one states, four territories, and the District of Columbia, and for the slave states and free states. The ratio of white illiterate to white population for 1850 was compared with the same data for 1840 for the six geographical divisions, for the slaveholding states as compared with the non-slaveholding states as well as for the country as a whole.[2] Illiteracy was

---
[1] *Sixth Census of the United States.*
[2] *Compendium of the Seventh Census*, Part III, pp. 152, 153, Tables CLV, CLVI, CLVII.

here considered, as in 1840, as the inability to read and write. In addition, data as to the number of whites and free colored, by totals and by sex, as well as the number of native and foreign-born, over twenty years of age who could not read or write, were given.[3] The opinion of Superintendent J. D. B. DeBow was that the statistics were "generally accurate."[4]

The 1860 Census tabulated the number of whites and free colored who could not read and write, by totals and by sex. A division into natives and foreign (no sex division being made) was also given. The data were tabulated for the thirty-four states, six territories, and the District of Columbia. No returns were received from the territory of Colorado.[5]

In 1870, the census enumerators for the first time classified as illiterate all persons ten years of age and over who could not write in any language. Hence the data became for the first time comparable with succeeding census reports. Futhermore, the census stated

that, great numbers of persons rather than admit their ignorance, will claim to read, who will not pretend that they can write. . . . If a man cannot write, it is fair to assume that he cannot read well; that is, that he really comes within the illiterate class. . . . Taking the whole country together, hundreds of thousands of persons appear in the class "cannot write" over and above those who confess that they cannot read. This is the true number of the illiterate of the country.[6]

Thus the data became not only comparable but also sufficiently reliable, in those categories utilized in this study.

---
[3] *Seventh Census of the United States*, p. LXI, Table XLIII.
[4] See p. 10, Introductory Remarks, *Ibid.*
[5] *Eighth Census of the United States*, vol. IV, p. 508.
[6] *Ninth Census, Population and Social Statistics*, XXX.

The trend of illiteracy in the United States has been steadily downward.[7] The relative decrease is from 20.0 per cent illiteracy in 1870 to 6.0 per cent in 1920. Expressed in another way, one out of every five persons ten years of age and over was classed as illiterate in 1870, while in 1920, approximately one person in every seventeen was classified as illiterate. The number of illiterates in 1920 (4,931,905) was approximately three-quarters of a million less than the number in 1870 (5,658,144), the high-water mark being reached in 1890, when the number rose to 6,324,702.

Figure I shows the illiteracy rates for the years 1870 to 1920, which the trend line follows closely. The actual data

TABLE I

ILLITERACY IN THE UNITED STATES, 1870 TO 1920

Year	Number of Persons 10 Years of Age and Over	Number of Illiterates[8]	Per Cent Illiterate
1870	28,228,945	5,658,144	20.0
1880	36,761,607	6,239,958	17.0
1890	47,413,559*	6,324,702*	13.3
1900	57,949,824	6,180,069	10.7
1910	71,580,270	5,516,163	7.7
1920	82,739,315	4,931,905	6.0

*Exclusive of persons in Indian Territory and on Indian Reservations. Such areas were especially enumerated in 1890, but illiteracy statistics are not available.

indicate a slower rate of decrease in the future, however, than is presented by the trend.

The United States Census Bureau classifies the various states into nine geographical divisions.[9] Illiteracy in the

---

[7]See Table I.

[8]*Fourteenth Census of the United States*, vol. II, chap. XII, Table I.

[9]New England, Middle Atlantic, East North Central, West North Central, South Atlantic, East South Central, West South Central, Mountain, and Pacific.

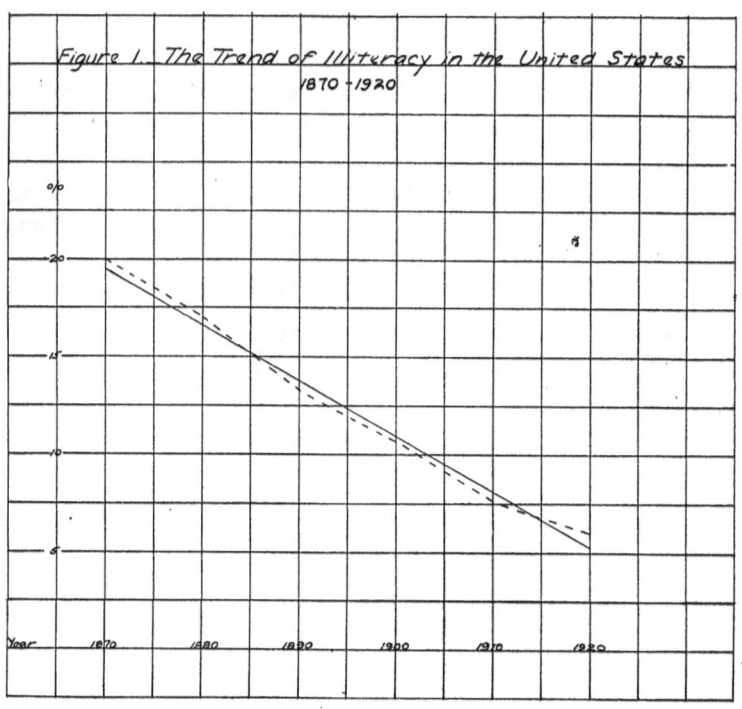

first of these, the New England Division, is increasing in numbers, but decreasing in percentage (Table II). Trend lines fitted to the data for the six New England states show a steady decrease in Rhode Island with slight decreases in Vermont and Massachusetts. Maine and Connecticut reveal but little decrease in the trend, while New Hampshire shows an increase for the total period. By observation, it is evident that the trend since 1890 is downward. The slowness of the decrease in the illiteracy percentage is partly a function of a relatively low illiteracy rate in 1870, and partly a result of the influx of illiterate immigrants, particularly since 1880. This latter factor will be discussed in a later chapter.

The trend for the Middle Atlantic Division as a whole, from 1870 to 1920, is clearly defined.[10] The trend lines for New Jersey and Pennsylvania show a slight though steady decrease. The illiteracy rate for New York, which was 7.1 per cent in 1870, dropped to 5.5 per cent in 1880, and remained at this level until the last census, when the downward trend was resumed. Only in 1880 however, did the actual number of illiterates decrease.

The East North Central Division, comprising the states of Ohio, Indiana, Illinois, Michigan, and Wisconsin, shows a gradual decrease, from an illiteracy rate of 8.2 per cent, in 1870, to a rate of 2.9 per cent in 1920, with the exception of 1890 when the illiteracy decrease slowed up, and the rate actually increased in Michigan and Wisconsin. Of the three divisions so far discussed, the East North Central Division is the only one to show a decrease in the actual number of illiterates in the half-century span.

From a 12.0 per cent illiteracy rate in 1870, the West North Central Division, comprising the states of Minne-

---

[10]See Table II and Figure 3.

TABLE II
ILLITERACY IN THE UNITED STATES, BY DIVISIONS, 1870 TO 1920[11]

Section	Year	Number of Persons 10 Years of Age and over	Number of Illiterates	Per Cent Illiterate
New England............	1870	2,773,337	195,963	7.1
	1880	3,219,856	198,506	6.2
	1890	3,859,728	243,404	6.3
	1900	4,524,602	272,402	6.0
	1910	5,330,914	280,806	5.3
	1920	5,945,989	289,700	4.9
Middle Atlantic..........	1870	6,657,455	516,314	7.8
	1880	8,050,234	500,863	6.2
	1890	10,028,649	616,585	6.2
	1900	12,167,559	704,134	5.8
	1910	15,446,515	873,812	5.7
	1920	17,666,354	865,832	4.9
East North Central.......	1870	6,586,383	542,448	8.2
	1880	8,339,175	507,286	6.1
	1890	10,317,783	588,965	5.7
	1900	12,443,302	534,299	4.3
	1910	14,568,949	491,850	3.4
	1920	17,130,786	495,470	2.9
West North Central.......	1870	2,706,051	323,469	12.0
	1880	4,421,666	345,734	7.8
	1890	6,591,830	373,303	5.7
	1900	7,838,564	324,023	4.1
	1910	9,097,311	263,138	2.9
	1920	9,889,740	193,221	2.0
South Atlantic...........	1870	4,207,398	1,943,166	46.2
	1880	5,286,645	2,129,830	40.3
	1890	6,415,921	1,981,888	30.9
	1900	7,616,159	1,821,346	23.9
	1910	9,012,826	1,444,294	16.0
	1920	10,513,447	1,212,942	11.5
East South Central.......	1870	3,109,016	1,393,195	44.8
	1880	3,831,101	1,565,762	40.9
	1890	4,608,235	1,433,669	31.1
	1900	5,474,227	1,364,935	24.9
	1910	6,178,578	1,072,100	17.4
	1920	6,677,229	845,459	12.7

TABLE II—Continued

Section	Year	Number of Persons 10 Years of Age and over	Number of Illiterates	Per Cent Illiterate
West South Central.......	1870	1,439,204	631,200	43.9
	1880	2,245,142	836,827	37.3
	1890	3,191,252	885,202	27.7
	1900	4,649,988	953,644	20.5
	1910	6,394,043	845,604	13.2
	1920	7,739,536	773,637	10.0
Mountain...............	1870	237,638	74,939	31.5
	1880	500,441	90,408	18.1
	1890	890,252	101,903	11.5
	1900	1,276,076	122,901	9.6
	1910	2,054,249	140,737	6.9
	1920	2,564,463	132,659	5.2
Pacific..................	1870	512,463	36,450	7.1
	1880	867,347	64,742	7.5
	1890	1,509,909	97,783	6.5
	1900	1,959,347	82,385	4.2
	1910	3,496,885	103,822	3.0
	1920	4,611,771	123,435	2.7

sota, Iowa, Missouri, North Dakota, South Dakota, Nebraska, and Kansas, achieved an illiteracy rate of 2.0 per cent in 1920, the lowest attained by any of the nine divisions in the United States.

The South Atlantic Division comprises the states of Delaware, Maryland, Virginia, West Virginia, North Carolina, South Carolina, Georgia, and Florida, as well as the District of Columbia.[12] The high percentage of

[11] *Fourteenth Census*, vol. II, chap. XII, Table V; *Thirteenth Census*, vol. I, chap. XIII, Table XXVI; *Thirteenth Census*, vol. I, chap. IV, Table XLIII (data computed); *Compendium of the Eleventh Census*, Part III, pp. 301-2 (data computed); *Ninth Census*, vol. I, Tables IX and XXVI (data computed).

[12] In general, data for the District of Columbia are omitted as it is not a comparable area.

illiteracy in 1870, 46.2 per cent, is partly due to the presence of a large Negro population, partly to the economic and social disorganization in most of this section in the preceding decade, partly to the rural conditions, and in large part to the less strongly entrenched cultural trait-complex of institutional education. Virginia, North Carolina, South Carolina, Georgia, and Florida had an illiteracy rate of over 50.0 per cent in 1870. The marginal states of Delaware, Maryland, and West Virginia had an illiteracy rate of approximately half that of the other states. The tremendous sweep of the downward trend lines shows the progress being achieved by all the South Atlantic States.

The states of Kentucky, Tennessee, Alabama, and Mississippi compose the East South Central Division. The illiteracy trend is fundamentally the same as that of the South Atlantic Division. The plotted data (Figure 7) reveal that the illiteracy trends dropped more rapidly after 1880 than before in each of the four states. This, as in the preceding division, is in large part a function of the greater disorganization and correspondingly greater recovery in the second as compared with the first decade after the outbreak of the Civil War.

The States of Arkansas, Louisiana, Oklahoma, and Texas comprise the West South Central Division. These states, the western marginal states of the South Eastern area of the United States, reveal high rates of illiteracy with the exception of Oklahoma. The comparatively low illiteracy of this state is due in part to the lower percentage of Negroes in the population.[13] The rise in 1900 for Okla-

---

[13]Negroes formed the following percentages of the population of the states of this division in 1920:

Arkansas	27.0
Louisiana	38.9
Oklahoma	7.4
Texas	15.9

homa, is due to the inclusion of Indians who were not included in 1890.[14]

The rapid progress of the Mountain Division is reflected in the drop from 31.5 per cent illiterate in 1870 to 5.2 per cent in 1920. The early settlement conditions and the large percentage of illiterate Mexicans and pre-literate American Indians probably account for much of the early high percentage of illiteracy.[15]

The rate of illiteracy on the Pacific Coast has never been high, comparatively speaking, while since 1880 in the case of Oregon and Washington, and since 1890 in California, the trend has been slowly downward. The steady increase in the number of illiterates in the Pacific Division is due in part to the high rate of illiteracy of the Japanese and Chinese immigrants, but chiefly to the Mexican and Mexican-descendant immigration.[16] Much of this immigration has used California as the state of entrance, hence its relatively larger proportion of illiteracy.

In conclusion, it may be stated that the actual rise in rate of illiteracy for many of the states in 1890 or a slowing up of the downward trend in a still greater number in that year may be chiefly ascribed to the high percentage of illiterates among the "new" immigration from southern and eastern Europe. This phenomenon, however, does not negate the general statement that the trend of illiteracy for the United States and its divisions, as well as for the forty-eight states, has been steadily downward.

---

[14]Persons in Indian Territory and on Indian Reservations were especially enumerated in 1890, but illiteracy statistics are not available.

[15]The data apparently present a number of inconsistencies which are symptoms of inaccurate census returns for some states prior to 1900.

[16]For proof of this, see chap. VI.

TABLE III
Percentages of Illiteracy in the United States, by States
1870 to 1920[17]

States	1870	1880	1890	1900	1910	1920
Maine................................	3.8	4.3	5.5	5.1	4.1	3.3
New Hampshire................	3.8	5.0	6.8	6.2	4.6	4.4
Vermont............................	6.8	6.0	6.7	5.8	3.7	3.0
Massachusetts..................	8.4	6.5	6.2	5.9	5.2	4.7
Rhode Island....................	12.6	11.2	9.8	8.4	7.7	6.5
Connecticut......................	7.0	5.7	5.3	5.9	6.0	6.2
New York..........................	7.1	5.5	5.5	5.5	5.5	5.1
New Jersey.......................	8.0	6.2	6.5	5.9	5.6	5.1
Pennsylvania....................	8.6	7.1	6.8	6.1	5.9	4.6
Ohio..................................	8.9	5.5	5.2	4.0	3.2	2.8
Indiana.............................	10.6	7.5	6.3	4.6	3.1	2.2
Illinois..............................	7.4	6.4	5.2	4.2	3.7	3.4
Michigan..........................	6.1	5.2	5.9	4.2	3.3	3.0
Wisconsin.........................	7.4	5.8	6.7	4.7	3.2	2.4
Minnesota........................	8.0	6.2	6.0	4.1	3.0	1.8
Iowa..................................	5.5	3.9	3.6	2.3	1.7	1.1
Missouri...........................	18.4	13.4	9.1	6.4	4.3	3.0
North Dakota...................	14.7	4.8	6.0	5.6	3.1	2.1
South Dakota...................	14.7	4.8	4.2	5.0	2.9	1.7
Nebraska..........................	5.5	3.6	3.1	2.3	1.9	1.4
Kansas..............................	9.5	5.6	4.0	2.9	2.2	1.6
Delaware..........................	24.9	17.5	14.3	12.0	8.1	5.9
Maryland..........................	23.5	19.3	15.7	11.1	7.2	5.6
Virginia............................	50.1	40.6	30.2	22.9	15.2	11.2
West Virginia...................	26.4	19.9	14.4	11.4	8.3	6.4
North Carolina.................	51.7	48.3	35.7	28.7	18.5	13.1
South Carolina.................	57.6	55.4	45.0	35.9	25.7	18.1
Georgia............................	56.6	49.9	39.8	30.5	20.7	15.3
Florida.............................	54.8	43.4	27.8	21.9	13.8	9.6
Kentucky..........................	35.7	29.9	21.6	16.5	12.1	8.4
Tennessee........................	40.9	38.7	26.6	20.7	13.6	10.3
Alabama...........................	54.2	50.9	41.0	34.0	22.9	16.1
Mississippi.......................	53.9	49.5	40.0	32.0	22.4	17.2

TABLE III—Continued

States	1870	1780	1890	1900	1910	1920
Arkansas......................	30.2	38.0	26.6	20.4	12.6	9.4
Louisiana.....................	52.5	49.1	45.8	38.5	29.0	21.9
Oklahoma.....................	......	......	5.4	12.1	5.6	3.8
Texas.........................	37.1	29.7	19.7	14.5	9.9	8.3
Montana.......................	5.1	5.3	5.5	6.1	4.8	2.3
Idaho.........................	25.7	7.1	5.1	4.6	2.2	1.5
Wyoming......................	7.5	3.4	3.4	4.0	3.3	2.1
Colorado......................	22.5	6.6	5.2	4.2	3.7	3.2
New Mexico...................	78.6	65.0	44.5	33.2	20.2	15.6
Arizona.......................	33.4	17.7	23.4	29.0	20.9	15.3
Utah..........................	13.0	9.1	5.6	3.1	2.5	1.9
Nevada........................	2.4	8.0	12.8	13.3	6.7	5.9
Washington....................	7.5	7.0	4.3	3.1	2.0	1.7
Oregon........................	6.8	5.7	4.1	3.3	1.9	1.5
California.....................	7.3	7.8	7.7	4.8	3.7	3.3

[17] *Fourteenth Census,* vol. II, chap. XII, Table VII; *Compendium of the Eleventh Census,* Part III, pp. 301, 302; *Ninth Census,* vol. I, Tables IX, XXVI.

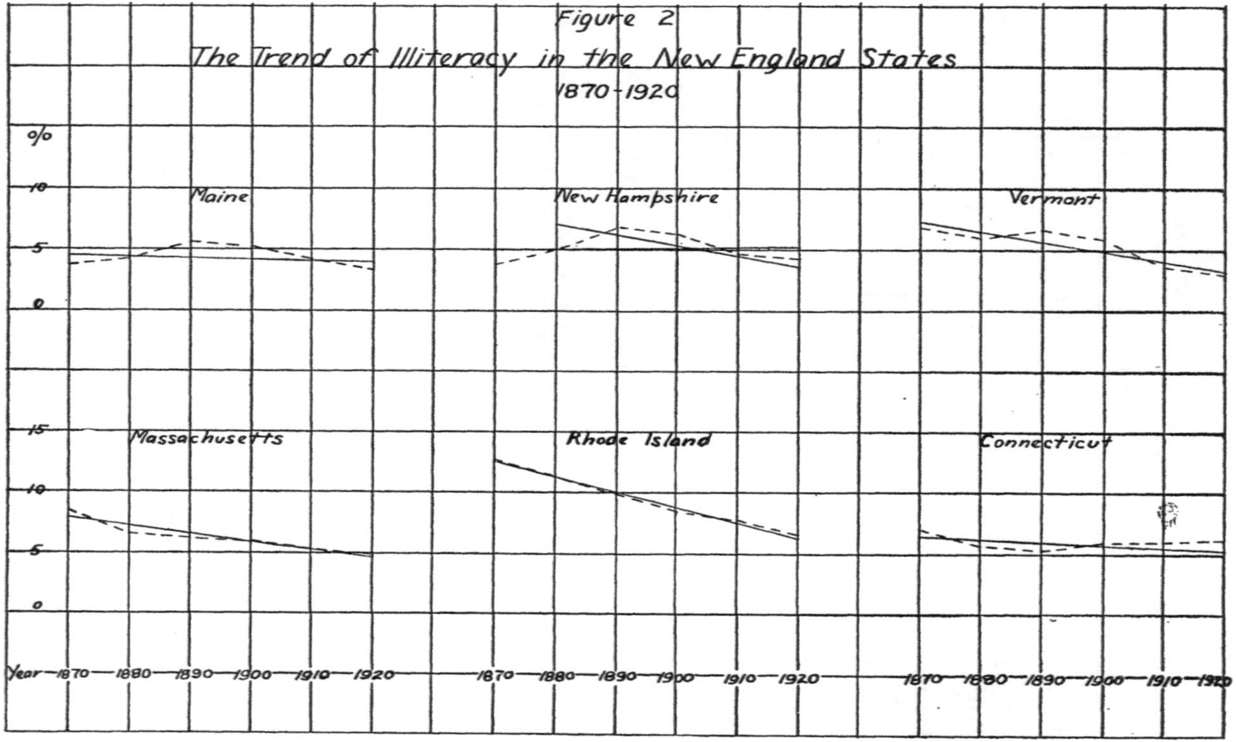
Figure 2
The Trend of Illiteracy in the New England States
1870-1920
%
10
5
0
Maine
New Hampshire
Vermont
15
10
5
0
Massachusetts
Rhode Island
Connecticut
Year—1870—1880—1890—1900—1910—1920
1870—1880—1890—1900—1910—1920
1870—1880—1890—1900—1910—1920

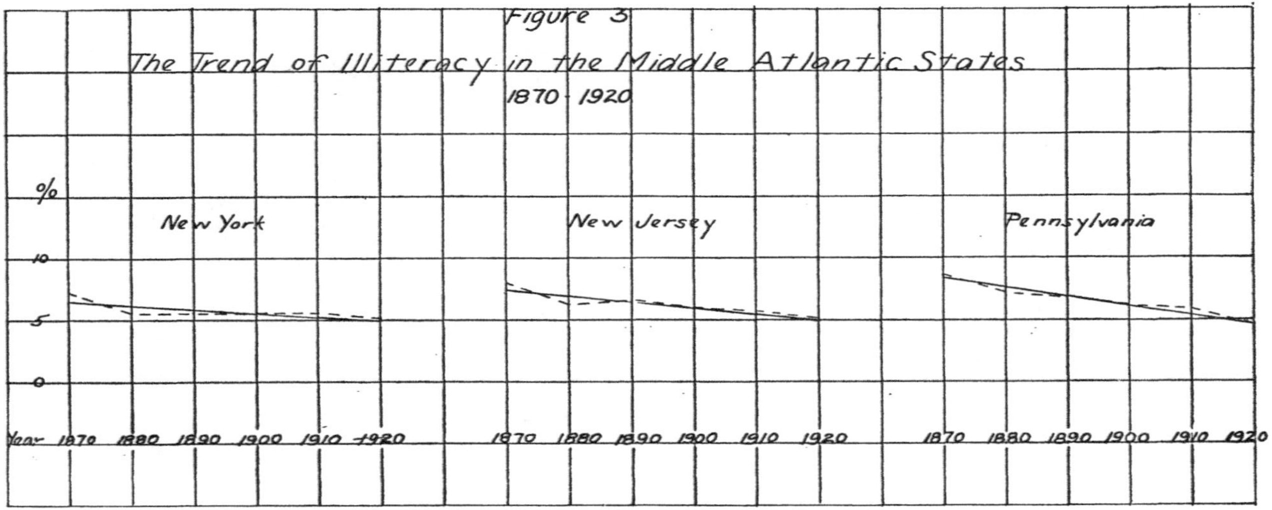

Figure 3
The Trend of Illiteracy in the Middle Atlantic States
1870-1920

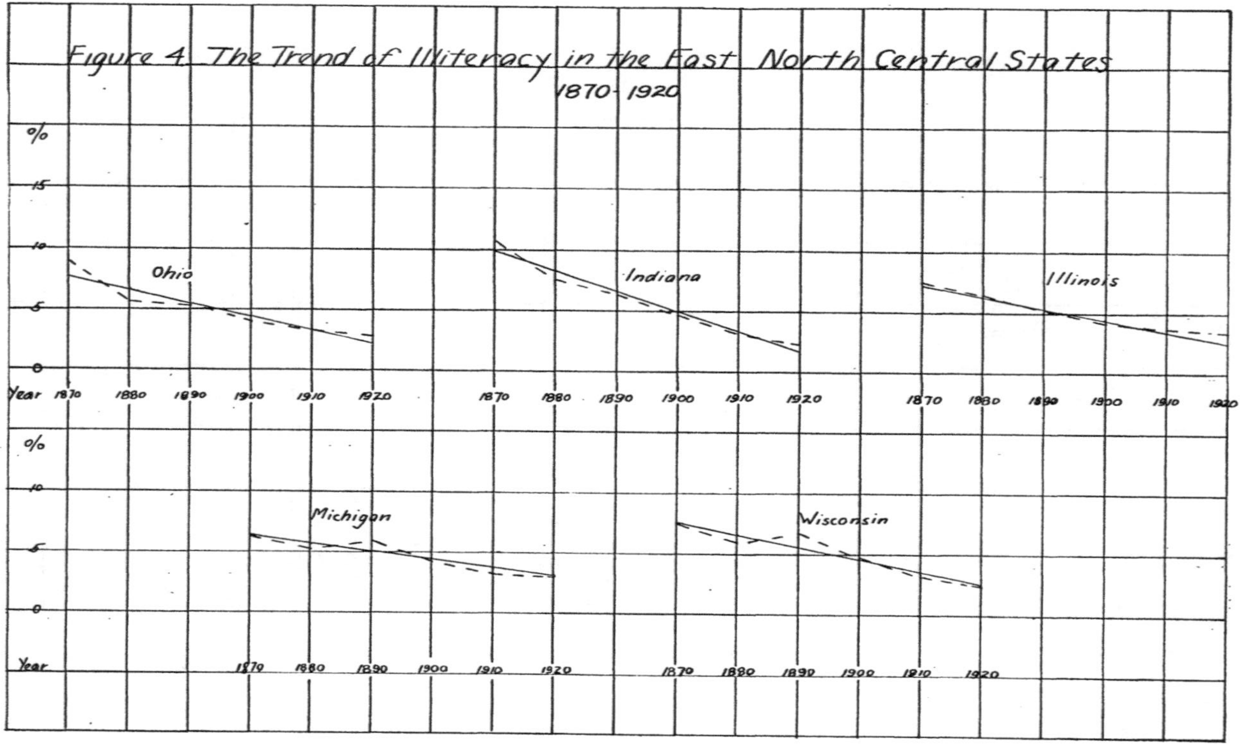

Figure 4. The Trend of Illiteracy in the East North Central States 1870-1920

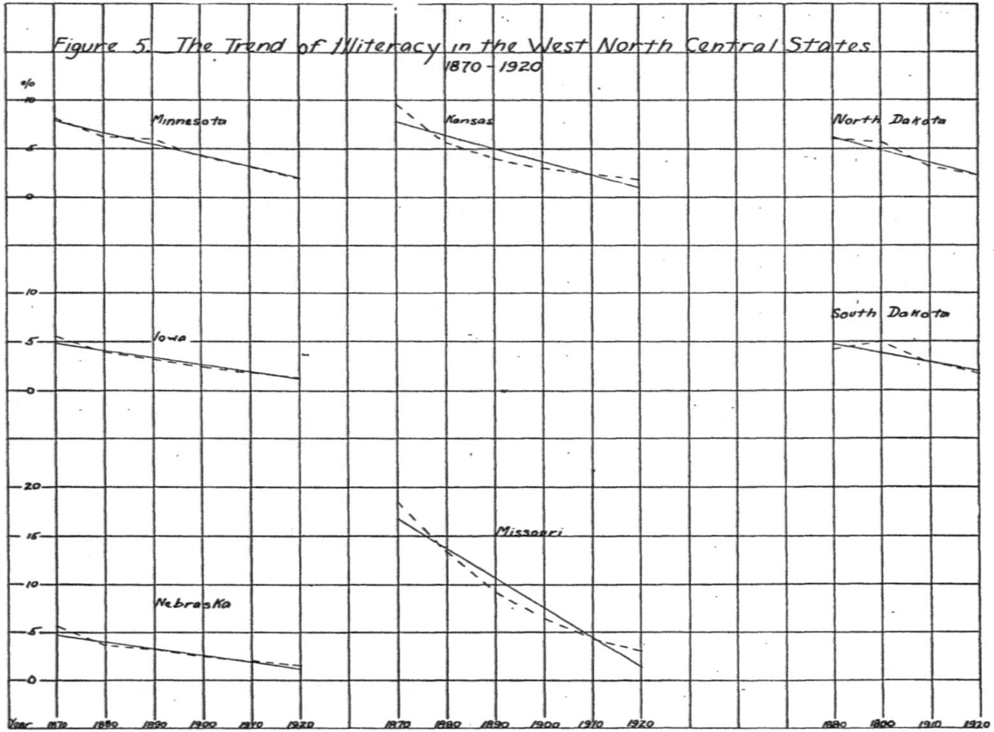

Figure 5. The Trend of Illiteracy in the West North Central States 1870-1920

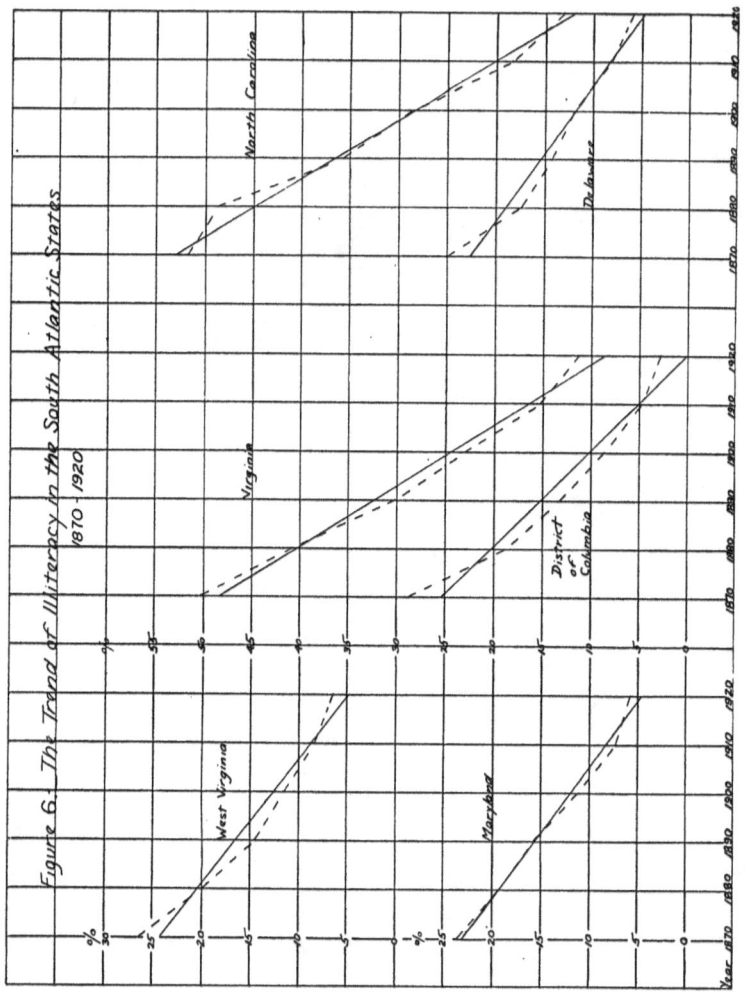

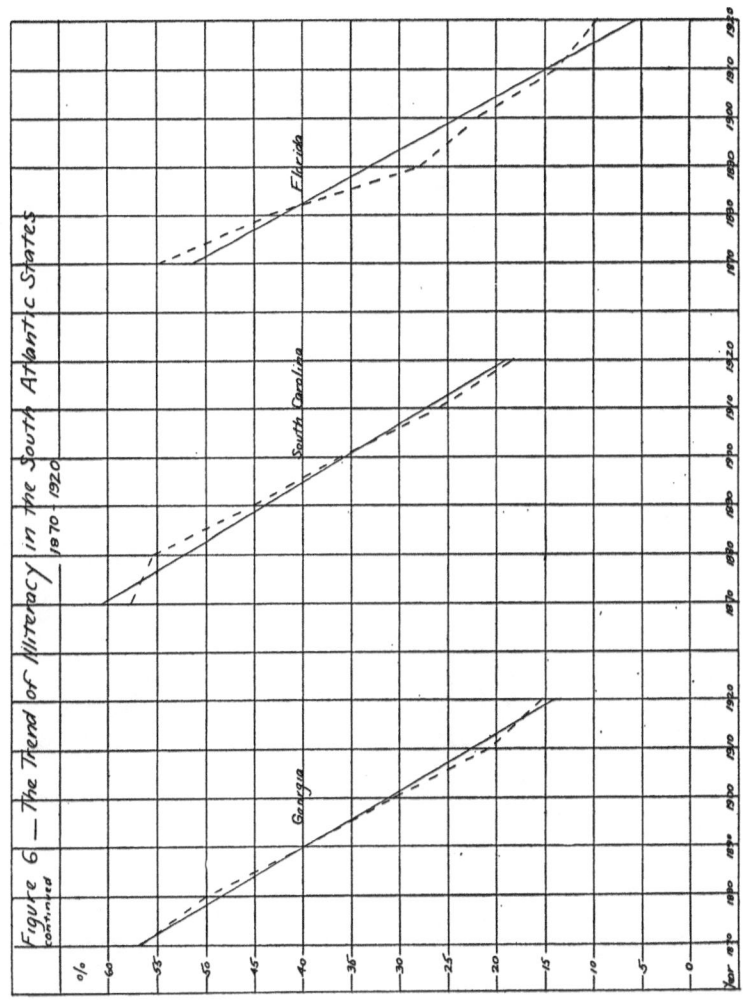

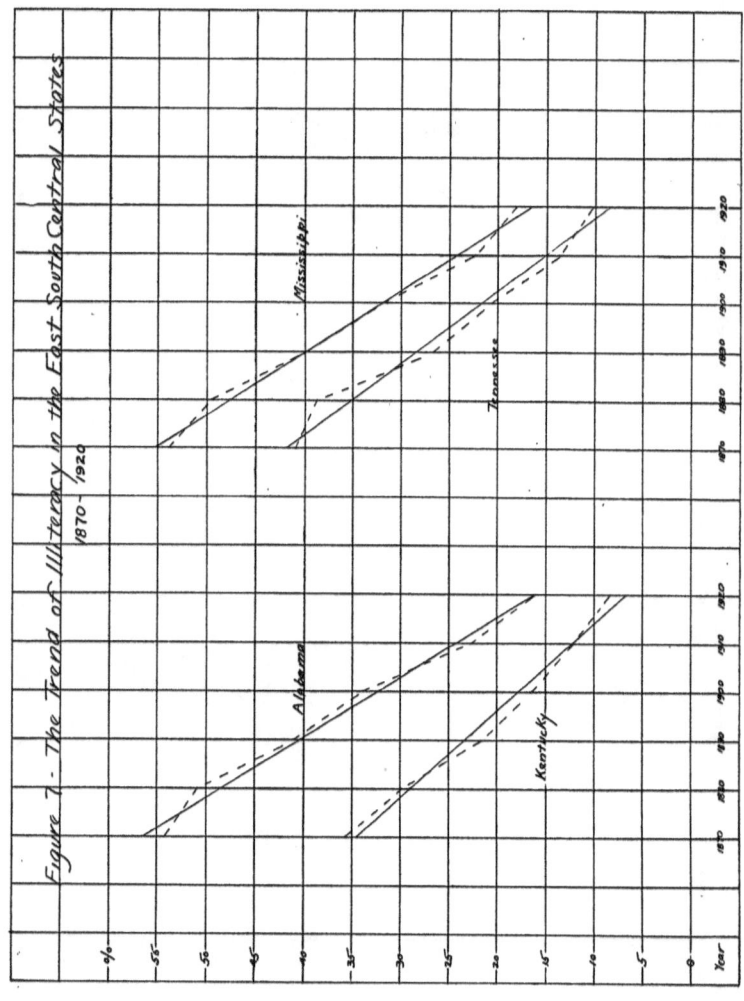

Figure 7 - The Trend of Illiteracy in the East South Central States 1870-1920

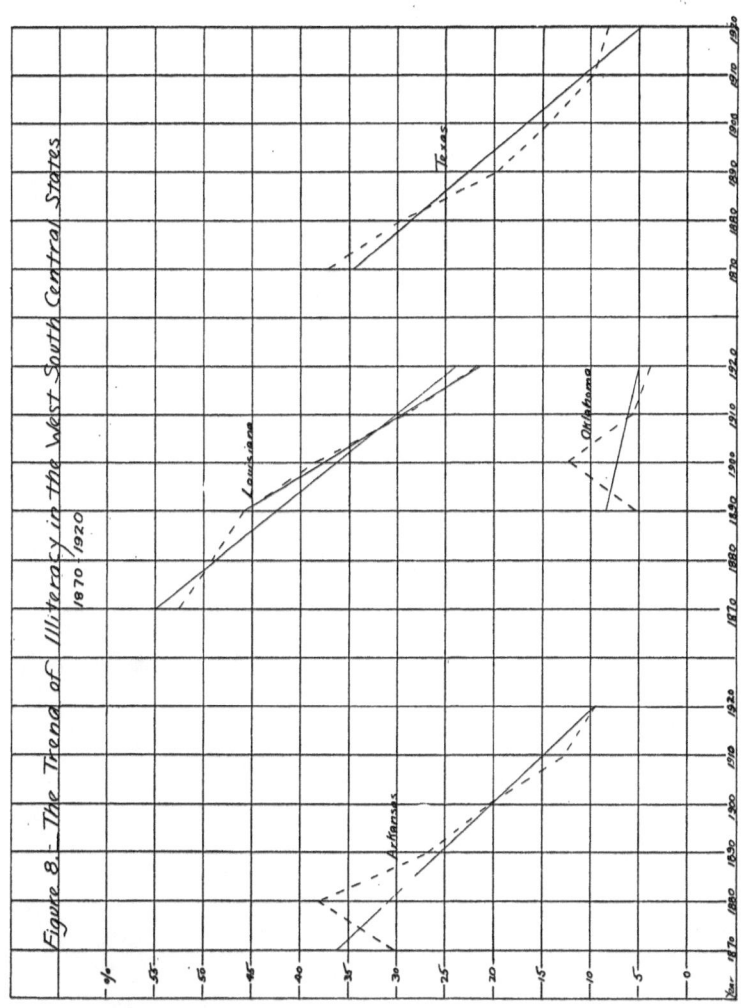

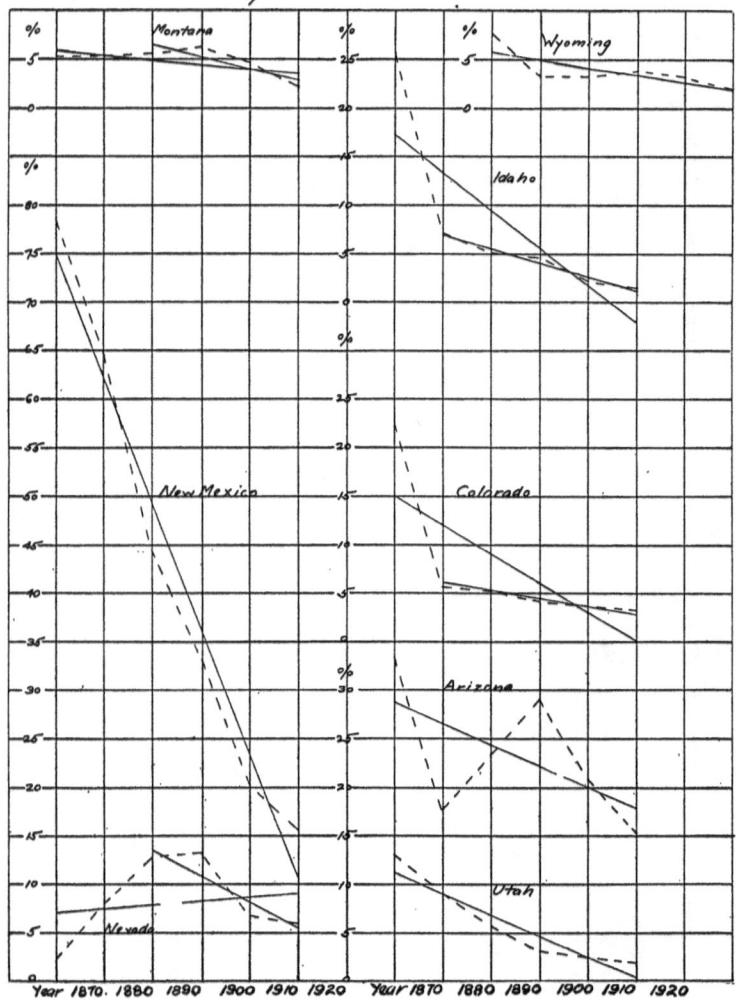

Figure 9.—Illiteracy in the Mountain States, 1870-1920

Figure 10.—The Trend of Illiteracy in the Pacific States
1870-1920

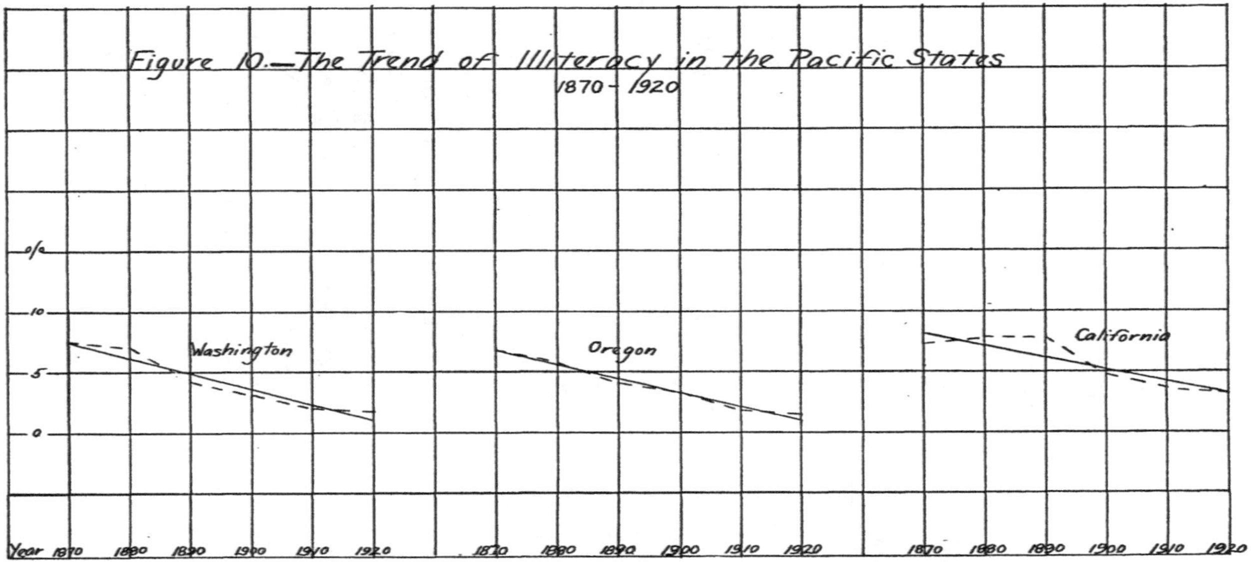

CHAPTER III

ILLITERACY AND SEX

The objective of this chapter is the analysis of the data on illiteracy and sex. The sources of error are, by the nature of the data, almost negligible when sex alone is considered. Table IV shows the number and percentage of both male and female illiterates for the United States as a whole. The folkways in reference to female education in the middle of the nineteenth century are reflected in the larger percentage of female illiteracy from 1870 to 1910. The trend is downward at a more rapid rate for females than for males, however, resulting in a slightly smaller percentage of female than of male illiteracy in 1920. It is to be noted that the decrease in actual number of illiterates began one decade earlier for women than for men.

Table V shows the actual number of illiterates and percentage of illiteracy for males and females, for the years 1870 to 1920, for the nine divisions of the United States. All show a greater percentage of female illiteracy in 1870, which slopes downward thereafter at a more rapid pace than male illiteracy, so that in only three divisions, the New England, the Middle Atlantic, and the Mountain divisions, is the percentage of female illiteracy greater than that of male illiteracy, in 1920. In the New England and Middle Atlantic divisions this may be largely explained by the higher percentage of females than males in the advanced age period[1] and also by the higher percentage of illiteracy among foreign-born females than males.[2]

---
[1] *Fourteenth Census of the United States*, vol. II, chap. XII, Table XII.
[2] The relation between age and illiteracy is fully discussed in the following chapter.

TABLE IV

ILLITERACY IN THE UNITED STATES,* BY SEX, 1870 TO 1920[3]

Year	Number of Males 10 Years of Age and Over	Number of Male Illiterates	Per Cent of Male Illiterates	Number of Females 10 Years of Age and Over	Number of Female Illiterates	Per Cent of Female Illiterates
1870	14,258,866	2,603,888	18.3	13,970,079	3,054,256	21.9
1880	18,735,980	2,966,421	15.8	18,025,627	3,273,537	18.2
1890	24,352,659	3,008,222	12.4	23,060,900	3,316,480	14.4
1900	29,703,440	3,011,224	10.1	28,246,384	3,168,845	11.2
1910	37,027,558	2,814,950	7.6	34,552,712	2,701,213	7.8
1920	42,289,969	2,540,209	6.0	40,449,346	2,391,696	5.9

*Figures for 1890 are exclusive of illiterate persons in Indian Territory and on Indian Reservations, areas especially enumerated but for which statistics are not available.
[3]*Fourteenth Census*, vol. II, chap. XII, Table I.

TABLE V
Illiteracy in the Divisions of the United States, by Sex, 1870 to 1920[a]

Division	Year	Number of Males 10 Years of Age and Over	Number of Male Illiterates	Per Cent of Male Illiterates	Number of Females 10 Years of Age and Over	Number of Female Illiterates	Per Cent of Female Illiterates
New England	1870	1,348,135	81,668	6.1	1,425,202	114,295	8.0
	1880	1,559,594	85,791	5.5	1,660,262	112,715	6.8
	1890	1,889,307	112,626	5.9	1,970,421	130,778	6.6
	1900	2,228,540	132,411	5.9	2,296,062	139,991	6.1
	1910	2,649,897	140,326	5.3	2,681,017	140,480	5.2
	1920	2,940,130	140,280	4.8	3,005,859	149,420	5.0
Middle Atlantic	1870	3,286,841	202,924	6.2	3,370,614	313,390	9.3
	1880	3,967,566	213,640	5.4	4,082,668	287,223	7.0
	1890	5,015,259	294,560	5.9	5,013,390	322,025	6.4
	1900	6,108,053	342,866	5.6	6,059,506	361,268	6.0
	1910	7,863,584	442,488	5.6	7,582,931	431,324	5.7
	1920	8,890,489	413,458	4.7	8,775,865	451,924	5.1
East North Central	1870	3,388,148	241,272	7.1	3,198,235	301,176	9.4
	1880	4,302,506	245,319	5.7	4,036,669	261,967	6.5
	1890	5,314,088	281,016	5.3	5,003,695	307,949	6.2

ILLITERACY AND SEX

West North Central	1900	6,387,365	259,427	4.1	6,055,937	274,872	4.5
	1910	7,529,768	262,137	3.5	7,039,181	229,713	3.3
	1920	8,837,101	262,638	3.0	8,293,685	232,832	2.8
	1870	1,452,486	154,013	10.6	1,253,565	169,456	13.5
	1880	2,381,598	170,253	7.2	2,040,067	175,481	8.6
	1890	3,513,995	176,777	5.0	3,077,835	198,526	6.5
	1900	4,140,550	153,176	3.7	3,698,014	170,847	4.6
	1910	4,807,164	138,030	2.9	4,290,147	125,108	2.9
	1920	5,112,443	101,744	2.0	4,777,297	91,477	1.9
South Atlantic	1870	2,030,149	904,627	44.6	2,177,249	1,038,539	47.7
	1880	2,588,035	1,003,565	38.8	2,698,610	1,126,265	41.7
	1890	3,178,769	929,096	29.1	3,237,152	1,055,792	32.6
	1900	3,798,278	879,065	23.1	3,817,881	942,281	24.7
	1910	4,528,942	723,570	16.0	4,483,884	720,724	16.1
	1920	5,282,930	637,980	12.1	5,230,517	574,962	11.0
East South Central	1870	1,532,085	653,063	42.7	1,576,931	740,132	46.9
	1880	1,900,639	746,439	39.3	1,930,462	819,323	42.4
	1890	2,313,978	674,991	29.2	2,294,257	758,678	33.1
	1900	2,758,148	665,392	24.1	2,716,079	699,543	25.8
	1910	3,116,286	542,291	17.4	3,062,292	529,809	17.3
	1920	3,348,984	447,071	13.3	3,328,245	398,388	12.0

TABLE V—Continued

Division	Year	Number of Males 10 Years of Age and Over	Number of Male Illiterates	Per Cent of Male Illiterates	Number of Females 10 Years of Age and Over	Number of Female Illiterates	Per Cent of Female Illiterates
West South Central	1870	733,720	307,354	41.9	705,484	323,846	45.9
	1880	1,169,117	414,185	35.4	1,076,025	422,642	39.3
	1890	1,663,636	423,764*	25.5	1,527,616	461,438	30.1
	1900	2,418,607	467,241	19.3	2,231,381	486,403	21.8
	1910	3,334,078	424,354	12.7	3,059,965	421,250	13.8
	1920	3,999,088	400,795	10.0	3,740,448	372,842	10.0
Mountain	1870	152,090	37,172	24.4	85,548	37,767	44.2
	1880	324,638	44,728	13.8	175,803	45,680	26.0
	1890	548,004	51,445	9.4	342,248	50,458	14.7
	1900	737,787	60,413	8.2	538,289	62,488	11.6
	1910	1,185,047	75,242	6.4	869,202	65,495	7.5
	1920	1,398,659	66,395	4.7	1,165,804	66,264	5.7
Pacific	1870	335,212	21,795	6.5	177,251	15,655	8.8
	1880	542,286	42,501	7.8	325,061	22,241	6.8
	1890	915,623	66,947	7.3	594,286	30,836	5.2

1900	1,126,112	51,233	4.6	833,235	31,152	3.7
1910	2,012,792	66,512	3.3	1,484,093	37,310	2.5
1920	2,480,145	69,848	2.8	2,131,626	53,587	2.5

*Figures for 1890 are exclusive of illiterate persons in Indian Territory and on Indian Reservations, areas especially enumerated, but for which statistics are not available.

⁴*Fourteenth Census*, vol. II, chap. XII, Table VII; *Compendium of the Eleventh Census*, Part III, pp. 301, 302; *Ninth Census*, vol. I, Tables IX, XXVI (data computed).

TABLE VI

ILLITERACY IN THE UNITED STATES, BY SEX, BY STATES, FOR 1920[5]

State	Number of Males 10 Years of Age and Over	Number of Male Illiterates	Per Cent of Male Illiterates	Number of Females 10 Years of Age and Over	Number of Female Illiterates	Per Cent of Female Illiterates
Maine	314,575	12,421	4.0	306,658	7,819	2.5
New Hampshire	181,286	8,246	4.6	180,644	7,542	4.2
Vermont	144,525	5,156	3.6	139,947	3,332	2.5
Massachusetts	1,514,904	68,423	4.5	1,591,865	78,184	4.9
Rhode Island	237,116	14,168	6.0	246,672	17,144	7.0
Connecticut	547,724	31,866	5.8	540,073	35,399	6.6
New York	4,186,818	188,353	4.5	4,215,968	236,669	5.6
New Jersey	1,256,332	61,546	4.9	1,237,914	66,115	5.3
Pennsylvania	3,447,339	163,559	4.7	3,321,983	149,140	4.5
Ohio	2,382,040	72,627	3.0	2,242,416	58,379	2.6
Indiana	1,198,722	28,864	2.4	1,157,492	23,170	2.0
Illinois	2,647,505	86,698	3.3	2,537,438	87,289	3.4
Michigan	1,536,629	48,173	3.1	1,358,977	39,873	2.9
Wisconsin	1,072,205	26,276	2.5	997,362	24,121	2.4

ILLITERACY AND SEX

State						
Minnesota	986,877	17,413	1.8	890,255	17,074	1.9
Iowa	980,360	11,353	1.2	932,795	9,327	1.0
Missouri	1,385,747	45,444	3.3	1,352,024	37,959	2.8
North Dakota	251,989	4,681	1.9	218,221	5,256	2.4
South Dakota	258,683	3,806	1.5	223,512	4,303	1.9
Nebraska	528,290	6,999	1.3	484,262	6,785	1.4
Kansas	720,497	12,048	1.7	676,228	10,773	1.6
Delaware	91,802	5,697	6.2	87,128	4,811	5.5
Maryland	582,933	33,435	5.7	576,020	30,999	5.4
Virginia	886,493	107,374	12.1	862,375	87,785	10.2
West Virginia	570,617	40,896	7.2	512,778	28,517	5.6
North Carolina	917,883	125,302	13.7	926,790	116,301	12.6
South Carolina	604,224	110,425	18.3	615,092	110,242	17.9
Georgia	1,069,254	173,254	16.2	1,080,976	155,584	14.4
Florida	386,150	37,252	9.6	365,637	34,559	9.5
Kentucky	933,175	86,495	9.3	904,259	68,519	7.6
Tennessee	885,962	98,852	11.2	884,810	83,777	9.5
Alabama	861,344	140,991	16.4	869,077	137,091	15.8
Mississippi	668,513	120,733	18.1	670,099	109,001	16.3
Arkansas	667,972	63,959	9.6	634,933	57,878	9.1
Louisiana	684,958	148,081	21.6	681,108	151,011	22.2
Oklahoma	797,753	32,347	4.1	716,198	24,517	3.4
Texas	1,848,405	156,408	8.5	1,708,209	139,436	8.2

TABLE VI—Continued

State	Number of Males 10 Years of Age and Over	Number of Male Illiterates	Per Cent of Male Illiterates	Number of Females 10 Years of Age and Over	Number of Female Illiterates	Per Cent of Female Illiterates
Montana	235,586	5,357	2.3	185,857	4,187	2.3
Idaho	179,948	3,085	1.7	146,103	1,839	1.3
Wyoming	88,316	2,180	2.5	62,677	969	1.5
Colorado	395,632	11,587	2.9	351,853	12,621	3.6
New Mexico	143,826	18,235	12.7	123,769	23,402	18.9
Arizona	143,651	19,984	13.9	111,810	19,147	17.1
Utah	172,295	3,678	2.1	159,235	2,586	1.6
Nevada	39,405	2,289	5.8	24,500	1,513	6.2
Washington	605,288	10,479	1.7	496,641	8,047	1.6
Oregon	343,059	5,589	1.6	295,928	3,728	1.3
California	1,531,798	53,780	3.5	1,339,057	41,812	3.1

[5]*Fourteenth Census of the United States*, vol. II, chap. XII, Table XII.

In the Mountain Division, the southwestern states with their high percentages of female illiterate foreign-born whites, Indians, and descendants of Mexicans raise the female rate above the male for the division as a whole.[6] In the West South Central Division, the virtual equality of the illiteracy rate is counterbalanced by the more downward slope of the trend line of the female illiteracy. The factor of nationality entering here is discussed in the chapter on race and nationality.

Upon further analysis of the sex difference in illiteracy, by states, it is observed that thirty-four of the forty-eight states have a higher percentage of male illiteracy than of female illiteracy in 1920 (see Table VI). Of the remaining fourteen states, three have a difference of 1/10 of 1 per cent. The fourteen states having a higher female illiteracy rate arrange themselves into four groups, group one containing Massachusetts, Rhode Island, Connecticut, New York, New Jersey, and Illinois. As has been stated in connection with the divisions, these highly industrialized areas contain a large percentage of foreign-born women, among whom the percentage of illiteracy is high, as well as a predominance of females among the aged. Group two contains the states of Minnesota, North Dakota, South Dakota, and Nebraska, states with low illiteracy rates, with a relatively large ratio of northwestern European immigrants or their immediate descendants. The females of these foreign-born have high illiteracy rates, particularly in old age.[7]

In group three, Louisiana is the only state listed. The higher female illiteracy rate is largely a function of the older Negro women and the older native white women of native parentage as well.[8] In group four, Colorado, New

---

[6] *Ibid.*, Table XII.   [7] *Ibid.*   [8] *Ibid.*

TABLE VII
ILLITERACY IN THE UNITED STATES AND ITS DIVISIONS, BY SEX, BY URBAN AND RURAL ENVIRONMENT, FOR 1920[9]

Section of United States	Males			Females		
	Number 10 Years of Age and Over	Number Illiterate	Per Cent Illiterate	Number 10 Years of Age and Over	Number Illiterate	Per Cent Illiterate
United States						
Urban..........	22,009,152	926,289	4.2	21,969,424	1,028,823	4.7
Rural...........	20,280,817	1,613,920	8.0	18,479,922	1,362,873	7.4
New England						
Urban..........	2,307,385	114,664	5.0	2,405,753	130,635	5.4
Rural...........	632,745	25,616	4.0	600,106	18,785	3.1
Middle Atlantic....						
Urban..........	6,636,690	316,673	4.8	6,683,251	374,553	5.6
Rural...........	2,253,799	96,785	4.3	2,092,614	77,371	3.7
East North Central						
Urban..........	5,386,447	179,490	3.3	5,157,081	172,138	3.3
Rural...........	3,450,654	83,148	2.4	3,136,604	60,694	1.9

Illiteracy and Sex

West North Central						
Urban	1,941,553	39,008	2.0	1,961,536	40,407	2.1
Rural	3,170,890	62,736	2.0	2,815,761	51,070	1.8
South Atlantic						
Urban	1,712,684	103,868	6.1	1,813,746	123,187	6.8
Rural	3,570,246	534,112	15.0	3,416,771	451,775	13.2
East South Central						
Urban	784,007	59,146	7.5	848,076	67,208	7.9
Rural	2,564,977	387,925	15.1	2,480,169	331,180	13.4
West South Central						
Urban	1,213,925	68,524	5.6	1,201,480	78,296	6.5
Rural	2,785,163	332,271	11.9	2,538,968	294,546	11.6
Mountain						
Urban	507,654	12,565	2.5	476,482	12,830	2.7
Rural	891,005	53,830	6.0	689,322	53,434	7.8
Pacific						
Urban	1,518,807	32,351	2.1	1,422,019	29,569	2.1
Rural	961,338	37,497	3.9	709,607	24,018	3.4

⁹*Ibid.*, Table XXII.

Mexico, Arizona, and Nevada are placed. The explanation for the illiteracy rate in these states has already been given in connection with the Mountain Division.

In comparing sex illiteracy by urban and rural environments for the United States as a whole, one notes (Table 7) the fact that the percentage of illiteracy is greater for females in the urban environment, while the reverse is true in the rural environment. This once more resolves itself into the relatively higher percentage of foreign-born female illiteracy, for the foreign-born largely congregate in the industrialized, urban centers, and into the higher percentage of aged women of all classes in urban areas, in general, as contrasted with rural areas.

Analyzing these differences by divisions, the greater female percentage of illiteracy in the urbanized areas is sound in every division except that of the Pacific Coast ftates, where the difference of 5/10 of 1 per cent is quite small. Contrariwise, in the rural areas, the ratio of female illiteracy is smaller in every division except that of the Mountain states where the much larger percentage of illiteracy on the part of the females has already been discussed.

Thus the apparent difference in illiteracy rates by sex largely resolves itself into the sex distribution according to urban and rural environments, age distributions, race and nationality distributions, and lastly the institutionalized educational facilities for the sexes both in the United States and in Europe. When these factors are adequately taken into consideration, sex differences in regard to illiteracy practically disappear.

Chapter IV

ILLITERACY AND AGE

With the general extension of the public school system in the United States, one would expect a diminishing percentage of illiteracy as one proceeds from the older age groups to the younger. Table VIII supports this conclusion for both sexes and for each sex taken separately. A comparison of the sexes in regard to age and illiteracy in the same table bears out the statement of the preceding chapter, namely, that several decades ago the educational opportunity for women was less than for men. The comparatively greater grasp of the opportunity by female children than males in recent years is also to be noted. There is a greater percentage of male illiteracy until the 25-34 year period.[1] From then on the percentage of illiteracy for males is less than for females.

The data for age are subject to certain qualifications. There are concentrations of numbers around five-year periods, and to a certain extent ages are reported as of even years, i.e., 12, 14, etc. It would appear that adult women tend to understate their ages and that there is a slight tendency on the part of young men to bring their ages up to twenty-one. Among the very aged there is a tendency to overstate the actual age. The census reports, as utilized in this study, largely negate these weaknesses. In general, the degree of inaccuracy is greater for adults than for youths and children. The broad age classifications, utilized in this study, are for five-year periods only up to,

---

[1]Census illiteracy data for five-year periods are available only up to the twenty-fifth year of age.

TABLE VIII

ILLITERACY IN THE UNITED STATES, BY AGE PERIODS, BY SEX, FOR 1920[2]

Age Period	Both Sexes			Males			Females		
	Total Population	Number Illiterate	Per Cent Illiterate	Total Population	Number Illiterate	Per Cent Illiterate	Total Population	Number Illiterate	Per Cent Illiterate
10–14 Years....	10,641,137	246,360	2.3	5,369,306	141,576	2.6	5,271,831	104,784	2.0
15–19 Years....	9,430,556	283,316	3.0	4,673,792	171,489	3.7	4,756,764	111,827	2.4
20–24 Years....	9,277,021	392,853	4.2	4,527,045	203,773	4.5	4,749,976	189,080	4.0
25–34 Years....	17,157,684	961,200	5.6	8,669,016	486,217	5.6	8,488,668	474,983	5.6
35–44 Years....	14,120,838	988,961	7.0	7,359,904	509,107	6.9	6,760,934	479,854	7.1
45–54 Years....	10,498,493	857,776	8.2	5,653,095	453,950	8.0	4,845,398	403,826	8.3
55–64 Years....	6,531,672	594,573	9.1	3,461,865	292,511	8.4	3,069,807	302,062	9.8
65 and Over....	4,933,215	591,385	12.0	2,483,071	273,000	11.0	2,450,144	318,385	13.0
Age Unknown...	148,699	15,481	10.4	92,875	8,586	9.2	55,824	6,895	12.4

[2] *Fourteenth Census of the United States*, vol. II, computed from chap. III, Table I, and chap. XII, Table XII.

but not including, twenty-five years, the years of greatest accuracy. From the twenty-fifth year up to, but not including, the sixty-fifth, the age groups are by ten-year periods. While this makes impossible certain comparisons on a five-year basis, it controls the tendency to concentrate around the ages of 30, 40, 50, and 60 years. The aged classification is "65 years and over," controlling the errors in age as reported after sixty-five. Moreover, the broad generalizations in regard to age are believed to be justifiable.

An analysis of Table IX further reveals, by divisions, the differential illiteracy according to age, with a gradual increase in the percentage of illiteracy as one approaches the age period of sixty-five years and over. The precipitous rise in percentage by the New England, Middle Atlantic, and East North Central Divisions after the two earliest age periods is due to the fact that immigrants are only in small part children, and the young adult (as well as the child) immigrant is more literate than his older immigrant-countrymen.[3]

The data in Table X may be utilized as a partial reflection of the educational opportunities during the decades preceding the taking of the Fourteenth Census. Native whites of native parentage are compared here, thus eliminating the colored and foreign-born population.

An interpretation of the 1920 data brings out the fact that, of those persons who were born in 1855 or prior to that year, 6.2 per cent of the survivors are illiterate. Of those born during the years 1906-1910, only 1.1 per cent of the survivors are illiterate.

---

[3]See *Fourteenth Census of the United States*, vol. II, chap. XII, Table XII, for statistical proof of this.

TABLE IX

PERCENTAGE OF ILLITERACY IN THE DIVISIONS OF THE UNITED STATES, BY AGE, BY SEX, FOR 1920[a]

Both Sexes

Age Period	New England	Middle Atlantic	East North Central	West North Central	South Atlantic	East South Central	West South Central	Mountain	Pacific
10-14 Years.....	0.3	0.3	0.2	0.4	4.9	6.2	5.9	2.2	0.4
15-24 Years.....	2.0	1.6	0.9	0.7	8.1	8.1	7.4	3.8	1.5
25-34 Years.....	6.4	6.0	3.1	1.5	9.5	10.4	8.6	4.8	2.9
35-44 Years.....	6.9	7.3	3.8	2.1	12.6	13.5	10.8	5.7	3.3
45-54 Years.....	6.3	6.9	3.9	2.7	17.1	19.4	14.4	6.9	3.2
55-64 Years.....	6.2	6.8	4.5	3.7	21.1	23.9	17.1	7.7	3.4
65 and Over.....	6.5	7.2	6.7	6.6	27.6	30.4	22.4	11.1	4.6

Males

Age Period	New England	Middle Atlantic	East North Central	West North Central	South Atlantic	East South Central	West South Central	Mountain	Pacific
10-14 Years.....	0.3	0.3	0.3	0.4	5.8	7.2	6.5	2.2	0.4
15-24 Years.....	1.7	1.4	0.9	0.9	9.9	10.1	8.3	3.7	1.6
25-34 Years.....	5.9	5.5	3.1	1.6	10.2	11.4	8.7	4.4	3.0
35-44 Years.....	7.0	7.2	4.2	2.3	12.4	13.4	10.2	5.1	3.4
45-54 Years.....	6.5	6.8	4.2	2.7	16.3	18.7	13.1	6.1	3.4

ILLITERACY AND AGE 45

Age									
55–64 Years	6.0	6.2	4.4	3.4	19.6	22.0	15.1	6.3	3.5
65 and Over	6.3	6.3	6.0	5.5	26.0	27.9	20.0	9.6	4.3
Females									
10–14 Years	0.2	0.2	0.2	0.3	4.0	5.1	5.4	2.2	0.4
15–24 Years	2.2	1.9	0.9	0.6	6.4	6.2	6.5	3.9	1.3
25–34 Years	6.8	6.4	3.0	1.3	8.8	9.4	8.4	5.3	2.7
35–44 Years	6.7	7.4	3.5	1.9	12.7	13.5	11.4	6.5	3.1
45–54 Years	6.0	7.0	3.6	2.7	17.9	20.2	16.0	8.1	3.0
55–64 Years	6.3	7.5	4.7	4.1	22.9	26.0	19.7	9.7	3.3
65 and Over	6.6	8.0	7.5	7.8	29.2	33.1	25.3	13.1	4.9

Fourteenth Census of the United States, vol. II, chap. XII, Table XII.

Of those native white of native parentage

born in 1855 or before,	6.2%	were illiterate in 1920
born in 1856-1865	4.9%	were illiterate in 1920
born in 1866-1875	3.7%	were illiterate in 1920
born in 1876-1885	2.6%	were illiterate in 1920
born in 1886-1895	1.9%	were illiterate in 1920
born in 1896-1905	1.6%	were illiterate in 1920
born in 1906-1910	1.1%	were illiterate in 1920

Thus were no further efforts made to reduce the illiteracy rate, and provided conditions remained the same, it may be assumed that the illiteracy rate for native whites of native parentage would approach 1 per cent, as those persons in the older age periods died.

Table X also presents interesting aspects when the illiteracy rate of one age group for one census year is compared

TABLE X

PERCENTAGE OF ILLITERACY IN THE UNITED STATES, BY AGE, FOR NATIVE WHITES OF NATIVE PARENTAGE, 1890 TO 1920[*5]

Age	1890	1900	1910	1920
10-14 Years	6.7	4.4	2.2	1.1
15-24 Years	5.7	4.3	2.6	1.6
25-34 Years	6.9	4.6	3.0	1.9
35-44 Years	8.1	6.4	3.8	2.6
45-54 Years	8.4	8.0	5.6	3.7
55-64 Years	10.2	8.0	6.7	4.9
65 Years and Over	12.7	10.7	7.6	6.2

*Data in the corresponding age groups are not available for 1870 and 1880.

with the next highest age group of the succeeding census. For example, in 1890, the age period 15-24 years had an illiteracy rate of 5.7 per cent. In 1900, the next age period,

[5]*Ibid.*, Tables III and XII; *Thirteenth Census*, vol. I, chap. XIII, Tables VI, VIII and XXVII; chap. IV, Table XVI.

25-34 years, composed of the survivors of the 15-24 year period, was only 4.6 per cent illiterate. Thus there was a decrease in rate of 1.1 per cent. In 1910 the 35-44 year period had an illiteracy rate of 3.8 per cent, a decrease of 0.8 per cent. In 1920 the survivors of the original group, now 45-54 years of age, were 3.7 per cent illiterate. Starting with other age periods in 1890, the same tendency to decrease is apparent. Is this due to schools for adults or to the fact that the necessities of adjustment to modern culture tend to result in the escape from illiteracy of a significantly high percentage in the course of a thirty or forty year period? The latter explanation appears more justifiable due to the late introduction of organized efforts to reduce the illiteracy rate in the various states. Thus starting with the indicated age period in 1890, each group became less illiterate with each succeeding census year.[6]

In conclusion, the statistics of illiteracy and age would seem to show that illiteracy is decreasing not only because of increased school facilities, but also as a result of the mortality of the aged. As has been shown, it is the aged groups who have the highest rates of illiteracy.

---

[6]The single apparent exception is the 10.2 per cent for the 55-64 year period in 1890 and the 10.7 per cent for 65 years and over in 1900. This latter rate is not comparable with the preceding rate due to the fact that it includes not only those 65-74 years of age but also those 75 years of age and over.

CHAPTER V

ILLITERACY AND URBAN AND RURAL ENVIRONMENT

The illiteracy rates differ so greatly between urban and rural communities that a separate discussion of the factors is entered into at this point. By "urban" and "rural," one may proceed only by the not always adequate census dichotomy. The United States Census Bureau classifies as urban "all incorporated places (and all towns in Massachusetts, Rhode Island, and New Hampshire) having 2,500 inhabitants or more."[1] The remainder of the country is treated as rural. Obviously this is merely a working basis as there is actually no clear line of demarcation. The statistical line has been drawn, however, after careful consideration by the Bureau of the Census, and is adequate for the needs of the present study.

An urban illiteracy rate of 4.4 per cent for the United States as a whole in 1920 is to be compared with a rural illiteracy rate of 7.7 per cent. The rural illiteracy rate of 7.7 per cent for 1920 compares favorably with the rural illiteracy rate of 10.1 per cent for 1910 as does the urban rate of 4.4 per cent with that of 5.1 per cent for the preceding census year. Illiteracy data according to urban and rural environment are not available for 1900 or preceding decades.

In an analysis of the available data according to the nine divisions, the same results are found. In each section the decrease in illiteracy is greater for rural than for urban

---

[1] *Fourteenth Census of the United States*, vol. II, chap. I, p. 20.

TABLE XI
ILLITERACY IN THE UNITED STATES, BY URBAN AND RURAL ENVIRONMENT, FOR 1910 AND 1920*[2]

Year	Urban		
	Total Population 10 Years of Age and Over	Number Illiterate	Per Cent Illiterate
1910	34,278,790	1,748,830	5.1
1920	43,978,576	1,955,112	4.4

Year	Rural		
	Total Population 10 Years of Age and Over	Number Illiterate	Per Cent Illiterate
1910	37,301,480	3,767,333	10.1
1920	38,760,739	2,976,793	7.7

*Earlier census reports do not give illiteracy according to urban and rural environment.

regions, comparing the 1920 with the 1910 results. There is an actual increase of 0.1 per cent of illiteracy in the urban rate for the Pacific division. Further analysis reveals that, of the three states in this division, the urban illiteracy rate of 2.4 per cent has remained the same for California from 1910 to 1920; for Oregon, the urban illiteracy rate has increased from 1.3 per cent in 1910 to 1.5 per cent in 1920; for Washington, the urban illiteracy rate has increased from 1.3 per cent in 1910 to 1.5 per cent in 1920. The apparent reversal of trend is traceable to the increase in the percentage of illiteracy of the foreign-born white in

---

[2]*Ibid.*, chap. XII, Table XXI.

TABLE XII

Illiteracy in the Divisions of the United States, by Urban and Rural Environment, for 1920 and 1910[a]

Division	1920			1910		
	Number 10 Years of Age and Over	Number Illiterate	Per Cent Illiterate	Number 10 Years of Age and Over	Number Illiterate	Per Cent Illiterate
New England						
Urban.......	4,713,138	245,299	5.2	4,064,027	227,841	5.6
Rural........	1,232,851	44,401	3.6	1,266,887	52,965	4.2
Middle Atlantic						
Urban.......	13,319,941	691,226	5.2	11,033,550	644,618	5.8
Rural........	4,346,413	174,156	4.0	4,412,965	229,194	5.2
East North Central						
Urban.......	10,543,528	351,628	3.3	7,831,590	277,444	3.5
Rural........	6,587,258	143,842	2.2	6,737,359	214,406	3.2
West North Central						
Urban.......	3,903,089	79,415	2.0	3,203,714	86,958	2.7
Rural........	5,986,651	113,806	1.9	5,893,597	176,180	3.0

ILLITERACY AND ENVIRONMENT

South Atlantic						
Urban	3,526,430	227,055	6.4	2,493,359	211,760	8.5
Rural	6,987,017	985,887	14.1	6,519,467	1,232,534	18.9
East South Central						
Urban	1,632,083	126,354	7.7	1,279,677	122,477	9.6
Rural	5,045,146	719,105	14.3	4,898,901	949,623	19.4
West South Central						
Urban	2,415,405	146,820	6.1	1,562,545	112,889	7.2
Rural	5,324,131	626,817	11.8	4,831,498	732,715	15.2
Mountain						
Urban	984,136	25,395	2.6	772,572	23,962	3.1
Rural	1,580,327	107,264	6.8	1,281,677	116,775	9.1
Pacific						
Urban	2,940,826	61,920	2.1	2,037,756	40,881	2.0
Rural	1,670,945	61,515	3.7	1,459,129	62,941	4.3

[3]*Ibid.*, Table XXI.

urban areas in all three Pacific division states.[4] The California urban illiteracy rate for foreign-born whites increased from 7.1 per cent in 1910 to 8.0 per cent in 1920; that for Oregon increased from 4.2 per cent in 1910 to 5.3 per cent in 1920; the rate for Washington increased from 4.0 per cent in 1910 to 4.5 per cent in 1920.

In the states of the New England, Middle Atlantic, East North Central, and West North Central Divisions (see Table XIII), the percentage of illiteracy in 1920 is higher for the urban than for the rural communities. In all four divisions this is traceable to the large proportion of illiterate foreign-born whites in the urban population.[5] Missouri, North Dakota, and South Dakota are the exceptions, all three having higher rural illiteracy rates due to the normally greater opportunity for education in urban communities. In Missouri and South Dakota, the higher foreign-born white urban illiteracy rates are more than offset by the small ratio of foreign-born whites to the population of these states.

Comparison of the urban and rural illiteracy rates for states in the remaining five divisions shows that all the states have larger rural illiteracy rates than urban illiteracy rates, with the exception of Oregon, where the difference is 1/10 of 1 per cent. The relatively larger foreign-born white illiteracy rate in urban than in rural areas for Oregon (5.3 per cent as compared with 5.0 per cent) is the important factor in this slight difference.

The results from the dichotomous division into urban and rural environment are further tested by a four-part division into (a) rural districts, (b) cities of from 2,500 to 25,000 inhabitants, (c) cities of from 25,000 to 100,000

---
[4]See *Thirteenth Census of the United States*, vol. I, chap. XIII, Table XXIII, and *Fourteenth Census of the United States*, vol. II, chap. XII, Table XXII.
[5]*Ibid.*

TABLE XIII
Percentage of Illiteracy in the United States, by States, by Urban and Rural Environment, 1920[6]

State	Urban	Rural	State	Urban	Rural
Maine................	3.5	3.1	Kentucky...........	5.1	9.8
New Hampshire.......	5.3	2.8	Tennessee...........	7.0	11.6
Vermont..............	3.9	2.6	Alabama............	10.4	17.8
Massachusetts........	4.8	3.0	Mississippi..........	11.3	18.2
Rhode Island.........	6.5	5.7			
Connecticut..........	6.6	5.3	Arkansas...........	4.9	10.3
			Louisiana...........	9.1	29.6
New York............	5.5	2.9	Oklahoma..........	1.9	4.5
New Jersey...........	5.3	4.6	Texas...............	6.5	9.3
Pennsylvania.........	4.6	4.6			
			Montana............	1.6	2.6
Ohio.................	3.2	2.2	Idaho...............	1.4	1.5
Indiana..............	2.6	1.8	Wyoming...........	2.1	2.1
Illinois...............	3.9	2.2	Colorado...........	2.3	4.2
Michigan.............	3.4	2.5	New Mexico........	7.1	17.6
Wisconsin............	2.6	2.3	Arizona.............	6.5	20.4
			Utah................	1.3	2.5
Minnesota...........	1.9	1.8	Nevada.............	1.8	7.0
Iowa.................	1.4	0.9			
Missouri.............	2.6	3.5	Washington.........	1.5	2.0
North Dakota........	1.5	2.2	Oregon.............	1.5	1.4
South Dakota........	1.1	1.8	California...........	2.4	5.4
Nebraska............	2.0	1.0			
Kansas...............	2.0	1.4			
Delaware.............	5.7	6.1			
Maryland............	4.4	7.4			
Virginia..............	7.1	13.0			
West Virginia........	3.2	7.6			
North Carolina.......	9.3	14.1			
South Carolina.......	10.3	20.0			
Georgia..............	9.5	17.5			
Florida...............	5.4	12.2			

[6]*Ibid.*, Table XXII.

TABLE XIV

PERCENTAGES OF ILLITERACY IN THE UNITED STATES, FOR NATIVE WHITES OF NATIVE PARENTAGE, BY STATES, FOR PRINCIPAL URBAN AND RURAL DIVISIONS, 1920[7]

State	Rural Districts	Places of			State	Rural Districts	Places of		
		2,500 to 25,000	25,000 to 100,000	100,000 and Over			2,500 to 25,000	25,000 to 100,000	100,000 and Over
Maine	1.6	0.5	0.4	.....	Kentucky	8.8	3.1	1.6	1.3
New Hampshire	0.6	0.7	0.2	.....	Tennessee	8.8	3.7	3.9	.....
Vermont	1.1	0.9	.....	.....	Alabama	7.7	3.3	0.6	0.7
Massachusetts	0.5	0.4	0.2	0.2	Mississippi	4.0	1.6	.....	.....
Rhode Island	2.2	0.5	0.5	0.2					
Connecticut	0.8	0.3	0.1	0.1	Arkansas	5.2	1.5	2.1	.....
					Louisiana	16.5	4.9	0.4	0.9
New York	1.0	0.6	0.5	0.2	Oklahoma	3.0	1.1	0.4	.....
New Jersey	1.5	0.6	0.2	0.3	Texas	2.7	1.4	0.7	0.8
Pennsylvania	1.3	0.6	0.5	0.3					
					Montana	0.4	0.2	.....	.....
Ohio	1.4	0.9	0.7	0.5	Idaho	0.3	0.3	0.2	.....
Indiana	1.6	1.2	1.3	0.8	Wyoming	0.4	0.3	.....	.....
Illinois	1.5	1.2	0.5	0.1	Colorado	2.5	1.3	0.9	0.3
Michigan	0.8	0.9	0.4	0.2	New Mexico	13.2	6.4	.....	.....

Wisconsin......	0.7	0.3	0.3	....	0.1	Arizona......	1.6	1.0	0.3	....
Minnesota.....	0.3	1.1	0.2	....	0.1	Utah.........	0.4	0.7	0.2	0.2
Iowa..........	0.5	0.7	0.4	....	0.4	Nevada.......	0.5	0.2	....	....
Missouri......	3.0	1.6	1.6	....	0.4	Washington...	0.4	0.4	0.2	0.1
North Dakota..	0.3	0.3	....	....	....	Oregon.......	0.4	0.6	....	0.2
South Dakota..	0.4	0.2	0.1	....	....	California...	0.7	0.4	0.2	0.2
Nebraska......	0.5	0.3	0.3	....	0.2					
Kansas........	0.6	0.6	0.3	....	0.9					
Delaware......	3.2	2.1	....	....	0.5					
Maryland......	3.3	1.9	1.7	....	0.6					
Virginia......	7.6	3.9	1.7	....	1.1					
West Virginia.	5.8	1.5	2.1	....	....					
North Carolina	9.2	4.5	2.9	....	....					
South Carolina	7.7	2.9	2.4	....	....					
Georgia.......	6.7	2.9	2.3	....	1.3					
Florida.......	4.3	0.5	0.8	....	....					

[7] *Ibid.*, computed from Tables XIV, XIX, XXII.

inhabitants, and (d) cities of 100,000 or more inhabitants. The data, when computed for all classes, are obscure, largely due to the incidence of colored and foreign-born. In order to eliminate these factors, the data are computed for native whites of native parentage. The general trend of a lower illiteracy rate as one goes from the rural to the quantitatively most urbanized communities is apparent (Table XIV).

Within the limits of the available data, however, it is evident that the difference between urban and rural rates is diminishing. For all classes the difference in 1910 was 5 per cent, in 1920 only 3.3 per cent. When race and nationality are eliminated by considering only native whites of native parentage, the difference between urban-rural rates of illiteracy in 1910 is found to be 4.5 per cent as compared with a difference of 3.0 per cent in 1920.[8]

Part II of the present study carries the investigation of the relation between illiteracy and urbanization further.[9]

---

[8]For native whites of native parentage, illiteracy rates in 1910 and 1920 were as follows:

	Urban	Rural
1910	0.9	5.4
1920	0.8	3.8

—*Fourteenth Census*, vol. II, chap. XII, Table XXI.

[9]Attention may be called here to page 40, above, which discusses the factor of age, in combination with sex and nationality, in a partial explanation of rural and urban illiteracy differences.

CHAPTER VI

ILLITERACY AND RACE AND NATIONALITY

There are important differences in the illiteracy rates for the various race and nationality[1] groups. It is the purpose of this chapter to analyze these differences and to show how they contribute to the illiteracy rates of the United States as a whole and of the various geographical divisions.

An analysis of the data presented in Table XV reveals the fact that taking each race and "nationality" (so far as the census differentiates) separately, all except three groups show a consistent downward trend from 1870 to 1920.

The illiteracy rate for the foreign-born whites is actually higher in 1920 than it was in 1880, the year when information on this group was first available. The trend is practically horizontal. In 1880 illiteracy rates were still high in all European countries while the progressive increase in the percentage of immigration from southern and eastern Europe, which lags behind western and northern Europe in educational opportunity, has seemed to keep the rate of illiteracy among the foreign-born practically the same throughout the period studied. Furthermore, the foreign-born are chiefly adults and do not readily learn to write after their arrival in America.[2]

The Chinese and Japanese illiteracy trends are downward over a span of three census years, but show increases

---
[1]The utilization of the terms "race" and "nationality" in this chapter necessarily follows the U. S. Bureau of the Census classifications.
[2]W. Talbot; *Adult Illiteracy*, p. 21.

TABLE XV

Percentage of Illiteracy in the United States, According to Race and Nationality, 1870 to 1920[3]

Year	White	Colored*	Negro	Native White	Native White of Native Parentage	Native White of For. or Mixed Parentage
1920	4.0	23.0	22.9	2.0	2.5	0.8
1910	5.0	30.5	30.4	5.0	3.7	1.1
1900	6.2	44.5	44.5	6.2	5.7	1.6
1890	7.7	56.8	57.1	7.7	7.5	2.2
1880	9.4	70.0		8.7		
1870	11.5	79.9	81.4			

Year	Native White of Foreign Parentage	Native White of Mixed Parentage	Foreign Born White	Indian	Chinese	Japanese	All Others**
1920	0.9	0.7	13.1	34.9	20.0	11.0	13.0
1910	1.2	0.9	12.7	45.3	15.8	9.2	39.9
1900			12.9	56.2	29.0	18.2	
1890			13.1				
1880			12.0				
1870							

*Persons of Negro descent, Indians, Chinese, Japanese, and "all others."
**"All Others" includes Hindus, Filipinos, Koreans, Maoris.
[3] *Fourteenth Census*, vol. II, chap. XII, Tables I and IV; *Thirteenth Census*, vol. I, chap. XIII, Table IV.

in 1920, as compared with 1910. The chances of error in collecting data are so great that no satisfactory explanation can be made. For example, in 1890, "it would appear that some assistant marshals committed the fault of returning as illiterate the Chinese who could not write English while they could read and write their own language."[4] Undoubtedly the data for 1920 are the most satisfactory.

The highest illiteracy rate, from 1900 to 1920, is recorded by the Indian group. The pre-literate culture of the Indians is still influencing the Indians' reactions to American culture. The older ones, who in their youth were not required to attend government schools, have very high rates. Furthermore, the great body of Indians is in the rural areas. The rate is rapidly decreasing, however, as the influence of the schools increases.

The Negro group has the next highest illiteracy rate. This is due partially to the fact that the Negro is still largely rural—66% living in rural areas in 1920—and partially to the fact that he lives largely in the southeastern section of the United States—where institutional education is not as important a part of the cultural complex as in other sections of the country. Two other factors, the attitude toward Negro education in parts of the South, and the very high rate of illiteracy among aged Negroes,[5] are traceable to the social situation arising from slavery and reconstruction days in the South. The rate of illiteracy has decreased practically 50 per cent from 1900 to 1920, and with greatly increased provisions for Negro education throughout the United States, there should be a further important decrease in the coming decades.

---

[4]*Ninth Census*, vol. I; footnote to Table IX.

[5]Forty-nine and four tenths per cent of the Negroes 55 to 64 years were illiterate in 1920; sixty-eight and three tenths per cent of the Negroes 65 years and over were illiterate at that time.

The numerically smallest group—Hindus, Filipinos, Koreans, and Maoris, grouped by the census under the classification "All Others"—has sharply decreased its illiteracy rate. This is due chiefly to the low illiteracy rate among the immigrants from 1910 to 1920.[6]

The Chinese, Japanese, and foreign-born whites have been discussed above.

Turning to those native whites who are the children of either foreign or mixed parentage, there is noted, in addition to the steady decrease in the illiteracy rate, the interesting fact that the illiteracy rate for this group is actually much lower than that of the native whites of native parentage. Analysis of the data bearing on this subject, however, brings out the fact that only 42.0 per cent of the native whites of native parentage resided in urban communities in 1920, whereas 69.2 per cent of native-born whites of foreign or mixed parentage lived in urban areas in the census year.[7] In addition, the white population of the southeastern section of the United States is overwhelmingly native white of native parentage.[8] This section of the United States, as has already been pointed out, is the section in which institutionalized education is least developed. Hence the heavy proportion of native whites of native parentage in this section penalizes this group as a whole. On the other hand, there is a small proportion of native whites of foreign or mixed parentage in this section

---

[6]Compare 1910 Census, vol. I, chap. XIII, Tables I and II, with 1920 Census, vol. II, chap. XII, Table I.

[7]*Fourteenth Census*, vol. II, chap. I, Table XX.

[8]Ninety-one per cent of the white population of the South Atlantic Division is native born of native parentage, as compared with three and seven tenths per cent for native whites of foreign or mixed parentage. Ninety-five and seven tenths per cent of the white population of the East South Central Division is native born of native parentage, as compared with one and eight tenths per cent for native born whites of foreign or mixed parentage. *Ibid.*, Table VII.

so that the general illiteracy rate for this group is but slightly affected. As a check on this reasoning, one finds, when the rural populations for the two groups are held constant, the difference is brought down to 32/100 of 1 per cent, which is the percentage by which the illiteracy rate of urban native white of native parentage exceeds the rate for native white of foreign or mixed parentage for the country as a whole.[9] Thus the difference between the two groups resolves itself largely into a function of educational opportunity. The slight difference in favor of native whites of mixed parentage as compared with native whites of foreign parentage may reasonably be ascribed to the probable better opportunity afforded the child of parents, one of whom is native born.

Table XVI is presented in further analysis of the differential illiteracy rates for the various race and "nationality" groups. The comparison of divisions for the native whites of native parentage reflects in large measure the educational opportunity afforded by the various sections. The high illiteracy rate for foreign-born whites, and for native born whites of foreign and mixed parentage in the West South Central Division, is traceable to the large numbers of illiterate Mexicans inhabiting this division, particularly the state of Texas.

The Negro group, forming approximately one-tenth of the population and biologically less easily assimilated than the white foreign-born, is important. In three divisions, the Middle Atlantic, the Mountain, and the Pacific, the Negro rate of illiteracy is less than the rate of illiteracy for native whites of native parentage in the South Atlantic and East South Central Divisions, showing the compara-

---

[9]The urban illiteracy rate for native whites of native parentage is 0.81 per cent; for native whites of foreign or mixed parentage it is 0.49 per cent. Computed from data furnished in *Fourteenth Census*, vol. II, chap. XII, Table XXII.

TABLE XVI

Percentage of Illiteracy in the Divisions of the United States, According to Race and Nationality, 1920[10]

Division	All Classes	Native White of Native Parentage	Native White of Foreign Parentage	Native White of Mixed Parentage	Foreign Born White
United States	6.0	2.5	0.9	0.7	13.1
New England	4.9	0.6	0.8	0.7	14.0
Middle Atlantic	4.9	0.7	0.5	0.4	15.7
East North Central	2.9	1.0	0.7	0.5	10.8
West North Central	2.0	1.1	0.6	0.4	6.4
South Atlantic	11.5	5.4	0.9	1.0	12.8
East South Central	12.7	6.6	1.2	1.8	9.1
West South Central	10.0	3.9	8.2	4.2	29.9
Mountain	5.2	2.4	1.2	0.7	12.7
Pacific	2.7	0.4	0.5	0.3	8.6

Division	Negro	Indian	Chinese	Japanese	All Others
United States	22.9	34.9	20.0	11.0	13.0
New England	7.1	12.9	22.3	5.0	2.0
Middle Atlantic	5.0	15.5	23.0	4.2	6.2
East North Central	7.3	20.7	20.0	3.4	4.6

West North Central..........	10.5	24.0	19.2	11.1	3.4
South Atlantic..............	25.2	35.3	18.8	2.5	2.9
East South Central..........	27.9	57.7	18.0	......	10.7
West South Central.........	25.3	18.6	25.9	6.6	26.3
Mountain...................	5.3	58.1	21.1	16.9	12.9
Pacific.....................	4.6	32.1	18.7	10.8	15.4

[10]*Ibid.*, Tables XI, and XII.

TABLE XVII

PERCENTAGE OF ILLITERACY IN THE UNITED STATES, ACCORDING TO RACE AND NATIONALITY, BY SEX, 1870 TO 1920[11]

Year	White		Colored*		Negro		Foreign Born White		Native White		Native White of Native Parentage	
	Male	Female	Male	Female	Male	Female	Male	Female	Male	Female	Male	Female
1920	4.1	4.0	23.4	22.5	23.5	22.3	11.7	14.8	2.2	1.8	2.7	2.3
1910	5.0	4.9	29.8	31.2	30.1	30.7	11.8	13.9	3.1	2.9	3.8	3.7
1900	6.0	6.6	42.8	46.2	43.1	45.8	11.3	14.7	4.6	4.7	5.6	5.9
1890	7.0	8.3	53.7	59.9	54.4	59.8	11.3	15.2	5.8	6.6	6.9	8.0
1880	8.6	10.2	67.3	72.7	....	....	....	....	....	....	....	....
1870	10.0	13.1	78.1	81.7	80.6	82.0	....	....	....	....	....	....

Year	Native White of Foreign or Mixed Parentage		Native White of Foreign Parentage		Native White of Mixed Parentage		Indian		Chinese		Japanese		All Others**	
	Male	Female	Male	Female	Male	Female	Male	Female	Male	Female	Male	Female	Male	Female
1920	0.8	0.7	0.9	0.8	0.8	0.6	32.8	37.2	19.7	23.1	8.7	16.2	13.0	12.5
1910	1.2	1.1	1.2	1.2	1.0	0.8	41.5	49.2	15.0	30.2	8.6	14.1	39.9	....

1900	1.7	1.6	
1890	2.3	2.2	
1880			
1870			

*Persons of Negro descent, Indians, Chinese, Japanese, and "all others."
**"All Other" includes Hindus, Filipinos, Koreans, Maoris.
[11] *Fourteenth Census*, vol. II, chap. XII, Tables I and II; *Thirteenth Census*, vol. I, chap. XIII, Table XIII.

tive educational progress of a formerly and still highly illiterate group, when considered as a whole.

In comparing the sexes of each race and "nationality" group, one observes that the sexes are about equal in illiteracy rates for the various native white groups and for the Negro group. In each case the difference in 1920 is one in favor of the female. For the three Mongoloid groups, the Indian, the Chinese and the Japanese, there is a much higher illiteracy rate for females. For the Chinese and Japanese, the selectivity of the male group must be taken into consideration, while in the case of the Indians this is another reflection of the culture. The foreign-born whites also show a higher illiteracy rate for females. This is ascribable, it is believed, to the selectivity of the male group, on the members of which is put the brunt of establishing a footing in the United States. It is also true, as has been previously pointed out, that education for women has lagged behind that for men in most European countries.

A comparison of the data for urban and rural environment (Table XVIII) reinforces the proof of more desirable educational opportunities in the urban communities. It is noteworthy that the foreign-born white group is the only one in which the difference in illiteracy rates between urban and rural areas is slight. This is traceable to the fact that the great majority of foreign-born whites emigrate after the age when they should have learned to write, and that, of those who were not literate (in the census definition) before emigrating, few have since learned.

It is also worthy of note that the difference between the urban and rural illiteracy rates in 1920 is less than the difference between the rates for these two divisions in 1910 for every race and "nationality" group presented.

TABLE XVIII

Percentage of Illiteracy in the United States, According to Race and Nationality, In Urban and Rural Environments, for 1910 and 1920[12]

Urban and Rural	All Classes	Native White of Native Parentage	Native White of Foreign Parentage	Native White of Mixed Parentage	Foreign Born White	Negro
1920						
Urban	4.4	0.8	0.5	0.4	13.0	13.4
Rural	7.7	3.8	1.6	1.1	13.3	28.5
1910			Native White of Foreign or Mixed Parentage			
Urban	5.1	0.9	0.7		12.5	17.6
Rural	10.1	5.4	1.9		13.3	36.0

[12] *Fourteenth Census*, vol. II, chap. XII, Table XXII.

CHAPTER VII

ILLITERACY AND SCHOOL SYSTEMS

It has long been recognized that a high relationship exists between illiteracy and educational facilities, on the basis of empirical observation. One would expect this relationship, not only for present day illiteracy and present day school systems but also for present day illiteracy and school systems of ten, twenty, and even fifty or sixty years ago. Illiteracy tends to lag an entire generation behind school systems so that illiteracy rates of 1920 are largely the evidence of poor school facilities in the past.

No single item in regard to school systems may be regarded as a completely adequate basis of comparison. Hence Leonard P. Ayres's *An Index Number for State School Systems* has been utilized. In his index Ayres combines the following ten factors:

1. Per cent of school population attending school daily.
2. Average days attended by each child of school age.
3. Average number of days schools were kept open.
4. Per cent that high school attendance was of total attendance.
5. Per cent that boys were of girls in high schools.
6. Average annual expenditure per child attending.
7. Average annual expenditure per child of school age.
8. Average annual expenditure per teacher employed.
9. Expenditure per pupil for purposes other than teachers' salaries.
10. Expenditure per teacher for salaries.

The index number is the average of the 10 figures corresponding to these 10 headings, after certain of them

ILLITERACY AND SCHOOL SYSTEMS 69

have been so multiplied or divided by constants as to bring each into comparability with a standard of 100.[1]

The years for which an index number is computed are 1890, 1900, 1910, and 1918. Thus a person ten years of age in 1890 would be included in the 35-44 year period by 1920.

Since influxes of immigrants or Negroes might produce a considerable change in the population of a given area during this thirty-eight year period, and since the school indices are a constant factor for any group, illiteracy in 1920 for native whites of native parentage alone was correlated with the indices of the various periods. The following correlations[2] were secured:

$$r = -.75, \text{ for } 1890$$
$$r = -.74, \text{ for } 1900$$
$$r = -.75, \text{ for } 1910$$
$$r = -.72, \text{ for } 1918$$

The four coefficients of correlation are not only quite high but they show only slight variations, the one for 1918 being slightly lower than the others. What has actually happened is that school systems have tended to develop in a relatively consistent manner so that the relationship with illiteracy for 1920 has remained about the same while the indices have risen over the period involved. The scatter of the indices has shown some variation, however, the greatest diversity being noted in 1918.

$$S_y = 5.1, \text{ for } 1890$$
$$S_y = 2.7, \text{ for } 1900$$
$$S_y = 2.2, \text{ for } 1910$$
$$S_y = 8.5, \text{ for } 1918$$

[1] *An Index Number for State School Systems*, pp. 14, 15.

[2] The corresponding errors of the coefficients of correlation (see Appendix A) are .06 for 1890, .07 for 1900, .06 for 1910, and .07 for 1918.

TABLE XIX

Percentage of Illiteracy for Native White of Native Parentage in 1920 and Index Numbers for School Systems for 1890, 1900, 1910, 1918, by States[3]

State	Per Cent Illiterate 1920	1890	1900	1910	1918	State	Per Cent Illiterate 1920	1890	1900	1910	1918
North Dakota	0.26	25.48	34.83	42.48	59.17	Vermont	1.05	30.22	35.44	42.11	51.51
Washington	0.29	30.80	37.14	61.21	63.67	Illinois	1.06	31.87	37.18	49.86	56.75
Massachusetts	0.30	45.86	49.52	56.32	61.04	Maine	1.27	29.88	33.70	39.68	47.36
Idaho	0.31*	22.81	29.25	44.57	58.57	Arizona	1.28	32.75	30.17	45.54	66.19
South Dakota	0.31	26.06	33.99	42.57	55.03	Indiana	1.36	29.82	36.33	45.95	58.80
Utah	0.34	28.64	37.51	50.92	61.39	Colorado	1.66	37.83	41.59	49.23	59.23
Montana	0.34	36.34	39.51	53.50	75.79	Maryland	1.99	33.30	35.49	38.47	43.22
Wyoming	0.35	36.27	31.91	42.59	56.71	Delaware	2.05	29.30	30.10	38.09	42.48
Minnesota	0.36	29.45	35.41	44.51	58.43	Texas	2.17	23.23	24.43	32.34	41.12
California	0.39	43.75	43.80	60.44	71.21	Missouri	2.20	21.88	20.89	26.39	30.04
Oregon	0.39	27.91	32.04	47.81	57.81	Oklahoma	2.38	.....	23.27	35.97	44.44
Nebraska	0.40	26.43	36.11	43.99	57.14	Florida	3.13	28.52	22.45	29.69	37.77
Connecticut	0.41	38.90	43.13	49.31	59.77	Mississippi	3.59	21.88	20.89	26.39	30.04
Nevada	0.42	34.47	42.37	56.01	59.05	Arkansas	4.57	20.07	20.99	26.70	30.28
Wisconsin	0.47	30.99	34.31	43.23	51.34	West Virginia	4.83	21.82	27.07	32.87	37.73
Rhode Island	0.51	39.27	43.05	50.84	56.33	Georgia	5.48	15.73	21.54	29.12	32.60
Iowa	0.52	30.96	34.49	41.45	61.85	Virginia	6.05	22.25	21.69	29.70	35.26

New Hampshire	0.55	30.95	33.82	42.47	54.37	Alabama	6.42	18.16	19.50	26.93	30.58
New York	0.56	40.92	46.57	51.87	59.35	South Carolina	6.63	12.46	20.75	24.87	29.39
Kansas	0.59	30.64	31.54	43.06	55.16	Kentucky	7.33	23.39	25.23	30.44	34.98
Michigan	0.61	31.86	35.60	45.19	60.43	Tennessee	7.40	21.01	22.33	29.49	35.14
New Jersey	0.72	37.49	40.26	54.47	65.93	North Carolina	8.21	17.80	17.51	25.71	30.59
Pennsylvania	0.82	34.70	36.97	47.25	57.65	Louisiana	11.39	18.40	21.55	30.94	33.86
Ohio	0.99	33.09	37.34	48.64	59.72	New Mexico	11.88	10.02	24.86	31.05	53.01

*In cases of apparent tie, the percentages were carried out to three or four places.

ᵃ*Fourteenth Census*, vol. II, chap. XII, Table XII; Ayres, *An Index Number for State School Systems*, pp. 31, 33, 35, and 37.

In conclusion, it may be stated that the general statement of the relation between illiteracy and school systems has been taken out of the realm of general statements and by statistical methods been reduced to the significant coefficient of correlation, $r = -.7$. In other words, high illiteracy rates are found in those states whose school systems have been below the average in the past and which continue to rank comparatively low at present.

CHAPTER VIII

ADJUSTED ILLITERACY RATES

The statistical tool, known as the method of standard population, is applicable to practically all sociological data which may be studied on the basis of age classifications. Since it makes it possible to hold the age distribution constant (i.e., the percentage of a given population that falls within a definite age period), the method of standard population permits a more accurate presentation of data than is usually given. The present chapter is devoted to presenting the applicability of the method as it applies to illiteracy data and to pointing out the changes in the alignment of states that result. Native whites of native parentage are studied in order that the race and "nationality" factor may be held constant.

Table XX presents the percentages of illiteracy for this group according to the actual census data. The percentages were carried to the hundredth place for the sake of accuracy in dealing with the extremely low rates of illiteracy in certain states. The percentage age distribution of the entire native white population of native parentage, ten years of age and over, for the United States as a whole was taken as the standard. The total populations for the various states were then distributed on this basis. The numbers falling within the specific age periods for each state were multiplied by the illiteracy rates according to the actual distribution and the percentage of illiteracy for the states was then computed.[1]

---

[1]Delaware offers a good example of the method. Her population in 1920 contained a much higher percentage of old people than did the population for the

In some states it is evident that the population distribution is practically average as the illiteracy rates show slight change after the population distribution is adjusted. In Connecticut and Nebraska the rates remained the same to the hundredth place. In at least half of the states the adjusted distribution makes a relatively significant change in the percentage of illiteracy. Some of these changes increase the rates, others decrease the rates. A change of one-tenth of 1 per cent may well be regarded as significant where the rates of illiteracy are extremely low as such a change may actually make a 20 or 25 per cent difference in the given rate.

Table XXI ranks the states according to the census figures of 1920 for illiteracy among native whites of native par-

United States as a whole which tended to raise her illiteracy rate. All figures are for native whites of native parentage.

Age Period	Percentage Distribution of U.S. Population 1920	Population Distribution for Delaware 1920	Adjusted Distribution for Delaware	Per Cent Illiterate 1920	Adjusted Number of Illiterates
(1)	(2)	(3)	(4)	(5)	(6)
10–14 Years	14.68	13,094	16,373	0.2	33
15–24 Years	24.50	24,581	27,326	0.6	164
25–34 Years	20.14	21,952	22,463	1.0	225
35–44 Years	15.72	18,228	17,533	1.8	316
45–54 Years	11.34	14,450	12,648	3.2	405
55–64 Years	7.39	10,566	8,242	4.6	379
65 Years and Over	6.23	8,664	6,949	7.0	486
		111,535	111,535		2,008

2,008 is to be compared with the actual number of illiterates in Delaware in 1920—2,290. The corresponding percentages of illiteracy are 2.05 and 1.80 (adjusted).

TABLE XX

PERCENTAGE OF ILLITERACY AMONG NATIVE WHITES OF NATIVE PARENTAGE ACCORDING TO CENSUS DATA AND ACCORDING TO THE RESULTS OF THE METHOD OF STANDARD POPULATION, FOR 1920[2]

State	Percentage of Illiteracy (Actual Data)	Percentage of Illiteracy (Adjusted Data)	State	Percentage of Illiteracy (Actual Data)	Percentage of Illiteracy (Adjusted Data)
Maine	1.27	1.25	West Virginia	4.83	5.02
New Hampshire	0.55	0.51	North Carolina	8.21	8.57
Vermont	1.05	0.95	South Carolina	6.63	7.00
Massachusetts	0.30	0.30	Georgia	5.48	5.76
Rhode Island	0.50	0.46	Florida	3.13	3.12
Connecticut	0.41	0.41			
			Kentucky	7.33	7.47
New York	0.56	0.54	Tennessee	7.40	7.53
New Jersey	0.72	0.56	Alabama	6.42	6.83
Pennsylvania	0.82	0.79	Mississippi	3.59	3.73
Ohio	0.99	0.94	Arkansas	4.57	4.81
Indiana	1.36	1.24	Louisiana	11.39	12.12
Illinois	1.06	1.08	Oklahoma	2.38	2.58
Michigan	0.61	0.61	Texas	2.17	2.29
Wisconsin	0.47	0.56			
			Montana	0.34	0.38
Minnesota	0.36	0.40	Idaho	0.31	0.35
Iowa	0.52	0.41	Wyoming	0.35	0.40
Missouri	2.20	2.18	Colorado	1.66	1.67
North Dakota	0.26	0.30	New Mexico	11.88	12.49
South Dakota	0.31	0.34	Arizona	1.28	1.35
Nebraska	0.40	0.40	Utah	0.34	0.44
Kansas	0.59	0.58	Nevada	0.42	0.44
Delaware	2.05	1.80	Washington	0.29	0.30
Maryland	1.99	1.94	Oregon	0.39	0.40
Virginia	6.05	6.09	California	0.39	0.37

[2] *Fourteenth Census*, vol. II, chap. XII, computed from data given in Table XII.

TABLE XXI

Rank of States According to Percentage of Illiteracy among Native Whites of Native Parentage, According to Census Data, and According to the Results of the Method of Standard Population, for 1920

Rank of States According to Census Data*		Rank of States According to Adjusted Data	Rank of States According to Census Data*		Rank of States According to Adjusted Data
State	Rank		State	Rank	
North Dakota	1	1	Vermont	25	25
Washington	2	3	Illinois	26	26
Massachusetts	3	2	Maine	27	28
Idaho	4	5	Arizona	28	29
South Dakota	5	4	Indiana	29	27
Utah	6	14	Colorado	30	30
Montana	7	7	Maryland	31	32
Wyoming	8	8	Delaware	32	31
Minnesota	9	11	Texas	33	34
California	10	6	Missouri	34	33
Oregon	11	9	Oklahoma	35	35
Nebraska	12	10	Florida	36	36
Connecticut	13	12	Mississippi	37	37
Nevada	14	15	Arkansas	38	38
Wisconsin	15	19	West Virginia	39	39
Rhode Island	16	16	Georgia	40	40
Iowa	17	13	Virginia	41	41
New Hampshire	18	17	Alabama	42	42
New York	19	18	South Carolina	43	43
Kansas	20	20	Kentucky	44	44
Michigan	21	21	Tennessee	45	45
New Jersey	22	22	North Carolina	46	46
Pennsylvania	23	23	Louisiana	47	47
Ohio	24	24	New Mexico	48	48

*In cases of apparent tie, the percentages on which the rankings are based were carried out to three or four places.

entage. North Dakota with a rate of only 0.26 ranks first while New Mexico with a rate of 11.88 is forty-eighth.[3] When the ranking according to the adjusted data is given, various changes are noted. North Dakota retains first place while Washington drops from second to third place and Massachusetts rises to second place. Utah drops from sixth to fourteenth place; Oregon rises from eleventh to ninth, Nebraska from twelfth to tenth; Wisconsin changes from fifteenth to nineteenth; Iowa rises from seventeenth in rank to thirteenth. Most of the succeeding states retain their former ranking, even though there are significant increases and decreases in the actual percentages of illiteracy. It is believed that the computed percentages are a more accurate index of the actual illiteracy rates for the native whites of native parentage of the various states than any which have hitherto been presented.

---

[3]The data according to which the ranking was made are presented in the preceding table.

CHAPTER IX

CONCLUSIONS TO PART I

The object of Part I has been an investigation of the general problem of illiteracy as it exists in the United States at the present time, together with the trend of illiteracy for the past fifty years. As a result of the investigation of the data certain conclusions present themselves. The preceding chapters contain analyses of the general results summarized below:

1. The trend of illiteracy in the United States has been steadily downward, decreasing from an illiteracy rate of 20.0 per cent in 1870 to a rate of 6.0 per cent in 1920.

2. The trend of illiteracy has been steadily downward in the nine geographical divisions of the United States from 1870 to 1920. The ranking of the divisions in 1920 was as follows:

Division	Percentage of Illiterates in 1920
West North Central	2.0
Pacific	2.7
East North Central	2.9
New England	4.87
Middle Atlantic	4.90
Mountain	5.2
West South Central	10.0
South Atlantic	11.5
East South Central	12.7

3. The trends of illiteracy in the various states from 1870 to 1920 are to be largely explained in terms of age distri-

bution, sex distribution, race and "nationality" groupings, percentage of urbanization, and school facilities.

4. Although the male illiteracy rate was lower than the rate for females from 1870 to 1910, in 1920 the female illiteracy rate for the United States was 5.9 per cent as compared with a male illiteracy rate of 6.0 per cent.

5. Thirty-four of the forty-eight states had a higher percentage of male illiteracy than of female illiteracy in 1920.

6. The percentage of illiteracy is greater for females than for males in urban environments, while the reverse is true in rural environments.

7. The apparent difference in illiteracy rates by sex largely resolves itself into the sex distribution according to urban and rural environments, age distributions, race and nationality distributions, and lastly the institutionalized educational facilities for the sexes both in the United States and in Europe. When these factors are adequately taken into consideration, sex differences in regard to illiteracy practically disappear.

8. As would be expected, there is a diminishing percentage of illiteracy as one proceeds from the older age groups to the younger.

9. If no further efforts were made to reduce the illiteracy rate and provided conditions remained the same, it may be assumed that the illiteracy rate for native whites of native parentage would approach 1 per cent as those persons in the older age periods die.

10. The slightly smaller percentage of illiteracy among females in 1920 is largely a function of the removal of larger percentages of illiterate older females than of illiterate older males from the population.

11. The urban illiteracy rate for the United States in 1920 was 4.4 per cent as compared with a rural illiteracy rate of 7.7 per cent.

12. In those states in which the urban illiteracy rate was higher than the rural illiteracy rate, there was a large proportion of illiterate foreign-born whites in the urban population as a dominant factor.

13. When the four-part division of (a) rural districts, (b) cities of from 2,500 to 25,000 inhabitants, (c) cities of from 25,000 to 100,000 inhabitants, and (d) cities of 100,000 or more inhabitants is utilized and when the factors of race and nationality are eliminated, the general trend of a lower illiteracy rate as one goes from the rural to the quantitatively most urbanized communities is apparent.

14. Within the limits of the available data, it is evident that the difference between urban and rural illiteracy rates is diminishing.

15. The illiteracy rate for the foreign-born whites was higher in 1920 than it was in 1880, the year when information on this group was first available.

16. In 1920 the Indians had the highest rate of illiteracy of any recorded race or "nationality" group in the United States (34.9 per cent) while the Negro group ranked second with a rate of 22.9 per cent.

17. The illiteracy rate of 1920 for native whites of foreign or mixed parentage was lower than the illiteracy rate of native whites of native parentage. (0.8 per cent as compared with 2.5 per cent).

18. In the Middle Atlantic, the Mountain, and the Pacific Divisions, the Negro rate of illiteracy in 1920 was lower than the rate for native whites of native parentage in the South Atlantic and East South Central Divisions.

19. The foreign-born white group is the only one of the race and "nationality" groups in which the difference in illiteracy rates between urban and rural areas is slight.

20. The coefficient of correlation for illiteracy and school systems is at least, $r = -.7$ for each of the years studied.

21. The method of standard population has been utilized in securing illiteracy rates for native whites of native parentage in such a way that actual conditions are more adequately presented than the unrefined data make possible.

PART II

ILLITERACY IN RELATION TO CERTAIN SOCIAL PHENOMENA

CHAPTER X

THE RELATION OF ILLITERACY TO BIRTH-RATE

The chief importance of the study of illiteracy as a societal phenomenon is its relation to other societal phenomena. It is the object of this and the succeeding chapters to utilize statistical and analytic techniques in the analysis of the relation of illiteracy to certain selected social factors. The methodology employed utilizes simple, partial, and multiple correlation in the endeavor to measure mathematically these several relationships. Regression equations are also presented as a basis of prediction. The use of statistical technique, properly guarded, places in the hands of the sociologist an instrument which enables him to approximate the manipulative methods of the more exact sciences. The first relationship to be considered will be that existing between illiteracy and the birth-rate.

Births are the basis and the necessary prerequisite of a continuing population. Any factor which, when varied, affects variances in the birth-rate is of importance. Illiteracy as a societal phenomenon—as has been pointed out above—achieves importance as it affects other phenomena. The object of the present chapter is the measurement and the analysis of the relation of illiteracy to the tremendously important factor of birth-rate.

The data utilized and the procedure involved follow. The rate of illiteracy per 1,000 women, of all classes, fifteen to forty-four years of age, and the number of legitimate births per 1,000 married women within the same age limits were first computed. The data on births were utilized for twenty-one of the twenty-three states included in the birth registration area of the United States in 1920. Utah was omitted because the high birth-rate was so clearly a departure from the normal due to the influence of Mormon culture. Maine was necessarily omitted due to the fact that births were not recorded in accordance with the age distribution of the mothers, and it was necessary to hold the important factor of age constant. In so far as possible only legitimate births were included though cases of unknown legitimacy were tabulated by the census as legitimate, while in California, Massachusetts, New Hampshire, and Vermont the birth certificates did not call for this information though it was sometimes given. The error, however, is slight, due to the facts that illegitimacy forms a small percentage of births, and that part of these illegitimate births are returned as such.

The validity of the results obtained from computations based upon twenty-one states might perhaps be questioned. Each item, however, is not a single datum in itself but is an average obtained from hundreds or even thousands of individual cases. Thus the statistical universe is much larger than a cursory survey of the data would reveal. However, these twenty-one states may not be regarded as wholly representative of the United States as the registration area does not include a proportionately equal number of states from the various sections. The character of the results obtained would seem to justify the utilization of such data for 1920 as are available. In general, these data appear reliable.

In an analytic study of the relation of illiteracy to birth-rate, certain important factors should also be included. That a definite relation exists between birth-rate and percentage of urbanization and between birth-rate and income has long been known. Hence these two factors were included in the more refined computations and the character of the results, it is believed, justifies their inclusion. The data utilized for the four variables are presented in Table XXII.

The notation employed in the correlations is as follows: X_a is the illiteracy rate for women of all classes, 15-44 years of age. X_c is the number of legitimate births per 1,000 married women of all classes, 15-44 years of age. X_d is the per cent of urbanization for the total population. X_e is the per capita current income, averaged for 1919, 1920, and 1921. Current income rather than total income is utilized, not only because the current income figures are more reliable[1] but also because it would appear to be more satisfactory for the purposes of this study.

Turning to the data, the linearity of the relation of illiteracy to birth-rate was first determined.

The coefficient of correlation[2] secured for illiteracy and birth-rate when data for all classes were utilized was,

$$r_{ac} = +.61$$

In order to refine the data by holding race and "nationality" constant, the data for native-born white women[3] were next computed. The relationship again being linear, the coefficient of correlation was found to be

$$r = +.75$$

This higher coefficient emphasizes the significant relationship which exists between illiteracy and high birth-

---
[1]Maurice Leven, *Income in the Various States*, chap. I.
[2]The errors for all coefficients of correlation are not included in the text to avoid possible confusion but are included in Appendix A, where the method of computation is also presented.
[3]See Appendix B.

TABLE XXII
Data Utilized in the Correlation of Illiteracy and Birth-rate, All Classes[4]

State	Illiteracy Rate Per 1,000 Females 15-44	Legitimate Births Per 1,000 Married Females 15-44	Percentage of Urbanization	Per Capita Current Income
	X_a	X_c	X_d	X_e
California.........	30.9	132.8	68.0	$ 909
Connecticut........	72.3	176.2	67.8	724
Indiana............	12.6	149.9	50.6	540
Kansas............	10.8	154.6	34.9	546
Kentucky..........	50.4	179.1	26.2	372
Maryland..........	38.6	167.3	60.0	670
Massachusetts......	51.2	177.7	94.8	835
Michigan..........	26.3	168.9	61.1	659
Minnesota.........	11.4	181.1	44.1	530
Nebraska..........	9.8	166.1	31.3	516
New Hampshire.....	42.9	174.6	63.1	612
New York..........	53.3	157.2	82.7	943
North Carolina......	96.6	224.8	19.2	329
Ohio...............	23.3	143.6	63.8	650
Oregon............	9.4	126.3	49.9	685
Pennsylvania.......	45.5	178.7	64.3	687
South Carolina.....	166.3	185.8	17.5	312
Vermont...........	17.5	161.3	31.2	544
Virginia...........	74.0	196.7	29.2	389
Washington........	13.2	131.8	55.2	710
Wisconsin..........	15.5	167.8	47.3	562

[4]Sources: X_a—*Fourteenth Census*, vol. II, chap. XII, computed from Table XII; X_c—Computed from Birth Statistics for 1920, Table V, and *Fourteenth Census*, vol. II, chap. IV., Table XI; X_d—*Fourteenth Census*, vol. II, chap. I, Table XX; X_e—Maurice Leven; *Income in the Various States*, p. 267.

rates, that is, that illiterate women tend to bear the larger number of children.

At this point, further analysis requires the holding constant of the factors of urbanization and per capita current income in order to study their effects separately and in combination. The method of partial correlation was employed, data for all classes being utilized.

The correlations of the zero order, the first order, and the second order are included in Table XXIII because of the light they throw upon the discussion, although it is obviously impossible to analyze each one separately. The correlations were calculated to the fourth place for algebraic reasons although they are only presented to two places. The accuracy of the correlations has been carefully checked and r_{ac} was calculated according to two methods as a further check. Tables by Truman Kelley[5] and John Rice Miner[6] were used to facilitate computation in this as in succeeding problems.

TABLE XXIII
Gross and Net Correlations

$r_{ac} = +.61$	$r_{ad.e} = +.20$	$r_{ac.de} = +.49$
$r_{ad} = -.27$	$r_{ae.c} = -.04$	$r_{ad.ce} = -.06$
$r_{ae} = -.38$	$r_{ae.d} = -.34$	$r_{ae.cd} = +.04$
$r_{cd} = -.38$	$r_{cd.a} = -.28$	$r_{cd.ae} = +.44$
$r_{ce} = -.59$	$r_{cd.e} = +.47$	$r_{ce.ad} = -.55$
$r_{de} = +.91$	$r_{ce.a} = -.48$	$r_{de.ac} = +.92$
$r_{ac.d} = +.57$	$r_{ce.d} = -.63$	
$r_{ac.e} = +.52$	$r_{de.a} = +.91$	
$r_{ad.c} = -.06$	$r_{de.c} = +.92$	

[5]*Tables: To facilitate the calculation of Partial Coefficients of Correlation and Regression Equations.*

[6]*Tables of $\sqrt{1-r^2}$ and $1-r^2$ for Use in Partial Correlation and in Trigonometry.*

Notation employed: $a =$ Illiteracy rate for women 15-44 years of age; $c =$ the number of legitimate births per 1,000 married women of all classes; $d =$ percentage of urbanization for total population; $e =$ current income per capita.

Whereas $r_{ac} = +.61$, $r_{ac.d} = +.57$. As has been pointed out, the gross correlation of illiteracy and birth-rate appears significant. The correlation of these two factors, holding percentage of urbanization constant, while slightly lower, is still significant. This bears out the hypothesis that urbanization is a factor affecting the birth-rate and should be held constant in order to study the relation of illiteracy to birth-rate more precisely. Furthermore, as was pointed out in Chapter VI, rates of illiteracy tend to be higher in rural than in urban areas. As a check on this analysis the correlation between birth-rate and urbanization is found to be $r_{cd} = -.38$ while the correlation between illiteracy and urbanization is $r_{ad} = -.27$.

Turning to the factor of per capita current income, the gross correlation of $+.61$ becomes a correlation of $+.52$ ($r_{ac.e} = -.52$). The importance of per capita current income is apparent. The simple correlations involved are $r_{ae} = -.38$ and $r_{ce} = -.59$.

Carrying the analysis a step further, the relation between illiteracy and birth-rate is obtained when both urbanization and per capita current income are held constant. The correlation when these two factors, both of which are negatively correlated with illiteracy and birth-rate, are assigned is further lowered so that $r_{ac.de} = +.49$. This correlation while lower than r_{ac} is actually more significant for the present purpose because two important factors are held constant. That is, when the effect of urbanization and the effect of current income are controlled, the relation between illiteracy and birth-rate may be stated in terms of the coefficient of correlation as $+.49$. Considering the fact that this is a net correlation, it assumes more significance, for the purposes of the present investigation, than the gross correlation of $+.61$. Thus illiterate women tend to have higher birth-rates than literate women.

In general, investigators of the factors affecting birth-rate have neglected the influence of illiteracy. Supporting the present conclusion, however, is the following statement in regard to English conditions. "It is worthy of note that the fall of the birth-rate in this country practically dates from the passing of the Education Act in 1870."[7] Hornell Hart in his study of "Differential Fecundity in Iowa" states that the poorly educated are more fecund than the better educated.[8] Del Vecchio has shown that for Italy the birth-rate is highest in the districts which contain the largest number of persons who have not learned to read.[9] In general, where educational status has been used at all, the approach to the problem has been an effort to determine the relation of education to lowered birth-rate. The present approach has been to determine instead the relation of illiteracy to high birth-rates. Thus this study is complementary to studies of the other type.

Obviously there is no value in attempting to predict the illiteracy rate on the basis of the birth-rate and the additional factors studied. It is important to predict the birth-rate, given a certain illiteracy rate. Interest chiefly centers around the prediction of the birth-rate when the illiteracy rate falls to a theoretical zero. The gross regression equation is $X_c = .373 X_a + 151.33$ with a corresponding error of estimate, $S_{ca} = 17.67$. According to this equation, when an illiteracy rate of zero is substituted for X_a, the birth-rate would become 151.3 ± 17.67 per 1,000 married mothers, 15-44. The net regression equation, however, offers a more accurate basis for prediction. $X_c = 201.12 + .237 X_a + .823 X_d - .142 X_e$. When X_d and X_e are held constant at the

---

[7]J. Anderson, "The Falling Birth-Rate," *Nature*, XCI, p. 84.

[8]*University of Iowa Studies in Child Welfare*, vol. II, no. 2. p. 35.

[9]Quoted in L. Brentano, "The Doctrine of Malthus and the Increase of Population During the Last Decades," *Economic Journal*, XXIX (1910), 382.

mean and zero is again substituted for X_a, the value of X_c becomes 157. This is a more precise estimate of the birth-rate as is indicated by the corresponding value of S. ($S_{c.ade}=3.005$). The mean of the given birth-rates is 166.8 while the mean for the illiteracy rate is 41.5.

The value of these predictions as well as the reliability of the partial correlations can easily be over-estimated. The reason is that the data are available for only a limited number of states. In spite of this limitation, however, the results appear sufficiently important to be considered as indicating definite trends. Hence it seems warrantable to state general conclusions on the basis of the results which have been secured from the application of certain statistical techniques to the data originally presented.

The decreasing birth-rate is a phenomenon that is of tremendous importance. Various factors have been found partially to account for this. The economic factor has been given due weight in previous studies and the results of this chapter support such conclusions. Some students have noted the effect of urbanization upon the birth-rate, while few have noted the effect of illiteracy[10] or of low educational status.

The present chapter was designed to test this hypothesis that illiteracy significantly affects the birth-rate but the result must only be considered a tentative one, subject to further investigation. To sum up briefly, one may say, then, that not only were low birth-rates found to be related to higher economic status, and to a high percentage of urbanization, but also to low illiteracy rates. Moreover, since urbanization and economic status were thought to be factors that disturbed the truer relationship of birth-rate

---

[10] Whenever the general term of illiteracy is used, it refers, of course, not to the actual number of illiterates but to the specific illiteracy rate as defined in the list of variables presented at the beginning of each chapter.

and illiteracy, these two affecting factors were mathematically controlled. When this was done, a significant relationship between illiteracy and birth-rates was still found to exist.

It would appear, then, that illiterate women tend to bear more children. To what degree this is due to lack of knowledge of birth control in its various forms, to what degree it is due to lack of other sources of interest, is a separate study in itself and need not be entered into here. If this relationship be true then, with the gradual decrease of illiteracy, and conversely, with the gradual increase in the educational status of women, it would appear that we have here an important factor in explaining the decreasing birth-rate in the United States. While mathematical prediction of the birth-rate, given a certain illiteracy rate, is statistically possible, nevertheless the results must be viewed with caution due to the paucity of the data. Yet the trend is definitely apparent. As the trend of illiteracy in the United States is downward, one may venture the prediction that, if other factors remain the same, the birth-rates of American families will also continue to tend downward. Increasing urbanization and the apparently increasing per capita current income will also work in the same direction, as the chapter indicates. Lastly, in connection with the results secured, it would appear that a complete study of the factors affecting birth-rates should certainly include illiteracy or some socio-educational equivalent.

CHAPTER XI

THE RELATION OF ILLITERACY TO INFANT MORTALITY

Death, like birth, is a process which though biological in character, is largely conditioned by societal phenomena. The first year of life, the period covered by the term "infant mortality," is admittedly hazardous. If the illiteracy rate affects the infant mortality rate, its importance is perhaps obvious. The present chapter undertakes to measure as well as to analyze, the relation of illiteracy to infant mortality in the United States.

Infant mortality refers to the ratio of deaths of infants under one year of age per 1,000 births, exclusive of stillbirths. Thirty-three states were utilized in the study. The infant mortality rate for twenty-three states was obtainable for 1920, while six additional states were obtainable for 1921 or 1922. Three states were included in the registration area for the first time in 1924, and one, West Virginia, was admitted in 1925 (see Table XXIV). These latter four states show returns which are normal. Birth and infant death reporting has been somewhat inaccurate in the past, but the states represented in the birth registration area are believed to have sufficiently accurate data, particularly for the period included in the scope of this study. The errors in reporting the age of a child do not affect the data, so long as they do not run past the one year age limit.

The variables under consideration, therefore, are illiteracy rates for all classes, 10 years of age and over,[1] and

---
[1] *Census of 1920*, vol. II, chap. XII, Table XII.

TABLE XXIV

Data Utilized in the Correlation of Illiteracy and Infant Mortality, All Classes[2]

State	Per Cent Illiterate, 10 Years of Age and Over X_f	Deaths of Infants under 1 Year of Age Per 1,000 Births X_q	Percentage of Urbanization X_d	Per Capita Current Income X_e
California	3.3	74	68.0	$ 909
Connecticut	6.2	92	67.8	724
Delaware	5.9	98	54.2	656
Florida	9.6	82	36.7	402
Illinois	3.4	76	67.9	764
Indiana	2.2	82	50.6	540
Iowa	1.1	55	36.4	524
Kansas	1.6	73	34.9	546
Kentucky	8.4	73	26.2	372
Maine	3.3	102	39.0	569
Maryland	5.6	104	60.0	670
Massachusetts	4.7	91	94.8	835
Michigan	3.0	92	61.1	659
Minnesota	1.8	66	44.1	530
Montana	2.3	70	31.3	573
Nebraska	1.4	64	31.3	516
New Hampshire	4.4	88	63.1	612
New Jersey	5.1	74	78.4	745
New York	5.1	86	82.7	943
North Carolina	13.1	85	19.2	329
North Dakota	2.1	67	13.6	426
Ohio	2.8	83	63.8	650
Oregon	1.5	62	49.9	685
Pennsylvania	4.6	97	64.3	687
Rhode Island	6.5	93	97.5	783

TABLE XXIV—Continued

State	Per Cent Illiterate, 10 Years of Age and Over	Deaths of Infants under 1 Year of Age Per 1,000 Births	Percentage of Urbanization	Per Capita Current Income
	X_f	X_g	X_d	X_e
Utah.............	1.9	71	48.0	$ 514
Vermont..........	3.0	96	31.2	544
Virginia...........	11.2	84	29.2	389
Washington........	1.7	66	55.2	710
West Virginia......	6.4	80	25.2	474
Wisconsin.........	2.4	77	47.3	562
Wyoming..........	2.1	79	29.5	826
South Carolina.....	18.1	116	17.5	312
Mean.............	4.7	81.8	49.1	$ 605

deaths of infants under one year of age per 1,000 births for all classes. The data are linear, and the coefficient of correlation is $r_{fg} = +.57$. This gross correlation coefficient appears significant.

The utilization of the method of partial correlation is the next step in the analysis of the data. As in Chapter X, the percentage of urbanization and the per capita current income would appear to be two factors of sufficient importance to affect the relationship between illiteracy and infant mortality.

---

[2]Sources: X_f—*Fourteenth Census*, vol. II, chap. XII, Table XII; X_g—*Birth, Stillbirth, and Infant Mortality Statistics for the Birth Registration Area of the United States*, 1924, pp. 31-32, and for 1925, p. 6; X_d—*Fourteenth Census*, vol. II, chap. I, Table XX; X_e—Leven, *Income in the Various States*, p. 267.

The notation utilized in the partial and multiple correlations is as follows:[3]

f = illiteracy for all classes, 10 years of age and over.

g = deaths of infants under 1 year of age per 1,000 births (exclusive of stillbirths.)

d = percentage of urbanization.

e = per capita current income.

Table XXV gives the correlations of the zero, first, and second orders.

TABLE XXV

Gross and Net Correlations

$r_{fg} = +.57$	$r_{gd.f} = +.37$
$r_{fd} = -.22$	$r_{gd.e} = +.28$
$r_{fe} = -.45$	$r_{ge.f} = +.37$
$r_{gd} = +.18$	$r_{ge.d} = -.21$
$r_{ge} = +.02$	$r_{de.f} = -.82$
$r_{de} = +.81$	$r_{de.g} = +.82$
$r_{fg.d} = +.63$	$r_{fg.de} = +.61$
$r_{fg.e} = +.64$	$r_{fd.ge} = +.14$
$r_{fd.g} = -.39$	$r_{fe.gd} = -.45$
$r_{fd.e} = +.28$	$r_{gd.fe} = +.13$
$r_{fe.g} = -.56$	$r_{ge.fd} = +.12$
$r_{fe.d} = -.47$	$r_{de.fg} = +.79$

The gross correlation between illiteracy and infant mortality as has been stated, is +.57. Holding the factor of percentage of urbanization constant, the coefficient of correlation becomes +.63 ($r_{fg.d} = +.63$).

Consideration of the correlations of the zero order shows that while the correlation between illiteracy and urbanization, $r_{fd} = -.22$, is negative, the correlation between infant mortality and urbanization, $r_{gd} = +.18$, is positive. Thus when the factor of urbanization which is differently cor-

[3] Table XXIV contains the data on which the computations were based.

related with the two primary factors is held constant, the net relationship is found to be higher than the gross correlation would indicate. When the factor of per capita current income is controlled, $r_{fg.e} = +.64$. The gross correlation of illiteracy and current income is negative ($r_{fe} = -.45$) while the gross correlation of infant mortality and current income is practically zero ($r_{ge} = +.02$). Therefore, when the influence of per capita current income on these two variables is controlled, the correlation between illiteracy and infant mortality rises significantly.

When both percentage of urbanization and per capita current income are held constant, the correlation is significantly high ($r_{fg.de} = +.61$). Thus it may be stated that the gross relationship between illiteracy and infant mortality is a significant one; but when the two important factors of percentage of urbanization and per capita current income are controlled, the refined relationship is found to be even more significant.

The most important studies, for purposes of comparison, are those made under the direction of the Children's Bureau. These studies, while important individually for their corroboration of the relation of illiteracy and infant mortality, increase in significance as they support each other. In a field study made in Baltimore, Maryland, the infant mortality rate for native white literate mothers was 94.1 per 1,000 births as compared with 189 per 1,000 births for native white illiterate mothers.[4] In a similar study conducted in Johnstown, Pennsylvania, the infant mortality for literate foreign mothers was found to be 148.0 as compared with 214.0 for illiterate foreign mothers.[5] In Mont-

---

[4] Anna Rochester, *Infant Mortality, Results of a Field Study in Baltimore, Md., Based on Births in One Year*, p. 332.

[5] Emma Duke, *Infant Mortality, Results of a Field Study in Johnstown, Pa., Based on Births in One Calendar Year*.

clair, New Jersey, it was found that the infant mortality rate where mothers were literate, was 76.9 while the rate where mothers were illiterate, was 108.4.[6] Similar studies were conducted in Pittsburgh, Pennsylvania, in Waterbury, Connecticut, in Akron, Ohio, in Brockton, Massachusetts, in Manchester, New Hampshire, and in Saginaw, Michigan, where approximately similar results were secured.

On the basis of the results previously secured, prediction of the rate of infant mortality, given a specified illiteracy rate, is important. The gross regression equation is $X_g = 2.052 X_f + 72.07$ while $S_{gf} = 11.12$. More precise results may be secured by utilization of the net regression equation, $X_g = 55.04 + 2.488 X_f + .113 X_d + .0156 X_e$. The standard error of estimate becomes $S_{g.fde} = 10.23$. Therefore, when urbanization and per capita current income are held constant at the mean and the illiteracy rate is theoretically reduced to zero, the infant mortality rate becomes 70.1 per 1,000 live births, for the total registration area. This must be regarded as only a tentative figure inasmuch as all the states were not included in the registration area when the data were computed. Moreover, the states included are, in general, those which do not have the highest rates of infant mortality. The general relationship of high illiteracy rates with high infant mortality is evident.

The first year of life is the most hazardous. The infant mortality rate covers this period. With the human organism so poorly equipped to survive, the importance of affecting factors is obvious. Illiteracy, particularly on the part of the mother, seems to be a factor affecting continuance of infant life. Apparently, at least as important as the economic factor is the factor of illiteracy. This latter

---

[6]Children's Bureau; U. S. Dept. of Labor. *A Study of Infant Mortality in a Suburban Community*, Montclair, N. J., p. 23.

is definitely contributory to the unsuitability of many mothers to adequately provide the necessary safeguards for their offspring. The relationship, of course, is not perfect; yet it would seem to be of tremendous importance. Ignorance in this matter can be successfully overcome by both private and public child welfare agencies.

The present chapter deals with the thirty-three states included in the registration area in 1925, data of non-registration states, even where available, being rejected on the score of doubtful validity. The results show a significant relationship between illiteracy and high infant mortality, a result to be expected if the foregoing relationship holds. The excellent studies of the Children's Bureau corroborate the findings of this chapter through their more intensive studies of smaller areas.

Prediction of the future so far as the factors under consideration are concerned may be made, subject to a certain margin of variance. In so far as society is concerned, the outlook is hopeful, for as the trend of illiteracy continues downward, it would appear that the infant mortality rate should be reduced.

Finally, it is evident, if the above holds true, that no analysis of the social factors affecting infant mortality can be complete unless illiteracy or some socio-educational equivalent is adequately taken into account.

Chapter XII

THE RELATION OF ILLITERACY TO EARLY AGE OF MARRIAGE

The object of this chapter is the measurement and analysis of the relation of illiteracy to early age of marriage. The rate of illiteracy for native whites of native parentage. ten years of age and over, is utilized as representing the former factor.[1] Early age of marriage is obtained by securing the ratio of females 15-19 ever married[2] to the total female population 15-19, native whites of native parentage being utilized.[3] Females are taken rather than males because the data for males are not as reliable and due to the nature of the investigation only one sex is necessary. The age period, 15 to 19, is utilized because prior to 15 years there is such a small percentage of marriages. The statistical universe is the forty-eight states.

Before proceeding with the study of the relation of illiteracy to early age of marriage for native whites of native parentage, the relationship of these factors, taking all classes into consideration,[4] was measured. The Pearsonian coefficient of correlation was found to be $r = +.64$, indicating a significant relationship. The data being slightly non-linear in nature, the index of correlation, or Rho, was computed on the basis of a second degree parabola.[5] The slight-

---
[1] *Fourteenth Census of the United States*, vol. II, chap. XII, Table V.
[2] Those women who are married, widowed, or divorced are under the same classification, inasmuch as they have all entered the marriage state.
[3] *Fourteenth Census of the United States*, vol. II, chap. IV, Table XI (computed).
[4] See Appendix B for data utilized.
[5] The formula used was

$$Rho^2_{yx} = \frac{a \Sigma(Y) + b \Sigma(XY) + c \Sigma(X^2Y) - Nc_y^2}{\Sigma(Y^2) - Nc_y^2}$$

ly better fit to the data was evidenced by the fact that the index of correlation was found to be $Rho = .68$ in comparison with the previously computed correlation coefficient, $r = +.64$.

Following this generalized picture of the relationship of illiteracy to early age of marriage, the more controlled group of native whites of native parentage was studied. These data were tested and found to be linear. The correlation was found to be $r = +.63$, which may be considered a significant one. This, however, is affected by other factors, and calls for the utilization of partial correlation methods in order to present a truer picture of the subject.

As in the preceding two chapters, percentage of urbanization and current income per capita were selected as the two most important measurable factors (in addition to illiteracy) affecting early age of marriage, and hence to be controlled. The percentage of urbanization[6] for native whites of native parentage ten years of age and over was selected as the third variable, because it was believed that the age factor should be controlled in the variable to this extent. The fourth variable, current income per capita, remains the same as in preceding chapters because of the impossibility of further refining this variable. However, it is utilized because of the fact that this carefully worked out index of current income is, as presented, possibly the most important indicator of economic wealth which in turn affects the age of marriage.

The notation utilized in the partial coefficients of correlation is as follows:

$b =$ illiteracy rate of native white of native parentage, 10 years of age and over.

---

[6]Computed from the *Fourteenth Census*, vol. II, chap. I, Table XX, and chap. II, Table XIII.

TABLE XXVI
Data Utilized in the Correlation of Illiteracy and Early Age of Marriage, Native Whites of Native Parentage[7]

State	Per Cent Illiterate, 10 Years of Age and Over	Percentage of Females, 15-19 Ever Married	Percentage of Urbanization 10 Years of Age and Over	Per Capita Current Income
	X_b	X_h	X_i	X_e
Maine................	1.3	11.5	31.7	$ 569
New Hampshire.....	0.6	10.1	49.1	612
Vermont.............	1.1	10.1	26.2	544
Massachusetts......	0.3	4.7	90.3	835
Rhode Island.......	0.5	5.5	93.9	783
Connecticut........	0.4	6.2	57.9	724
New York..........	0.6	7.3	67.1	943
New Jersey.........	0.7	8.0	68.4	745
Pennsylvania.......	0.8	9.7	56.3	687
Ohio...............	1.0	11.6	55.0	650
Indiana............	1.4	13.6	45.5	540
Illinois.............	1.1	10.8	52.1	764
Michigan...........	0.6	12.7	55.2	659
Wisconsin..........	0.5	5.6	44.1	562
Minnesota..........	0.4	6.1	47.0	530
Iowa...............	0.5	10.5	38.3	524
Missouri............	2.2	14.1	38.9	542
North Dakota.......	0.3	7.6	20.2	426
South Dakota.......	0.3	9.3	21.3	500
Nebraska...........	0.4	10.7	32.6	516
Kansas.............	0.6	12.6	36.2	546
Delaware...........	2.0	13.7	45.9	656
Maryland..........	2.0	12.4	54.6	670
Virginia............	6.1	13.8	28.6	389
West Virginia.......	4.8	17.7	25.0	474
North Carolina.....	8.2	16.3	19.6	329
South Carolina.....	6.6	17.3	22.1	312
Georgia............	5.5	20.9	27.5	722
Florida.............	3.1	19.6	32.4	402

TABLE XXVI—*Continued*

State	Per Cent Illiterate, 10 Years of Age and Over	Percentage of Females, 15-19 Ever Married	Percentage of Urbanization 10 Years of Age and Over	Per Capita Current Income
	X_b	X_h	X_i	X_e
Kentucky	7.3	20.6	22.2	$ 372
Tennessee	7.4	19.5	23.6	336
Alabama	6.4	20.8	21.6	291
Mississippi	3.6	17.3	16.6	263
Arkansas	4.6	22.4	17.3	306
Louisiana	11.4	16.1	36.0	395
Oklahoma	2.4	21.6	28.1	466
Texas	2.2	17.6	32.7	497
Montana	0.3	11.6	31.4	573
Idaho	0.3	13.5	28.9	549
Wyoming	0.4	15.4	28.7	826
Colorado	1.7	14.2	48.6	670
New Mexico	11.9	18.0	18.8	445
Arizona	1.3	17.9	40.4	640
Utah	0.3	10.0	46.9	514
Nevada	0.4	13.7	23.6	874
Washington	0.3	14.6	54.2	710
Oregon	0.4	14.1	47.3	685
California	0.4	11.4	68.1	909
Mean	2.4	13.3	40.0	$ 564

Sources: X_b—*Fourteenth Census*, vol. II, chap. XII, Table V; X_h—*Ibid.*, chap. IV, computed from Table XI; X_i—*Ibid.*, computed from chap. I, Table XX and chap. II, Table XIII; X_e—Leven, *op. cit.*, p. 267.

$h=$ per cent of females, 15-19, ever married, native white of native parentage.

[7]Except data on per capita current income which is necessarily for all classes.

i = per cent of urbanization, native white of native parentage, 10 years of age and over.

e = current income per capita.

All the correlations of the zero order, the first order, and the second order are to be found in Table XXVII.

TABLE XXVII
Gross and Net Correlations

$r_{bh} = +.63$	$r_{hi.b} = -.50$
$r_{bi} = -.49$	$r_{hi.e} = -.38$
$r_{be} = -.65$	$r_{he.l} = -.33$
$r_{hi} = -.65$	$r_{he.i} = -.23$
$r_{he} = -.60$	$r_{ie.b} = +.65$
$r_{ie} = +.75$	$r_{ie.h} = +.59$
$r_{bh.i} = +.48$	$r_{bh.ie} = +.43$
$r_{bh.e} = +.40$	$r_{bi.he} = +.17$
$r_{bi.h} = -.13$	$r_{be.hi} = -.44$
$r_{bi.e} = +.01$	$r_{hi.be} = -.41$
$r_{be.h} = -.43$	$r_{he.bi} = -.0006$
$r_{be.i} = -.49$	$r_{ie.bh} = +.60$

The gross correlation of illiteracy and early age of marriage is $+.63$, which is indicative of an important relationship, to be further tested. When the factor of urbanization is held constant, the correlation is $r_{bh.i} = +.48$, a significant correlation, with the influence of urbanization mathematically controlled. The correlation between illiteracy and urbanization is found to be $r_{bi} = -.49$, showing the important negative relationship of illiteracy and urbanization. The correlation between urbanization and early age of marriage is $r_{hi} = -.65$, showing the importance of the former factor which was controlled in obtaining the correlation, $r_{bh.i} = +.48$.

The gross correlation of $+.63$ was then refined by holding the current income per capita constant, the resulting correlation being $r_{bh.e} = +.40$, a not particularly high, yet statistically significant, correlation. The gross correlation of $r_{be} = -.65$ between illiteracy and current income per capita, and the gross correlation of $r_{he} = -.60$ between early age of marriage and current income per capita emphasize the important negative relationships which influence the simple correlation, $r_{bh} = +.63$.

Although both affecting factors are so clearly important, the relationship between illiteracy and early age of marriage, holding both percentage of urbanization and current income per capita constant, appears significant. $r_{bhie} = +.43$.

In their study of the families of Mid-Western college students, Baber and Ross found that for men of the "present generation," "While education does have a retarding effect on marriage, the postponement from this cause is not very great."[8] For women, also of the "present generation," "As they climb the educational stairs the postponement of their wedding day becomes not only absolutely but also relatively later as though the stairsteps were of increasing height."[9]

When it is desired to predict the percentage of married females, 15-19, from a given illiteracy rate, the gross and net regression equations are as follows:

$$X_h = .988 X_b + 10.93$$
$$X_h = 16.40 + .645 X_b - .1156 X_i - .000013 X_e.$$

The standard errors of estimate are $S_{hb} = 3.57$ and $S_{h.bie} = 3.08$. When percentage of urbanization and current income per capita are held constant at their means and zero is substituted for X_b in the net regression equation, 11.77 is

---
[8] Ray E. Baber, and Edward A. Ross; *Changes in the Size of American Families in One Generation.* p. 31.
[9] *Ibid.*, p. 32.

Illiteracy and Early Marriage

secured as the percentage of married females, 15-19, native white of native parentage.

Thus it is evident that there are a number of social factors which affect the age at which populations marry. While the sociologist who looks at the family from a long range standpoint has no fears but that some form of family life will continue to exist, it must be noted that there are various factors which tend to compete, in early years at least, with entrance into the family relationship. Urbanization is an example of this, offering as it does various alternatives to marriage. Higher economic status would also appear to be an important factor with its various intellectual inducements to at least postpone marriage. The results of the present chapter confirm both of these hypotheses, there being significant negative correlations between early age of marriage, on the one hand, and the factors of urbanization and economic status, on the other.

But the main concern here is with the relationship of illiteracy, as an index of low educational status, to the phenomenon of early marriage. A significant correlation (+.63) is found, and when the highly important correlated factors of urbanization and current income are controlled, the mathematical relationship, while naturally lower, is of sufficient importance to be noted. When both factors are controlled, the resulting correlation is still important.

One appears warranted in stating, then, that the illiterate woman, the woman of lowest educational status, tends to marry earlier than her literate sister. To what degree this is due to circumscribed environment brought about in part, or concomitant with, little education, (formal or otherwise) is interesting to speculate upon. Our concern is with the facts, and the correlation shows not only an important relationship, but also the use of the regression equation enables us to predict that the raising of the educational status of women will be one factor tending to postpone the age at which they marry, even though other factors, such as birth-control, for instance, may tend to operate in the opposite direction. Presumably, then, illiteracy or its equivalent is a factor to be definitely taken into account in any study of early age of marriage although its importance has apparently, in most cases, been overlooked by previous investigators in this field.

CHAPTER XIII

THE RELATION OF ILLITERACY TO SIZE OF FAMILY

The object of the present chapter is the measurement and analysis of the possible relationship of illiteracy to size of family. On empirical grounds it would appear that such a relationship does exist.

"Size of family," as such, is not computed by the Census. However, the average number of living children of mothers of 1920 is available for twenty states. A preliminary investigation of this problem was made as follows. "Size of family" was approximated through obtaining the average number of living children of native white mothers of 1920 for those twenty states of the registration area for which such information was obtainable.[1] This was correlated with the illiteracy rate per 1,000 native white women, 15-54.[2] The resulting Pearsonian coefficient of correlation was $+.72$.[3] The correlation is apparently significant, but one may question the degree to which the factor "average number of living children of native white mothers of 1920" is sufficiently representative of the sought factor, "size of family."

A second and perhaps more fruitful approach (in addition to possible corroboration of the above results) was

---

[1] Data for Maine and New Hampshire are not available for "children living."

[2] Computed from data obtained in U. S. Census, 1920, vol. II, chap. XII, Table XII. The data on which the computations were based is included in Appendix B.

[3] $r = +.70$, when the illiteracy rate per 1,000 native white women, 15-44, was used.

determined upon. With the illiteracy rate per 1,000 native white women 15-54, was correlated the number of children under 15 years of age per native white woman, ever married, 15-54.[4]

This approximation to "size of family"[5] was utilized because it gives what is believed to be a more accurate picture of actual conditions. The broad age span for women ever married was taken so as to include not only mothers of the child-bearing period but also mothers of fairly advanced years who still have young children. If mothers 15 to 44 had been utilized together with all children under fifteen years of age, the number of children per married woman would have been larger than is actually the case.

The gross coefficient of correlation is $+.62$. This is significant, and indicates a high degree of relationship, and in addition this is corroborative of the results of the incomplete sample utilized in the preceding correlation. One may infer, then, that there is an apparently important degree of relationship between illiteracy and the number of children under fifteen years of age, per 1,000 native white women, ever married, 15-54.

The factors of current income and urbanization may partially account for this apparently high degree of relationship, however, and hence the method of partial correlation is again utilized to keep these factors, separately and together, constant.

The notation employed in the following partial and multiple correlations is as follows:

X_j = illiteracy per 1,000 native white women, 15-54.

X_k = number of children under fifteen years of age per native white women, ever married, 15-54.

---

[4]U. S. Census, 1920, vol. II, chap. III, computed from Table I.

[5]Males were not included as obviously the number of ever married native white males would not correspond numerically to the same classification of females.

TABLE XXVIII
Data Utilized in the Correlation of Illiteracy and Size of Family, Native Whites[6]

State	No. Illiterate Per 1,000 Native White Women 15-54	No. of Children Under 15 Years Per Ever Married Native White Woman 15-54	Percentage of Urbanization of Native White Persons	Per Capita Current Income
	X_j	X_k	X_l	X_e
Alabama.........	50.5	2.14	21.1	$ 291
Arizona..........	24.8	1.35	39.7	640
Arkansas.........	31.5	2.06	16.7	306
California........	3.6	.88	68.4	909
Colorado.........	15.6	1.29	47.5	670
Connecticut......	3.8	.96	65.4	724
Delaware.........	9.9	1.26	52.6	656
Florida...........	22.0	1.63	34.5	402
Georgia..........	39.8	2.03	26.4	322
Idaho............	2.3	1.74	27.5	549
Illinois...........	4.6	1.22	62.7	764
Indiana..........	6.7	1.38	47.9	540
Iowa.............	2.7	1.42	35.7	524
Kansas...........	3.6	1.52	33.5	546
Kentucky........	52.1	1.91	23.6	372
Louisiana........	106.2	1.92	38.5	395
Maine............	11.0	.63	36.3	569
Maryland........	10.8	1.42	59.6	670
Massachusetts....	3.3	.98	93.9	835
Michigan.........	4.2	1.19	57.8	659
Minnesota........	3.3	1.34	42.5	530
Mississippi.......	24.8	2.13	16.2	263
Missouri.........	11.3	1.44	42.9	542
Montana.........	2.2	1.36	31.1	573
Nebraska.........	2.8	1.50	29.5	516
Nevada..........	3.1	1.06	21.8	874
New Hampshire...	6.0	1.08	59.2	612
New Jersey.......	4.5	1.07	76.3	745

TABLE XXVIII—Continued

State	No. Illiterate Per 1,000 Native White Women 15-54	No. of Children Under 15 Years Per Ever Married Native White Woman 15-54	Percentage of Urbanization of Native White Persons	Per Capita Current Income
	X_j	X_k	X_l	X_e
New Mexico	145.7	1.93	18.8	$ 445
New York	3.7	.98	78.7	943
North Carolina	66.4	2.30	18.6	329
North Dakota	3.6	1.54	14.1	426
Ohio	4.9	1.27	60.3	650
Oklahoma	15.5	1.89	26.5	466
Oregon	2.3	1.18	48.4	685
Pennsylvania	5.2	1.38	61.6	687
Rhode Island	7.3	.94	96.9	783
South Carolina	60.0	2.19	21.3	312
South Dakota	3.2	1.59	16.6	500
Tennessee	53.1	1.94	22.9	336
Texas	25.9	1.75	31.5	497
Utah	2.4	1.91	47.0	514
Vermont	8.9	1.31	29.8	544
Virginia	41.6	1.96	28.1	389
Washington	1.9	1.12	54.2	710
West Virginia	35.7	2.04	24.8	474
Wisconsin	4.5	1.41	45.7	562
Wyoming	2.2	1.42	28.8	826
Mean	20.0	1.50	41.3	$ 564

Sources: X_j—*Fourteenth Census of the United States*, vol. II, chap. XII, computed from Table XII; X_k—*Ibid.*, chap. III, computed from Table I; X_l—*Ibid.*, chap. I, Table XX; X_e—Leven, *op. cit.*, p. 267.

[6]With the exception of per capita current income which is necessarily for all classes.

ILLITERACY AND SIZE OF FAMILY

X_l = percentage of urbanization of native white persons.
X_e = per capita current income.
Table XXIX gives the correlation coefficients of the zero, first, and second orders. $r_{jk} = +.62$, while $r_{jk.l} = +.57$ and $r_{jk.e} = +.35$.

TABLE XXIX

Gross and Net Correlations

$r_{jk} = +.62$	$r_{kl.j} = -.68$
$r_{jl} = -.42$	$r_{kl.e} = -.28$
$r_{je} = -.55$	$r_{ke.j} = -.78$
$r_{kl} = -.74$	$r_{ke.l} = -.75$
$r_{ke} = -.86$	$r_{le.j} = +.69$
$r_{le} = +.75$	$r_{le.k} = +.23$
$r_{jk.l} = +.57$	$r_{jk.le} = +.36$
$r_{jk.e} = +.35$	$r_{jl.ke} = +.11$
$r_{jl.k} = +.09$	$r_{je.kl} = -.08$
$r_{jl.e} = -.002$	$r_{kl.je} = -.30$
$r_{je.k} = -.04$	$r_{ke.jl} = -.60$
$r_{je.l} = -.40$	$r_{le.jk} = +.34$

The interpretation of these statistical results is that there is an important gross correlation between illiteracy and the variable utilized for size of family.[7] When urbanization is held constant, the correlation is still important. When current income per capita is held constant the correlation, while a low one, is considered significant. The checks, $r_{kl} = -.74$ and $r_{ke} = -.86$, show the necessity of holding the X_l and X_e factors constant since they show important negative correlations with size of family. In addition, $r_{jl} = -.42$ and $r_{je} = -.55$, indicating important negative correlations between X_j and X_l and between X_j and X_e. These correlations also indicate the necessity of hold-

---

[7] Hereafter this variable will be called, for brevity's sake, "size of family."

ing percentage of urbanization and per capita current income constant. When either of these two significant factors is assigned, the net correlation between illiteracy and size of family is lowered.

When both percentage of urbanization and per capita current income are held constant, $r_{jk.le} = +.36$. This indicates a tendency for high rates of illiteracy and large families to be found together, for the contributing factors of urbanization and current income are mathematically controlled.

Various studies have noted the fact that there is a relationship between size of family and educational status. S. J. Holmes found that "education has a potent effect in reducing family size."[8] Better educated women tend to have fewer children than do those with less education, according to the findings of Mary R. Smith.[9] Baber and Ross also found that on the average the more poorly trained groups have the larger families.[10] In addition, many of the studies of economic status and size of family show small families for those occupations which require the greater educational preparation.

One may utilize regression equations for prediction of size of family. When equations, $X_k = .0088 X_j + 1.32$ and $X_k = 2.38 + .003 X_j - .0043 X_l - .00135 X_e$, are utilized, the number of children per native white woman, ever married, 15-54, may be predicted from a given illiteracy rate. When the net regression equation is used, and X_l and X_e are held constant at their mean values, a zero illiteracy rate gives 1.4 children. The standard errors of estimate are $S_{k.jle} = .18$

---

[8]"Size of College Families," *Journal of Heredity*, October, 1924, p. 410.

[9]"Statistics of College and Non-College Women," *Journal of the American Statistical Association*, VII (1900), 9.

[10]*Op. cit.*, chap. VII.

for the net regression equation and $S_{kj}=.31$ for the gross regression equation.

In measuring the relationship between illiteracy and size of family, we have again a biological reaction of man, affected by social factors. It is to be noted that the index of size of family utilized in this chapter, i.e., the number of children under fifteen years of age per ever married woman, 15 to 54 years of age, is a statistical approximation, in lieu of the practical impossibility of accurately determining the actual family size for all families in the United States.

Size of family, as numerous studies in various countries have noted, is adversely affected by higher economic status. In addition, the number of children per family is lowered by increasing urbanization as various investigators have shown. The present chapter corroborates these findings. Moreover, the high negative correlations show the necessity of mathematically holding constant these two factors, which affect both illiteracy and size of family, if a truer picture of the relationship between these latter phenomena is to be obtained. The simple correlation between illiteracy and size of family is significant. When the effect of urbanization is controlled, the relationship is still important, and when the effect of economic status is controlled, there yet remains a tendency for illiterate mothers to have larger families than mothers of higher educational status. When both disturbing factors are controlled, the net correlation of $+.36$ continues to show an evident relationship between low educational status and large families.

The regression equations once more offer a possibility of predicting that the size of family which is already quite small will continue to grow smaller with the increase in educational status. Moreover, the growing urbanization rate and the apparent increase in the average income will hasten this shrinkage. Not a rosy picture, surely, for those who foresee the possible danger in this phenomenon!

Lastly the importance of some socio-educational factor in analyzing the factors affecting the lowering size of family is borne out in this generalized study of the subject.

CHAPTER XIV

THE RELATION OF ILLITERACY TO MOBILITY TO OTHER STATES

Present day society is characterized by a high degree of mobility. Probably one of the most important characteristics of contemporary culture is this intensive shifting of individuals from one locality to another.[1] The following chapter has for its object the measurement of the relation of one type of horizontal mobility to the factor of illiteracy. Interstate mobility is determined from the census which gives data pertaining to the percentage of various color and nationality classes who were born in a specified state, but who were, in 1920, living in other states. For the purposes of this study, native whites of native parentage were utilized not only because the race and nationality factors are thus held constant, but also because interstate mobility of native whites of native parentage gives a more reliable statistical picture of actual mobility in the United States.

The variable X_b is correlated with the variable, X_m, where X_b is the per cent of native whites of native parentage, ten years of age and over, who are illiterate,[2] and X_m is the per cent of native whites of native parentage born in a specified state, but living in other states.[3] The coefficient of correlation is —.40, the data being linear in character. This is interpreted as meaning that there is a low but significant negative relationship between illiteracy and

---
[1] Pitirim Sorokin, *Social Mobility*, p. 9.
[2] U. S. Census, 1920, vol. II, chap. XII, Table V.
[3] U. S. Census, 1920, vol. II, chap. V, Table XVI.

TABLE XXX
DATA UTILIZED IN THE CORRELATION OF ILLITERACY AND MOBILITY TO OTHER STATES, NATIVE WHITES OF NATIVE PARENTAGE[4]

State	Per Cent Illiterate, 10 Years of Age and Over	Percentage of Inhabitants Born in State and Living in Other States	Percentage of Urbanization 10 Years of Age and Over	Percentage of Male Wage Earners in Manufacturing 15 Years of Age and Over
	X_b	X_m	X_i	X_n
Maine.............	1.3	26.4	31.7	24.5
New Hampshire.....	0.6	37.2	49.1	35.6
Vermont...........	1.1	37.5	26.2	22.4
Massachusetts......	0.3	20.1	90.3	36.4
Rhode Island.......	0.5	27.0	93.9	42.6
Connecticut........	0.4	24.2	57.9	45.4
New York..........	0.6	19.8	67.1	23.5
New Jersey........	0.7	17.6	68.4	35.0
Pennsylvania.......	0.8	17.2	56.3	30.3
Ohio..............	1.0	22.5	55.0	29.4
Indiana...........	1.4	27.2	45.5	22.3
Illinois............	1.1	30.6	52.1	19.9
Michigan..........	0.6	18.8	55.2	30.5
Wisconsin..........	0.5	24.9	44.1	28.1
Minnesota.........	0.4	26.2	47.0	11.1
Iowa..............	0.5	37.0	38.3	7.9
Missouri...........	2.2	33.2	38.9	12.1
North Dakota......	0.3	32.6	20.2	1.9
South Dakota......	0.3	32.7	21.3	2.5
Nebraska..........	0.4	33.9	32.6	6.8
Kansas............	0.6	38.0	36.2	8.7
Delaware..........	2.0	31.2	45.9	30.3
Maryland..........	2.0	20.7	54.6	20.5
Virginia...........	6.1	22.7	28.6	13.2
West Virginia......	4.8	18.1	25.0	15.3
North Carolina.....	8.2	14.3	19.6	15.4
South Carolina.....	6.6	15.3	22.1	12.4

TABLE XXX—Continued

State	Per Cent Illiterate, 10 Years of Age and Over	Percentage of Inhabitants Born in State and Living in Other States	Percentage of Urbanization 10 Years of Age and Over	Percentage of Male Wage Earners in Manufacturing 15 Years of Age and Over
	X_b	X_m	X_i	X_n
Georgia	5.5	18.0	27.5	11.2
Florida	3.1	13.7	32.4	20.6
Kentucky	7.3	25.7	22.2	7.4
Tennessee	7.4	26.6	23.6	10.2
Alabama	6.4	22.6	21.6	13.6
Mississippi	3.6	27.1	16.6	10.0
Arkansas	4.6	30.5	17.3	8.6
Louisiana	11.4	12.9	36.0	15.3
Oklahoma	2.4	23.1	28.1	4.1
Texas	2.2	16.2	32.7	6.3
Montana	0.3	32.1	31.4	7.9
Idaho	0.3	29.4	28.9	8.6
Wyoming	0.4	39.8	28.7	8.3
Colorado	1.7	34.5	48.6	9.1
New Mexico	11.9	21.8	18.8	4.6
Arizona	1.3	30.7	40.4	6.6
Utah	0.3	22.6	46.9	11.1
Nevada	0.4	53.9	23.6	8.4
Washington	0.3	23.6	54.2	23.0
Oregon	0.4	27.0	47.3	17.4
California	0.4	11.6	68.1	14.7
Mean	2.4	26.0	40.0	16.9

[4]Sources: X_b—*Fourteenth Census of the United States*, vol. II, chap. XII, Table V; X_m—*Ibid.*, chap. V, Table XVI; X_i—*Ibid.*, computed from chap. I, Table XX, and chap. II, Table XIII; X_n—*Ibid.*, computed from chap. III, Table XIII, and vol. VIII, Table XV.

interstate mobility. The significance of the result is more apparent when it is pointed out that certain factors, important in themselves, tend to obscure the actual correlation.

The urbanization of a state would tend to affect the correlation, due to the fact that where a state is highly urbanized, this acts as an attracting factor to that state's rural population, and hence acts as a partial deterrent, it is believed, to migration to other states; moreover, the presence of a nearby urbanized state would act as an attracting factor to inhabitants of other states. Therefore, it is a factor which should be held constant, and this should raise—not lower—the net correlation over the gross correlation. A second factor of importance, related to the factor just discussed, yet different from it, is the amount of industry within a state. Where a state is highly industrialized, it acts as a deterrent to migration elsewhere, it is contended, as well as an attracting stimulus-situation to nearby less industrialized states.

Partial correlation is therefore resorted to, as the next logical step in the analysis of illiteracy in its relation to mobility to other states.

The notation employed is as follows:

X_b = percentage of illiteracy, native white of native parentage, 10 years of age and over.

X_m = percentage of native whites of native parentage born in a specified state and living in other states.

X_i = percentage of urbanization of native whites of native parentage, 10 years of age and over.

X_n = percentage of male wage earners in manufacturing, 15 years of age and over.

The last variable was utilized as an index of industrialization. The percentage of actual wage earners was considered a more fitting index than the amount of capital employed in industry because it is after all the opportunity afforded men that is the factor necessary to hold constant.[5]

Table XXXI presents the correlations of the zero, first, and second orders.

TABLE XXXI

Gross and Net Correlations

$r_{bm} = -.40$ $r_{mi.b} = -.51$
$r_{bi} = -.49$ $r_{mi.n} = -.06$
$r_{bn} = -.28$ $r_{mn.b} = -.40$
$r_{mi} = -.22$ $r_{mn.i} = -.11$
$r_{mn} = -.24$ $r_{in.b} = +.76$
$r_{in} = +.78$ $r_{in.m} = +.76$

$r_{bm.i} = -.59$ $r_{bm.in} = -.58$
$r_{bm.n} = -.50$ $r_{bi.mn} = -.55$
$r_{bi.m} = -.64$ $r_{bn.mi} = +.14$
$r_{bi.n} = -.45$ $r_{mi.bn} = -.36$
$r_{bn.m} = -.42$ $r_{mn.bi} = -.006$
$r_{bn.i} = +.18$ $r_{in.bm} = +.71$

When the percentage of urbanization is held constant, the gross correlation of $-.40$ becomes a correlation of $-.59$, $(r_{bm.i} = -.59)$ a result to be expected, if the preceding argument holds. When the percentage of male wage earners in manufacturing is held constant, the result is a correlation of $-.50$ $(r_{bm.n} = -.50)$ which is also to be expected.

When both percentage of urbanization and percentage of male wage earners in manufacturing are held constant, $r_{bm.in} = -.58$. This correlation emphasizes the important negative relationship existing between illiteracy and mobility to other states since two of the strongest affecting factors are controlled. Further analysis of the net correla-

---

[5]Computed from data obtained from U. S. Census, 1920, vol. VII, Table XV, and vol. II, chap. III, Table XIII.

tions reveals the fact that this partial correlation is higher than any other combination of factors except percentage of urbanization with percentage of male wage earners in manufacturing ($r_{in.bm} = +.71$). It appears, therefore, that the degree of relationship between mobility to other states and illiteracy is higher than both the relationship between mobility to other states and percentage of urbanization and than the relationship between mobility to other states and the percentage of male wage earners in manufacturing, 15 years of age and over.

Hornell Hart's analysis of data secured for the state of Iowa also reveals this important negative relationship between illiteracy and mobility.[6] Robert E. Park points out that education is one of the factors which has operated to vastly increase the mobility of modern peoples.[7] In analyzing English labor conditions of the nineteenth century, Redford found that "Peasants, especially uneducated peasants, are immobile except under the spur of extreme necessity. They do not migrate whenever it is to their economic interest, but only when they must."[8]

Since the primary interest is the prediction of mobility to other states on the basis of a given illiteracy rate, the following equations may be utilized.

$$X_m = -1.109X_b + 28.75$$
$$X_m = 40.55 - 1.849X_b - .248X_i + .0435X_n$$

The corresponding standard errors of estimate are $S_{mb} = 7.61$ and $S_{m.bin} = 6.53$. When the net regression equation is utilized and when X_i and X_n are held constant at their respec-

---
[6]"Selective Migration as a Factor in Child Welfare in the United States with Especial Reference to Iowa," *University of Iowa Studies in Child Welfare*, vol. I, no. 7, p. 56.

[7]"The City: Suggestions for the Investigation of Human Behavior in the City Environment," *American Journal of Sociology*, XX (1915), 589.

[8]Arthur Redford, *Labour Migration in England, 1800-1850*, p. 82.

tive means, the substitution of an illiteracy rate of zero gives 30.55 as the predicted percentage of mobility to other states.

By way of summary, it may be pointed out that the present day shifting of individuals from one state to another is correlated with various factors. The present chapter has shown that migration to other states is partially hindered when a particular state offers certain attracting alternatives. For purposes of this study, degree of urbanization and individual opportunity have been selected as factors which act as deterring agents to migration to other states.

In order to obtain a true picture of the possible relationship existing between illiteracy and mobility to other states, it would be necessary, first, to eliminate race and foreign birth factors, and, second, to control the factors of urbanization and industrial opportunity. Race and foreign birth may be statistically eliminated by utilizing the sub-classifications of the Census Bureau. The urbanization and industrial factors are controlled through the utilization of the method of partial correlation.

The simple coefficient of correlation between illiteracy and mobility to other states is a low but significant one. When either percentage of urbanization or the percentage of male wage earners engaged in manufacturing (which is utilized as the index of industrialization) is held constant, the correlation between the primary factors of illiteracy and mobility to other states rises, bearing out the hypothesis that the deterring factors disturb the relationship between illiteracy and mobility. When both affecting factors are controlled, the net relationship is important enough to support the hypothesis on which the present chapter is based, namely, that illiterates, or persons of low educational status, tend to be more stagnant than persons of higher educational status. There are various factors—which need not be entered into here—which tend to restrict more severely the average horizon of the person of low educational status, causing him to remain in a more fixed locality, often at the expense of finding greater opportunity, especially for one of his status, elsewhere.

Regression equations enable one to predict that as illiteracy decreases and educational status rises, mobility will tend to increase, particularly from states with lesser opportunity for obtaining the primary needs of life.

It would appear that the analysis of factors leading to greater or less mobility must take into consideration some index of socio-educational status, if the analysis is to be a complete one.

Chapter XV

THE RELATION OF ILLITERACY TO SUICIDE

Suicide is a form of adjustment which results in death. From the socio-psychological standpoint, suicide is behavioristically a reaction to the complexity of social stimuli. From the standpoint of the present social group, suicide is an undesirable phenomenon, striking as it does at the all-important (from the standpoint of the group) social organization. The hypothesis advanced in this chapter is that there is an inverse relationship of illiteracy with suicide.[1]

Since suicide data are not presented by the census according to race and nationality, data for all classes were utilized in the present investigation. The percentage of illiteracy for all classes ten years of age and over was correlated with the number of suicides per 100,000 population. Since suicides do not occur in large numbers the suicides for 1919, 1920, and 1921[2] were averaged for each of the thirty-four registration states and used as the basis of computation.

The gross correlation for these two variables is $-.74$, which is indicative of a high negative relationship. The data were previously tested and found to be linear.

It was necessary to refine the data to a greater degree by the utilization of partial correlations. The percentage

---

[1]This does not imply a causal relationship. In fact, the concept of "cause" is foreign to any discussion in this study. Factorization, of which the end result is but a function, and that within the limits of the data, is always implied.

[2]*Mortality Statistics, 1919, 1920, 1921*, Table VIII.

TABLE XXXII
Data Utilized in the Correlation of Illiteracy and Suicide, All Classes[3]

State	Percentage of Illiteracy, 10 Years of Age and Over	No. of Suicides* Per 100,000 Population	Percentage of Urbanization 10 Years of Age and Over	Percentage Not in Married State, 15 Years of Age and Over	Percentage Not Native White of Native Parentage
	X_f	X_o	X_p	X_q	X_s
California.......	3.3	24.0	69.2	42.6	51.0
Colorado........	3.2	14.9	50.9	39.8	35.8
Connecticut.....	6.2	13.3	67.7	41.4	67.5
Delaware........	5.9	9.1	54.6	39.4	37.3
Florida..........	9.6	7.3	38.6	37.6	45.0
Illinois..........	3.4	13.5	68.6	40.3	52.7
Indiana.........	2.2	12.8	51.4	36.9	20.5
Kansas..........	1.6	11.5	36.2	37.7	26.0
Kentucky.......	8.4	7.3	28.6	38.2	15.6
Louisiana.......	21.9	5.6	37.5	40.6	47.6
Maine...........	3.3	12.6	39.6	40.4	35.4
Maryland.......	5.6	10.8	61.2	41.9	38.4
Massachusetts...	4.7	11.2	94.7	44.7	68.1
Michigan........	3.0	10.6	61.9	37.6	54.5
Minnesota.......	1.8	12.5	45.5	44.5	65.3
Mississippi......	17.2	3.2	14.6	37.7	53.8
Missouri........	3.0	12.7	48.7	39.3	25.5
Montana........	2.3	15.9	33.0	40.2	49.8
Nebraska........	1.4	12.3	32.8	39.7	41.6
New Hampshire..	4.4	12.0	62.8	42.1	49.1
New Jersey......	5.1	12.7	78.3	39.8	61.6
New York.......	5.1	12.6	82.6	42.4	64.7
North Carolina ..	13.1	3.8	20.8	39.4	31.0
Ohio............	2.8	11.9	64.6	38.5	36.3
Oregon..........	1.5	14.1	51.4	39.4	36.5

TABLE XXXII—Continued

State	Percentage of Illiteracy, 10 Years of Age and Over	No. of Suicides* Per 100,000 Population	Percentage of Urbanization 10 Years of Age and Over	Percentage Not in Married State, 15 Years of Age and Over	Percentage Not Native White of Native Parentage
	X_f	X_o	X_p	X_q	X_s
Pennsylvania....	4.6	10.0	65.4	40.3	45.5
Rhode Island....	6.5	9.7	97.4	44.2	71.3
South Carolina...	18.1	3.9	19.2	39.8	52.5
Tennessee.......	10.3	6.3	28.3	37.9	21.6
Utah............	1.9	8.8	50.2	39.2	45.3
Vermont.........	3.0	13.0	31.6	40.1	35.2
Virginia.........	11.2	7.0	31.3	41.3	33.5
Washington......	1.7	17.6	56.7	40.4	47.5
Wisconsin.......	2.4	11.7	48.4	42.0	59.9
Mean...........	5.9	11.1	50.7	40.2	44.8

*Average number of suicides for 1919, 1920, 1921.

of urbanization[4] for all classes, ten years of age and over, was adopted as the third variable. Since it is a known fact that suicide rates are higher among the non-married[5] than among the married, the percentage not included in the married state, fifteen years of age and over,[6] was taken as

[3]Sources: X_f—*Fourteenth Census of the United States*, vol. II, chap. XII, Table XII; X_o—*Mortality Statistics, 1919, 1920, 1921*, Table VIII; X_p—*Fourteenth Census of the United States*, vol. II, chap. XII, computed from Tables XII and XXII; X_q—*Ibid.*, chap. IV, computed from Table XI; X_s—*Ibid.*, chap. I, computed from Table VII.
[4]*Ibid.*, chap. XII, computed from Tables XII and XXII.
[5]Single, widowed, and divorced.
[6]*Fourteenth Census*, vol. II, chap. IV, computed from Table XI.

the next variable. Since suicide rates differ significantly according to race and nationality groupings,[7] this factor was controlled by taking as a fifth variable, the percentage not native white of native parentage.[8]

The system of notation employed is as follows:

f = Percentage of illiteracy for all classes 10 years of age and over.

o = Suicides per 100,000 population, all classes.

p = Percentage of urbanization of all classes, 10 years of age and over.

q = Percentage not in the married state, all classes, 15 years of age and over.

s = Percentage not native white of native parentage, all ages.

The correlations of the zero, first, second and third orders are presented in the following table:

TABLE XXXIII

Gross and Net Correlations

$r_{fo} = -.74$	$r_{fp.o} = -.13$	$r_{oq.p} = +.07$
$r_{fp} = -.43$	$r_{fp.q} = -.44$	$r_{oq.s} = +.37$
$r_{fq} = -.14$	$r_{fp.s} = -.52$	$r_{os.f} = +.24$
$r_{fs} = +.006$	$r_{fq.o} = +.19$	$r_{os.p} = -.15$
$r_{op} = +.47$	$r_{fq.p} = +.19$	$r_{os.q} = -.19$
$r_{oq} = +.35$	$r_{fq.s} = -.23$	$r_{pq.f} = +.65$
$r_{os} = +.16$	$r_{fs.o} = +.18$	$r_{pq.o} = +.57$
$r_{pq} = +.64$	$r_{fs.p} = +.33$	$r_{pq.s} = +.39$
$r_{ps} = +.56$	$r_{fs.q} = +.18$	$r_{ps.o} = +.63$
$r_{qs} = +.77$	$r_{op.f} = +.26$	$r_{ps.o} = +.56$
$r_{fo.p} = -.67$	$r_{op.q} = +.34$	$r_{ps.q} = +.15$
$r_{fo.q} = -.74$	$r_{op.s} = +.47$	$r_{qs.f} = +.78$
$r_{fo.s} = -.75$	$r_{oq.f} = +.37$	$r_{qs.o} = +.77$

---

[7] For example, Negroes have low rates; Japanese have high rates; North Europeans generally have high rates, etc. See A. D. Frenay, *The Suicide Problem in the United States*, chap. XI.

[8] *Fourteenth Census*, vol. II, chap. I, computed from Table VII.

TABLE XXXIII—Continued

$r_{qs.p} = +.61$	$r_{op.fs} = +.15$	$r_{qs.fo} = +.77$
$r_{fo.pq} = -.70$	$r_{op.qs} = +.38$	$r_{qs.fp} = +.63$
$r_{fo.ps} = -.67$	$r_{oq.fp} = +.28$	$r_{qs.op} = +.66$
$r_{fo.qs} = -.73$	$r_{oq.fs} = +.31$	
$r_{fp.oq} = -.30$	$r_{oq.ps} = +.21$	$r_{fo.pqs} = -.68$
$r_{fp.os} = -.32$	$r_{os.fp} = +.10$	$r_{fp.oqs} = -.32$
$r_{fp.qs} = -.48$	$r_{os.fq} = -.09$	$r_{fq.ops} = +.16$
$r_{fq.op} = +.32$	$r_{os.pq} = -.25$	$r_{fs.opq} = +.14$
$r_{fq.os} = +.08$	$r_{pq.fo} = +.61$	$r_{op.fqs} = +.05$
$r_{fq.ps} = -.02$	$r_{pq.fs} = +.32$	$r_{oq.fps} = +.28$
$r_{fs.op} = +.31$	$r_{pq.os} = +.26$	$r_{os.fpq} = -.10$
$r_{fs.oq} = +.06$	$r_{ps.fo} = +.60$	$r_{pq.fos} = +.30$
$r_{fs.pq} = +.28$	$r_{ps.fq} = +.26$	$r_{ps.foq} = +.26$
$r_{op.fq} = +.03$	$r_{ps.oq} = +.24$	$r_{qs.fop} = +.63$

The gross correlation between illiteracy and suicide is $r_{fo} = -.74$. When the factor of urbanization is controlled, $r_{fo.p} = -.67$. When the factor of percentage not in the married state is held constant, $r_{fo.q} = -.74$. Finally, when the percentage not native white of native parentage is controlled, $r_{fo.s} = -.75$. In the correlations of the second order, $r_{fo.pq} = -.70$, $r_{fo.ps} = -.67$, and $r_{fo.qs} = -.73$. That there is a high negative degree of relationship between illiteracy and suicide appears to be substantiated by each of these correlations. Furthermore, in his analysis of European data, Morselli also shows the negative relationship between illiteracy and suicide.[9]

Since there is an inverse relationship between illiteracy and suicide, the probable suicide rate may be predicted from the following equations when the illiteracy rate falls to an approximate zero.

$$X_o = -5.885 X_f + 45.82, \text{ and}$$
$$X_o = -3.05 - .604 X_f + .0225 X_p + .4743 X_q - .0557 X_s.$$

---

[9] *Suicide*, chap. IV. Suicide, of course, refers to the suicide rate per 100,000 population, as defined on page 129, above.

The standard errors of estimate are $S_{of} = 2.77$ and $S_{o.fpqs} = 1.26$ respectively. Substituting the mean values of X_p, X_q, and X_s and reducing X_f (illiteracy) to zero, X_o or the suicide rate becomes 14.66 per 100,000. In other words, if conditions remained the same as utilized here and if the illiteracy rate dropped to zero, the chances are that in 68 out of 100 cases, the suicide rate would fall within the limits of 14.66 ± 1.26.

In summing up, it may be pointed out that suicide is a form of—from the standpoint of the group—anti-social behavior. Hence the mores operate more or less in an unconscious endeavor to prevent the taking of one's own life. Does low educational status, as reflected in illiteracy, reduce suicide or is the opposite true? This is the question raised in the present chapter and an answer is attempted.

When the relationship of illiteracy to suicide is measured, a high negative correlation,—.74, is obtained. Apparently illiterates do not commit suicide, as compared with persons of higher educational status. It is claimed, however, that suicides are committed in urban areas, and since a large percentage of illiterates live in rural areas, the above correlation is affected. The method of partial correlation enables one to control the factor of urbanization, giving a resulting correlation of $-.67$, which is still significant.

There is another factor of importance to be taken into consideration. Suicide rates are higher among the non-married (single, widowed, or divorced) than among the married, and hence it is desirable to control this differential factor. When the percentage not included in the married state, fifteen years of age and over, is held constant, the correlation first obtained, $-.74$, is unchanged.

Again suicide rates in the United States differ significantly according to the races, and also according to country of birth. These latter two factors may be controlled at the same time by holding constant mathematically the percentage *not* native white of native parentage. When this is done, the resulting correlation remains practically unchanged. Various correlations of the higher orders are presented in the tables for purposes of completeness, but due to the small number of cases, their validity is questionable. The net coefficient of correlation between illiteracy and suicide, with all the disturbing factors mentioned above controlled, however, is consistent with the results arrived at previously, and is found to be $-.68$, an apparently significant correlation.

It would appear, then, that the illiterate, as compared with persons of higher educational status, do not commit suicide to an important degree. When the regression equations are utilized, the suicide rate may be predicted as rising as educational status rises. To what degree this is due to the rise of educational status, and to what degree it is due to the increased complexity of stimuli which confront the person of higher educational status is an important study in itself.

It may be pointed out that from the results obtained it is evident that the inverse relationship between illiteracy and suicide is so high that no investigator of the social factors affecting suicide can neglect the phenomenon of illiteracy or some socio-educational equivalent.

CHAPTER XVI

THE RELATION OF ILLITERACY TO URBANIZATION AND TO SCHOOL SYSTEMS

The present chapter has for its objective the measurement of the relationship of illiteracy to urbanization and to school systems. Figures have been given[1] which show the higher rate of illiteracy in rural than in urban areas for the United States in both 1910 and 1920. The correlations secured in each chapter of Part II indicate a relationship between illiteracy and urbanization as well as a relationship between the other primary factor being studied and urbanization.

Is literacy, then, strictly speaking, a function of urbanization? Or is it rather that urbanization possibly provides the opportunity to society of maintaining adequate school systems which in turn operate to reduce the rate of illiteracy? Theoretically, illiteracy may be reduced to an approximate zero because the human organism is capable of attaining that degree of education which would classify him as literate according to the census terminology. The exceptions to this include the relatively small percentage of those who are idiots and low grade imbeciles, as well perhaps as a few other physical defectives. Insanity, almost without exception, occurs sufficiently late in life so that if a person were capable of becoming literate he would already have become so provided there were adequate educational opportunity. Germany, Holland, and Switzerland, for example, have practically negligible rates of illit-

[1] See above, Chap. V.

TABLE XXXIV
Data Utilized in the Correlation of Illiteracy and Urbanization*

State	Per Cent Illiterate 10 Years of Age and Over	Percentage of Urbanization 10 Years of Age and Over	Index Numbers for State School Systems 1918	Index Numbers for State School Systems 1890
	X_b	X_i	X_t	X_z
Maine............	1.3	31.7	47.4	29.9
New Hampshire.....	0.6	49.1	54.4	31.0
Vermont..........	1.1	26.2	51.5	30.2
Massachusetts......	0.3	90.3	61.0	45.9
Rhode Island.......	0.5	93.9	56.3	39.3
Connecticut........	0.4	57.9	59.8	38.9
New York..........	0.6	67.1	59.4	40.9
New Jersey.........	0.7	68.4	65.9	37.5
Pennsylvania.......	0.8	56.3	57.7	34.7
Ohio..............	1.0	55.0	59.7	33.1
Indiana...........	1.4	45.5	58.8	29.8
Illinois............	1.1	52.1	56.8	31.9
Michigan..........	0.6	55.2	60.4	31.9
Wisconsin..........	0.5	44.1	51.3	31.0
Minnesota.........	0.4	47.0	58.4	29.5
Iowa..............	0.5	38.3	61.9	31.0
Missouri...........	2.2	38.9	49.6	25.5
North Dakota......	0.3	20.2	59.2	25.5
South Dakota.......	0.3	21.3	55.0	26.1
Nebraska..........	0.4	32.6	57.1	26.4
Kansas............	0.6	36.2	55.2	30.6
Delaware..........	2.0	45.9	42.5	29.3
Maryland..........	2.0	54.6	43.2	33.3
Virginia...........	6.1	28.6	35.3	22.3
West Virginia......	4.8	25.0	37.7	21.8
North Carolina.....	8.2	19.6	30.6	17.8
South Carolina.....	6.6	22.1	29.4	12.5
Georgia............	5.5	27.5	32.6	15.7
Florida............	3.1	32.4	37.8	28.5

TABLE XXXIV—Continued

State	Per Cent Illiterate 10 Years of Age and Over	Percentage of Urbanization 10 Years of Age and Over	Index Numbers for State School Systems 1918	Index Numbers for State School Systems 1890
	X_b	X_i	X_t	X_z
Kentucky	7.3	22.2	35.0	23.4
Tennessee	7.4	23.6	35.1	21.0
Alabama	6.4	21.6	30.6	18.2
Mississippi	3.6	16.6	30.0	21.9
Arkansas	4.6	17.3	30.3	20.1
Louisiana	11.4	36.0	33.9	18.4
Oklahoma	2.4	28.1	44.4	20.5
Texas	2.2	32.7	41.1	23.2
Montana	0.3	31.4	75.8	36.3
Idaho	0.3	28.9	58.6	22.8
Wyoming	0.4	28.7	56.7	30.3
Colorado	1.7	48.6	59.2	37.8
New Mexico	11.9	18.8	53.0	10.0
Arizona	1.3	40.4	66.2	32.8
Utah	0.3	46.9	61.4	28.6
Nevada	0.4	23.6	59.1	34.5
Washington	0.3	54.2	63.7	30.8
Oregon	0.4	47.3	57.8	27.9
California	0.4	68.1	71.2	43.8
Mean	2.4	40.0	51.0	28.4

*Sources: X_b—*Fourteenth Census of the United States*, vol. II, chap. XII, Table V; X_i—*Ibid.*, computed from chap. I, Table XX, and chap. II, Table XIII; X_t—Ayres, *An Index Number for State School Systems*, p. 37; X_z—*Ibid.*, p. 31.

The data on illiteracy and urbanization are for native whites of native parentage. The data on school systems are not given according to any race or "nationality" classification.

eracy.[2] The methods by which this is ascertained, while not comparable with those of the United States, do give results which support the statements made above.

The next logical step is a consideration of the adequacy of school systems as they exist in the United States today and as they have existed in past decades. The data presented by Leonard P. Ayres in "An Index Number for State School Systems" is utilized as forming the most adequate basis for analysis as was previously pointed out in Chapter VII.

Before utilizing these educational data in the present chapter, the degree of gross relationship between illiteracy and urbanization was first investigated. The Pearsonian coefficient of correlation for illiteracy and urbanization, for all classes, was found to be $-.36$.[3] Since the data were slightly non-linear in character, the index of correlation was computed on the basis of the following formula:

$$Rho^2{}_{yx} = \frac{a\Sigma(Y)+b\Sigma(XY)+c\Sigma(X^2Y)-Nc_y{}^2}{\Sigma(Y^2)-Nc_y{}^2}$$

$Rho = .39$ which indicates that a second degree parabola affords a slightly better fit for the data than does a straight line.

The data were then refined by utilizing only native whites of native parentage, ten years of age and over.[4] The coefficient of correlation was found to be $r_{bi} = -.49$. Since the data appeared on inspection to be somewhat non-linear in character, the index of correlation was next computed on the basis of a second degree parabola, the formula given in connection with the discussion of the data for all classes being utilized. The result was $Rho_{bi} = .58$. The non-

---

[2]*Illiteracy and School Attendance in Canada* (Dominion Bureau of Statistics, 1926), p. 30.
[3]See Appendix B for data utilized.   [4]Table XXXIV.

linear character of the data was further studied by means of an exponential curve. The formula,

$$Rho^2{}_{yx} = \frac{\log a \Sigma y + \log b \Sigma x \cdot \log y - Nc_{\log y}{}^2}{\Sigma(\log y)^2 - Nc_{\log y}{}^2}$$

was utilized. Proof of the fact that the data for illiteracy and urbanization, native white of native parentage, 10 years of age and over, fall along an exponential curve is given by the result, $Rho_{bi} = .74$. Inasmuch as this is a gross correlation, it appears necessary to refine the data and determine whether the apparent high relationship between illiteracy and urbanization holds.

L. P. Ayres's index numbers for school systems for the years 1918 and 1890 were utilized as the third and fourth variables. Since the relationship between each of these variables and illiteracy is linear, the four variables were utilized in the partial and multiple correlations on the assumption of general linearity. This could be done because when the non-linear relationship between urbanization and illiteracy, for native whites of native parentage, was tested for linearity where utilized in partial correlation, by computing the derivative and plotting against the dependent variable, the non-linear relationship was found not to be of significant effect. The size of the sample is also operative here.

The notation employed was as follows:

$b =$ illiteracy rate for native whites of native parentage, 10 years of age and over.

$i =$ percentage of urbanization, native white of native parentage, 10 years of age and over.

$t =$ index numbers for state school systems, 1918.

$z =$ index numbers for state school systems, 1890.

TABLE XXXV
Gross and Net Correlations

$r_{ui} = -.49$ $r_{it.b} = +.32$
$r_{bi} = -.72$ $r_{it.z} = -.08$
$r_{oz} = -.75$ $r_{iz.b} = +.74$
$r_{it} = +.55$ $r_{iz.t} = +.69$
$r_{iz} = +.79$ $r_{tz.b} = +.42$
$r_{tz} = +.73$ $r_{tz.i} = +.58$

$r_{bi.t} = -.16$ $r_{bi.tz} = +.25$
$r_{bi.z} = +.26$ $r_{bi.iz} = -.38$
$r_{bt.i} = -.62$ $r_{bz.it} = -.50$
$r_{bt.z} = -.39$ $r_{it.bz} = +.03$
$r_{iz.i} = -.68$ $r_{iz.bt} = +.70$
$r_{bz.t} = -.41$ $r_{tz.bi} = +.28$

Since not only urbanization but also school systems are of primary interest here, the three gross correlations of $r_{bi} = -.49$, $r_{bt} = -.72$, and $r_{bz} = -.75$ may first be considered. The gross relationships of illiteracy and school systems for both 1918 and 1890 are higher than the gross relationship of illiteracy with urbanization.

The correlation of illiteracy and school systems of 1918, holding percentage of urbanization constant, is $r_{bt.i} = -.62$. The correlation of illiteracy and school systems of 1890, holding percentage of urbanization constant, is $r_{bz.i} = -.68$. As in the gross correlations of illiteracy with school systems for these years, a significant inverse correlation is found. Furthermore, in the correlations of both the zero and first orders, the data for school systems of 1890 give a slightly higher correlation with illiteracy for 1920 than do the data for school systems of 1918.

In the partial correlations of the second order, $r_{bi.tz} = +.25$. When the effects of the school systems of 1918 and 1890 are controlled, the relationship between illiteracy and urbanization becomes positive. This, however, is chiefly a function of the index numbers for school systems in 1890 when the United States was less highly urbanized. When the school systems in 1918 alone are controlled $r_{bi.t} = -.16$, which appears to be the truer indication of the actual relationship at the present time.

The coefficient of the multiple correlation is $R_{b.itz} = .81$. This is indicative of a high degree of relationship between the dependent variable, illiteracy, and the independent series in combination.

In the preceding chapters of Part II, the regression equations have been presented at this point. Since the data for illiteracy and urbanization are exponential in character, similar predictions in this chapter would not be warranted. In fact, the regression equations were analyzed but the figures secured as a basis of prediction were obviously inaccurate. In speaking of the validity of such results where there is a departure from linearity, Mills says, "There would be no fallacy involved in the use of the equation under these conditions, but it would not furnish as good a basis for estimates as one which took account of the true relationship."[5]

In summary, the chapter pursues somewhat further the analysis of the already observed negative relationship between illiteracy and urbanization. There is, moreover, a significant relationship between illiteracy and the adequacy of state school systems for the various census years. The correlation remains important when percentage of urbanization is held constant. When the adequacy of school systems is controlled, however, the relationship between illiteracy and urbanization loses its significance. It would appear, therefore, that while illiteracy may be thought of as being negatively related to urbanization, more correctly

---

[5] *Statistical Methods*, p. 499.

speaking, the lower illiteracy rate is rather a function of the adequacy of urban school systems, in comparison with rural school systems.

Finally, multiple correlation is resorted to in order to determine the effect of school systems and urbanization, in combination, upon educational status. The result, $R=.81$, indicates the important relationship of the factors of urbanization and adequate school systems upon educational status.

CHAPTER XVII

CONCLUSIONS TO PART II

Illiteracy in the United States is a steadily decreasing phenomenon. Nevertheless, in 1920 there were in round numbers 4,900,000 persons in the United States over ten years of age who were illiterate. While the rate for the United States as a whole was six per cent, certain great groups of the population had a much higher rate.

The human organism is a mechanism biologically equipped and culturally trained to make adjustments to life situations. Other factors being equal, it seems evident that the literate individual, on the average, is better equipped than the illiterate to adapt himself to existing situations or to problems as they arise. Modern culture is so dependent upon communication by means of written symbols that the illiterate individual is more definitely circumscribed in his ability to adjust to the surrounding culture than he would have been twenty or thirty or forty years ago.

In Part II of the present study, an attempt has been made to analyze by statistical procedure the relationships which exist between illiteracy and certain selected social phenomena.

First among these phenomena studied was birth-rate. Any factor which tends to either increase or decrease the birth-rate is a matter of significance. Various studies have been made in which the effect of education upon the birth-rate has been pointed out. For example, the lowered birth-rate among college graduates has practically become a truism. At least as significant an approach to the problem,

Conclusions to Part II 141

and certainly a more comprehensive one inasmuch as only small groups of college graduates have been studied, is an investigation of the relation of illiteracy to birth-rate for the country as a whole. Thus, when the two important affecting factors of urbanization and per capita current income were mathematically controlled, it was found that the net coefficient of correlation, indicating the degree of relationship between illiteracy and birth-rate, was $r = +.49$. This is indicative of the fact that high illiteracy rates and high birth-rates tend to go together. Furthermore, if other conditions remained the same and the illiteracy rate should fall to zero, it is possible to predict, by means of the regression equations, that there would be a significant decrease in the birth-rate for the country as a whole.

After determining that the birth-rate is positively correlated with the illiteracy rate, the relation of this latter factor to deaths of infants under one year of age was next investigated. High infant mortality rates are to a great extent due to ignorance with regard to the proper care of children. It is obvious that the illiterate mother or father will be more ignorant in regard to modern methods of child care than the literate mother or father who has access to the great bulk of published material of a relatively scientific nature, dealing with the general question of proper care of infants. When the relationship existing between illiteracy and infant mortality is reduced to measurable terms, it is found that after urbanization and per capita current income are controlled, the net coefficient of correlation for the two factors of illiteracy and infant mortality is $+.61$. In other words, high infant mortality rates are associated with high illiteracy rates. Further analysis of the existing data points to the fact that if other conditions were to remain the same while the illiteracy rate fell to an approximate zero, a significant decrease in the infant mortality rate of the United States would occur. Thus illiteracy is a factor which must be considered not only with regard to the birth-rate of the country but also with regard to the percentage of infants who do not survive the first year of life.

The third social phenomenon to be investigated with regard to its relation to illiteracy was early age of marriage, considered in terms of the number of females, ever married, 15 to 19 years of age, for native whites of native parentage. The percentage of such early marriages in the population is a matter of definite social significance. "Our civilization is today so complex that the judgments and experience necessitated by family life are not always acquired early. Marriage today also involves in many cases restrictions to opportunities and limitations on activities. Many occupations requiring long-time preparation in education or apprenticeship tend to discourage early marriage."[1] While these relationships are not specifically measured, nevertheless the above statements appear valid. It is possible, however, to measure the degree of relationship which exists between illiteracy and early age of marriage. When percentage of urbanization and per capita current income were held constant, the net coefficient of correlation between illiteracy and early age of marriage was found to be $r = +.43$. This means that there is a positive relationship between the percentage of illiteracy and the percentage of females between the ages of 15 and 19, native white of native parentage, who are married. Thus, it is to be expected (as the regression equations indicate) that if other conditions were to remain the same, a significant lowering of the illiteracy rate would be definitely connected with a decrease in the percentage of early marriage

---

[1] E. R. Groves and Wm. F. Ogburn, *American Marriage and Family Relationships*, p. 219.

among native white females of native parentage.

The phenomenon next studied was that of size of family as defined in terms of the number of children under fifteen years of age for native white women, 15 to 54, ever married. This was believed to be a closer equivalent to the actual number of children per family than the census approximation. While size of family has been investigated from various standpoints, its relation to illiteracy has received but scant attention. According to the results of the present investigation, however, when the affecting factors of urbanization and per capita current income are mathematically controlled, the degree of relationship between illiteracy and size of family, as here considered, may be expressed in terms of the net coefficient of correlation as $r = +.36$. Thus, where illiteracy is high, the number of children per married woman tends to be relatively large. On the basis of the regression equations computed it is possible to predict that a decrease in the illiteracy rate, other conditions remaining the same, would lead to a decrease in the number of children per native white married woman within the specified age limits.

A phenomenon which perhaps more definitely affects the redistribution of population than any of those hitherto considered is that of mobility. This factor has been analyzed here in terms of the percentage of native white persons of native parentage who were born in a specified state but were living in other states in 1920. When the two factors of percentage of urbanization and percentage of male wage earners employed in manufacturing are held constant, the net coefficient of correlation for illiteracy and mobility to other states, for native whites of native parentage, becomes $-.58$. In other words, the illiterate individual tends to be less mobile than the literate person. Therefore, if the illiteracy rate of the United States should approximate zero, and if other conditions should remain the same, the percentage of mobility to other states would apparently increase, with a resultant intensification of geographical redistribution of individuals in the United States.

As in the case of mobility, suicide, the next phenomenon investigated, operates inversely with illiteracy. Various investigators have pointed out the fact that a relation seems to exist between suicide and degree of education. Thus suicide appears to be a form of adjustment which the literate tend to make rather than the illiterate. In measuring the relationship between illiteracy and suicide the gross coefficient of correlation for all classes was found to be $r = -.74$. Of the various social factors affecting suicide rates, the percentage of urbanization, marital status, and race and nationality were held constant in the partial correlations. When these three variables were controlled, the net coefficient of correlation became $r = -.68$. This high negative figure emphasizes the fact that low illiteracy rates and high suicide rates are found together. Therefore, one may predict on the basis of the regression equation that if other conditions should remain the same and if the illiteracy rate should fall to zero, the suicide rate would increase.

Although the factor of percentage of urbanization was taken into consideration in every social phenomenon studied, a more intensive analysis of this factor and of school systems was deemed advisable. From the unanalyzed data, it would appear that an important relationship exists between the illiteracy rate and percentage of urbanization. When the gross coefficient of correlation was computed for these two variables, for native whites of native parentage, it was found to be $r = -.49$. When index numbers for state school systems for 1918 were held constant, the coefficient of partial correlation for illiteracy and percentage of urbanization dropped to $r = -.16$. The coefficient of partial correlation for illiteracy and index numbers for state school systems of 1918, holding percentage of urbanization constant, was $r = -.62$. The coefficient of partial correlation for illiteracy and school systems of 1890, again holding percentage of urbanization constant, was $r = -.68$. In other words, it would appear that the lower illiteracy rate for the urban areas of the United States as a whole is a function of the adequacy of urban school systems both at present and in past decades in comparison with rural school systems rather than a function of urbanization *per se*.

In the analysis of the various societal phenomena which were studied, no cause and effect relationships were assumed. A process of factorization was followed and in each case, whether all classes, native whites, or native whites of native parentage were studied, at least two of the important factors affecting the phenomenon were controlled in the partial correlations, after the two primary factors had previously been refined as far as possible. Thus a measuring of relationships was the general objective and the reliability of these relationships was statistically determined by computation of the error.[2]

The phenomena studied in relation to illiteracy include birth-rate, infant mortality, early age of marriage, size of family, mobility and suicide. As a general conclusion, it may be stated that the rate of illiteracy is a factor which is related to each of these societal phenomena and which has, in general, not been adequately considered in previous investigations. It is believed, on the basis of the results obtained, that no comprehensive analysis of any one of these subjects can omit the important, measurable factor of illiteracy or some socio-educational equivalent. Within the

---

[2] A table of the errors of coefficients of correlation is included in Appendix A.

limits of the present investigation, the importance of education as related to various types of social data has been demonstrated.

APPENDIXES

APPENDIX A

METHODOLOGY

Appendix A contains a brief statement of the statistical techniques employed in the analysis of illiteracy and certain related factors. To some extent, the classificatory procedure utilized by the census bureau provided a method of refining data. Part I of the present study utilizes this in the analysis of illiteracy data, according to sex, age, race and nationality, urban and rural environment. It may be added that this method of refining data sometimes obviates the use of partial correlation.

In Chapter II, straight line trends were put through the data for the United States as a whole and for each state for the period, 1870 to 1920.[1] From observation of the plotted data, it was evident that the trends of illiteracy over the period studied were in general linear in character. A straight line was fitted to the six points corresponding to the six decades by the method of least squares, the following equations being used:

$$\Sigma(y) = na + b\Sigma(x)$$
$$\Sigma(xy) = a\Sigma(x) + b\Sigma(x^2)$$

Solving these two equations, the most probable relationship between the variables studied was obtained.[2]

---

[1] In some cases straight lines were also computed for shorter periods while the data for a few states appeared somewhat curvilinear. In these latter cases a second degree parabola was utilized, but it was found that it afforded no better fit to the data.

[2] For a discussion of the theory on which the method is based see Frederick C. Mills's *Statistical Methods*, pp. 273–78. Also, see C. G. Dittmer's *Introduction to Social Statistics*, pp. 149–52.

The statistical tool known as the method of standard population was utilized in Chapter VIII. At that point a discussion of the methods employed was given in some detail.[3] Utilization of this method enables the investigator to control the important factor of age distribution.

The methodology employed in Part II consisted in the utilization of certain additional statistical tools. The results obtained with these techniques were discussed as they were presented.

As a preliminary investigation, the Pearsonian coefficient of correlation was computed for illiteracy and each of the social phenomena studied[4] as an abstract measure of the degree of relationship existing between the two variables. The value of r, the symbol for the coefficient of correlation, fluctuates between 0 and ± 1. A correlation of zero indicates no relationship while a correlation of one indicates a perfect relationship which may be either positive or negative.[5] Owing to the complexity of social data, a valid, perfect correlation is practically an impossibility. In general, the higher the correlation and the lower the error, the more significant does the former become. The formula utilized in computing the Pearsonian coefficient of correlation was

---

[3] For further discussion, consult G. C. Whipple's *Vital Statistics*, pp. 292-303.

[4] Divorce was investigated but proved unsatisfactory for the present study owing to the lack of standardization in divorce laws. Insanity also appeared unsatisfactory as the rates are so dependent on the states' provisions for the care of persons with mental diseases. Statistics on crime are largely dependent on the various state laws and criminal procedures so that they, also, could not be utilized. In all three cases the Pearsonian coefficients of correlation were computed but the errors were so large that the correlations were not significant.

[5] For a clear discussion of the meaning and methodology of the Pearsonian coefficient, see Edmund E. Day's *Statistical Analysis*, pp. 193-99. A more extended discussion of linear correlation is found in G. Udny Yule's *An Introduction to the Theory of Statistics*, chap. IX.

Methodology 151

$$r = \frac{\dfrac{\Sigma(x'y')}{N} - c_x c_y}{\sqrt{\dfrac{\Sigma(x')^2}{N} - c_x^2} \sqrt{\dfrac{\Sigma(y')^2}{N} - c_y^2}}$$

In certain instances, however, the relationship between the two variables was found, upon plotting, to be non-linear in character. The measure of non-linear relationship is called the index of correlation and is represented by the symbol *Rho*. The index of correlation[6] was computed for curves that were parabolic in nature and also for exponential curves. The formula utilized when a second degree parabola was fitted to the data was

$$Rho^2{}_{yx} = \frac{a\Sigma(X) + b\Sigma(XY) + c\Sigma(X^2Y) - Nc_y^2}{\Sigma(Y^2) - Nc_y^2}$$

When the data were exponential in character, logarithms were utilized in the following formula for the computation of the index of correlation:

$$Rho^2{}_{yx} = \frac{\log a \Sigma y + \log b \Sigma x . \log y - Nc_{\log y}^2}{\Sigma(\log y)^2 - Nc_{\log y}^2}$$

In computing the coefficients of partial and multiple correlation, two methods were followed. When five variables were utilized, it was considered perhaps more economical to step the coefficients of correlation up from the zero order, to the first order, and so on.[7] For example, after computing the *r's* of the zero order, the *r's* of the first order were computed from the formula,

---

[6] See Frederick C. Mills's *op. cit.*, pp. 436-41.
[7] For an analysis of the theory and methodology, consult G. Udny Yule's *An Introduction to the Theory of Statistics*, chap. XV. Also, see Frederick C. Mills's *Statistical Methods*, pp. 507-12.

$$r_{12.3} = \frac{r_{12} - r_{13} \cdot r_{23}}{(1 - r^2_{13})^{\frac{1}{2}} (1 - r^2_{23})^{\frac{1}{2}}}$$

This formula was further expanded for the computation of the coefficients of correlation of the second and third orders. The coefficients of regression were computed from equations of the form $b_{12.345} = r_{12.345} \dfrac{S_{1.345}}{S_{2.345}}$. The standard error of estimate for five variables was obtained by means of the formula,

$$S^2_{1.2345} = (1 - r^2_{12})(1 - r^2_{13.2})(1 - r^2_{14.23})(1 - r^2_{15.234})$$

In computing the coefficient of multiple correlation denoted by R, which measures the degree of relationship between the single dependent variable and the series of independent variables, in combination, the equation

$$R^2_{1.2345} = 1 - \frac{S^2_{1.2345}}{\sigma_1^2}$$

was utilized.

The coefficients of partial and multiple correlation were, in general, computed for only four variables, however. In those cases the first method of computingt he coefficients given by Frederick C. Mills in his *Statistical Methods*[8] was followed. The coefficients of net correlation were computed on a basis of the coefficients of regression. For example,

$$r_{12.34} = \sqrt{b_{12.34} \cdot b_{21.34}}$$

The b's were previously computed from the normal equations according to the Doolittle Method of solution.[9] The estimating or regression equation took the form,

---

[8]Chapter XIV. This chapter includes a discussion of the various tools of analysis utilized.
[9]Mills, *op. cit.*, pp. 577–81.

$$X_1 = a + b_{12.34} X_2 + b_{13.24} X_3 + b_{14.23} X_4$$

The reliability of estimates based on this equation was determined by the computation of the standard error of estimate from the formula.,

$$S^2_{1.234} = \sigma_1^2 - b_{12.34}\, p_{12} - b_{13.24}\, p_{13} - b_{14.23}\, p_{14}$$

The coefficient of multiple correlation which is dependent on the relation between S and σ was computed from the formula,

$$R^2_{1.234} = 1 - \frac{S^2_{1.234}}{\sigma_1^2}$$

The standard error of the correlation coefficient[10] is computed according to the formula, $\sigma_r = \dfrac{1 - r^2}{\sqrt{N}}$

This formula holds for the coefficient of multiple correlation and coefficients of partial correlation as well as for the simple coefficient of correlation. The following table gives the errors for the various numbers of states employed:

According to W. F. Ogburn,[11] the coefficient of correlation should be at least three times as large as its error be-before one can be sure it is significant. Other authorities[12] make comparable statements. Some prefer to state the error in terms of the probable error or .6745 times the error as computed above.

At this point, some further explanation as to the theory of correlation should perhaps be added. Day states this concisely. "By correlation is meant, in brief, a definite

---

[10] Yule, *op. cit.*, p. 352; also, Mills, *op. cit.*, p. 556.

Note: Scatter diagrams were prepared for all intercorrelations as a test for linearity. The single exception to linearity or approximate linearity is dealt with on page 136 above.

[11] Groves and Ogburn, *American Marriage and Family Relationships*, p. 474.

[12] See Harry Jerome, *Statistical Method*, p. 285.

tendency for two or more variables to vary together. The variables may move in the same or in opposite directions, but if they are correlated they are never indifferent to one another, they are either mutually attractive or mutually repellent. Correlation involves a one-to-one correspond-

r	Error When $N=48$	Error When $N=34$	Error When $N=33$	Error When $N=21$
0.05	0.144	0.171	0.174	0.218
0.10	0.143	0.170	0.172	0.216
0.15	0.141	0.168	0.170	0.213
0.20	0.139	0.165	0.167	0.209
0.25	0.135	0.161	0.163	0.205
0.30	0.131	0.156	0.158	0.199
0.35	0.127	0.150	0.153	0.191
0.40	0.121	0.144	0.146	0.183
0.45	0.115	0.137	0.139	0.174
0.50	0.108	0.129	0.131	0.164
0.55	0.101	0.120	0.121	0.152
0.60	0.092	0.110	0.111	0.140
0.65	0.083	0.099	0.101	0.126
0.70	0.074	0.087	0.089	0.111
0.75	0.063	0.075	0.076	0.095
0.80	0.052	0.062	0.063	0.079
0.85	0.040	0.048	0.048	0.061
0.90	0.027	0.033	0.033	0.041
0.95	0.014	0.017	0.017	0.021

ence between the paired variables."[13] The essential point is the mutual relationship between two variable phenomena. The closeness of this relationship determines the size of the coefficient of correlation, r. Yule, in discussing the coefficient of correlation, says, "The constant r is of very great importance. It is evidently a pure number and its magnitude is unaffected by the scales in which x and y are

---
[13]Edmund E. Day, *Statistical Analysis*, pp. 188–89.

measured, for these scales will affect the numerator and denominator to the same extent."[14]

Multiple and partial correlation methods enable the investigator to carry his analysis much farther than in simple correlation alone and to more nearly approach the work of the exact scientist who controls his various factors. "The coefficient of multiple correlation is an index of the degree of relationship between a single dependent variable and a number of independent variables, in combination. It measures the degree to which variations in the dependent variable are related to the combined action of the other factors. Its significance may be clearer if all the independent variables are looked upon as constituting a single independent series. The coefficient is then seen to be a measure of the relationship between the dependent variable and the independent series, which is precisely what the coefficient of correlation is in the simpler case of two variables."[15]

Partial or net correlation signifies the degree of relationship between two variables when other specified factors are held constant. That is, the investigator can theoretically determine, within the limits of the error, the degree of association between two variables when other affecting variables (most often one or two) are abstracted. The importance of this statistical tool is perhaps obvious. The caution should be included, however, that where the number of cases is small, as in the present study, too much reliance upon the mathematical values of the partial correlations is both unwarranted and dangerous. Because of the recognition of this fact, the interpretations in the body of the study must be regarded as empirical, inferential probabilities, based upon a thorough knowledge of the data.

[14] G. Udny Yule, *An Introduction to the Theory of Statistics*, p. 173.
[15] Mills, *op. cit.*, pp. 497-98.

It is admittedly hazardous to lay down any specific rules for the interpretation of a coefficient of correlation as the type of data studied and the number of cases involved must be considered as well as the actual size of the coefficient itself. "Furthermore, it is more hazardous to attempt to appraise the partial dependence of one variable on each of several others than to estimate the degree of relationship between two variables."[16] In addition, the inferences drawn from the use of such methodology must be carefully stated. All careful statisticians emphasize the fact that generalizations must not only be consistent with the data but also that they must be kept within the limits of the data presented. Furthermore, the present study does not pretend to give a complete description of the data. Only those aspects necessary for the development of the hypotheses presented were utilized. In the problem, therefore, attempts at interpretation were definitely limited to such generalizations as the data clearly justified. Other possible interpretations were rigidly excluded as being inconsistent with the purpose of the investigation.

Finally, for the technical justification for correlating ratios and unweighted averages, reference may be made to Frank A. Ross's monograph, "School Attendance in 1920".[17]

---

[16] W. L. Crum, and A. C. Patton, *An Introduction to the Methods of Economic Statistics*, p. 263.

[17] U. S. Bureau of the Census, Monograph V, pp. 210–11. See also, M. R. Neifield, "A Study of Spurious Correlation," *Journal of the American Statistical Association*, XXII, 331–38, and G. Udny Yule, "On the Interpretation of Correlation, between Indices or Ratios," *Journal of the Royal Statistical Society*, vol. LXXIII (1910), pp. 644–47.

APPENDIX B

Appendix B contains supplementary tables, the data having been utilized only in simple correlations. All other data are included in the chapters of which they form the basis.

TABLE XXXVI

Data for Correlation of Illiteracy and Birth-Rate, for Native White Females, 15-44[1]

State	Illiteracy Rate* Per 1,000 Females	Legitimate[2] Births** Per 1,000 Married Females
California...............	3.4	119.4
Connecticut..............	3.5	153.3
Indiana..................	5.1	150.1
Kansas...................	3.2	157.3
Kentucky.................	43.5	188.9
Maryland.................	9.1	170.8
Massachusetts............	3.0	169.4
Michigan.................	3.7	167.4
Minnesota................	2.9	189.3
Nebraska.................	2.6	170.1
New Hampshire............	5.6	167.1
New York.................	3.4	146.8
North Carolina...........	56.0	231.1
Ohio.....................	3.8	140.9
Oregon...................	2.1	125.8
Pennsylvania.............	4.5	171.6
South Carolina...........	68.6	205.8
Vermont..................	7.2	157.9
Virginia.................	36.4	230.5
Washington...............	1.6	131.6
Wisconsin................	3.8	172.8

[1]Sources: *Fourteenth Census of The United States, vol. II, chap. XII, computed from Table XII.

**Birth Statistics for the Birth Registration Area of the United States, 1920, Table V, and Fourteenth Census, vol. II, chap. IV, Table XI.

[2]Unknown legitimacy is tabulated as legitimate while the birth certificates of California, Massachusetts, New Hampshire and Vermont do not require this information although it is sometimes given.

TABLE XXXVII
Data for the Correlation of Illiteracy and Early Age of Marriage, all Classes[3]

State	Per Cent* Illiterate, 10 Years of Age and Over	Per Cent of** Females, 15-19 Ever Married	State	Per Cent* Illiterate, 10 Years of Age and Over	Per Cent of** Females, 15-19 Ever Married
Maine...........	3.3	10.2	West Virginia....	6.4	18.4
New Hampshire...	4.4	8.0	North Carolina..	13.1	16.1
Vermont.........	3.0	9.8	South Carolina...	18.1	17.0
Massachusetts....	4.7	5.0	Georgia..........	15.3	22.9
Rhode Island.....	6.5	5.7	Florida..........	9.6	21.8
Connecticut......	6.2	6.3			
			Kentucky........	8.4	20.1
New York........	5.1	6.5	Tennessee.......	10.3	20.2
New Jersey.......	5.1	7.6	Alabama........	16.1	20.4
Pennsylvania.....	4.6	10.0	Mississippi......	17.2	21.1
Ohio.............	2.8	11.5	Arkansas........	9.4	23.2
Indiana..........	2.2	13.3	Louisiana........	21.9	18.2
Illinois...........	3.4	9.3	Oklahoma.......	3.8	21.1
Michigan.........	3.0	11.4	Texas...........	8.3	18.6
Wisconsin........	2.4	5.7			
			Montana........	2.3	10.8
Minnesota.......	1.8	5.3	Idaho...........	1.5	13.1
Iowa.............	1.1	9.4	Wyoming........	2.1	15.3
Missouri.........	3.0	13.5	Colorado........	3.2	13.6
North Dakota.....	2.1	6.7	New Mexico.....	15.6	18.9
South Dakota.....	1.7	8.0	Arizona.........	15.3	22.2
Nebraska.........	1.4	9.4	Utah............	1.9	10.1
Kansas...........	1.6	12.1	Nevada.........	5.9	13.8
Delaware.........	5.9	13.9	Washington......	1.7	13.0
Maryland........	5.6	12.3	Oregon..........	1.5	12.7
Virginia..........	11.2	13.7	California.......	3.3	12.0

[3]Married, widowed, and divorced.
Sources: *Fourteenth Census of the United States, vol. II, chap. XII, Table V; **Ibid., chap. IV, computed from Table XI.

TABLE XXXVIII
Data for the Correlation of Illiteracy and Size of Family, Native White Females, 15-54[4]

State	Illiteracy Rate* Per 1,000 Females	Average Number** of Living Children Per Mother of 1920
California	3.6	2.2
Connecticut	3.8	2.3
Indiana	6.7	2.7
Kansas	3.6	2.8
Kentucky	52.1	3.1
Maryland	10.8	2.7
Michigan	4.2	2.6
Minnesota	3.3	2.8
Nebraska	2.8	3.0
New York	3.7	2.3
North Carolina	66.4	3.3
Ohio	4.9	2.5
Oregon	2.3	2.4
Pennsylvania	5.2	2.7
South Carolina	60.0	3.2
Utah	2.4	3.1
Vermont	8.9	2.8
Virginia	41.6	3.2
Washington	1.9	2.4
Wisconsin	4.5	2.8

[4]Sources: *Fourteenth Census of the United States*, vol. II, chap. XII, computed from Table XII;
**Birth Statistics for the Birth Registration Areas of the United States, 1920*, p. 15.

TABLE XXXIX

DATA FOR THE CORRELATION OF ILLITERACY AND URBANIZATION, ALL CLASSES, 10 YEARS OF AGE AND OVER[5]

State	Per Cent Illiterate*	Per Cent of **Urbanization	State	Per Cent Illiterate*	Per Cent of **Urbanization
Maine............	3.3	39.6	West Virginia....	6.4	27.1
New Hampshire...	4.4	62.8	North Carolina...	13.1	20.8
Vermont.........	3.0	31.6	South Carolina...	18.1	19.2
Massachusetts....	4.7	94.7	Georgia.........	15.3	27.6
Rhode Island.....	6.5	97.4	Florida..........	9.6	38.6
Connecticut......	6.2	67.7			
			Kentucky........	8.4	28.6
New York........	5.1	82.6	Tennessee.......	10.3	28.3
New Jersey.......	5.1	78.3	Alabama.........	16.1	23.6
Pennsylvania.....	4.6	65.4	Mississippi......	17.2	14.6
Ohio.............	2.8	64.6	Arkansas........	9.4	18.1
Indiana..........	2.2	51.4	Louisiana........	21.9	37.5
Illinois...........	3.4	68.6	Oklahoma.......	3.8	28.7
Michigan.........	3.0	61.9	Texas...........	8.3	34.7
Wisconsin........	2.4	48.4			
			Montana........	2.3	33.0
Minnesota........	1.8	45.5	Idaho...........	1.5	28.9
Iowa.............	1.1	37.9	Wyoming........	2.1	30.8
Missouri..........	3.0	48.7	Colorado........	3.2	50.9
North Dakota.....	2.1	14.8	New Mexico.....	15.6	19.1
South Dakota.....	1.7	17.1	Arizona.........	15.3	36.5
Nebraska.........	1.4	32.8	Utah............	1.9	50.2
Kansas...........	1.6	36.2	Nevada.........	5.9	20.3
Delaware.........	5.9	54.6	Washington......	1.7	56.7
Maryland........	5.6	61.2	Oregon..........	1.5	51.4
Virginia..........	11.2	31.3	California.......	3.3	69.2

[5]Sources: *Fourteenth Census of the United States*, vol. II, chap. XII, Table XII; **Ibid.*, computed from chap. III, Table XIII and chap. XII, Table XXII

BIBLIOGRAPHY

I. GENERAL

Anderson, J., "The Falling Birth-rate," *Nature*, Vol. I, (1913), 84-85.

Ayers, Leonard P., *An Index Number for State School Systems*, Russell Sage Foundation, New York City, 1920.

Baber, Ray E., and Ross, Edward A., *Changes in the Size of American Families in One Generation*, (University of Wisconsin Studies in the Social Sciences and History, No. 10), Madison, 1924.

Birth Statistics for the Birth Registration Area of the United States, 1920, U. S. Bureau of the Census, Dept. of Commerce.

Birth, Stillbirth, and Infant Mortality Statistics of the Birth Registration Area of the U. S., 1924, 1925, U. S. Bureau of the Census, Dept. of Commerce.

Bloch, Louis, "Results of Two Years' Operation of the Literacy Test for Admission of Immigrants," *Q. Pub. Am. Stat. Assn.*, XVII, (1920-1921) pp. 333-35.

Boas, F., *The Census of the North American Indians*, Am Ed. Assn. N. S. 1899.

Brentano, L., "The Doctrine of Malthus and the Increase of Population During the Last Decades," *Economic Journal*, XX, (1910), 371-93.

Canada, Dominion of, Dominion Bureau of Statistics, *Illiteracy and School Attendance in Canada*, Ottawa, Canada, 1926.

Cavan, R. S., *Suicide*, Chicago, University of Chicago Press, 1928.

Chapman, J. C., and Wiggins, D. M., "Relation of Family Size to Intelligence of Offspring and Socio-economic Status of Family," *Pedagog. Sem.* XXXII, (1925), 414-21.

Children's Bureau, U. S. Dept. of Labor, *Infant Mortality*,

A Study of Infant Mortality in a Suburban Community, Montclair, N. J., Series No. 4, Pub. No. 1, pp. 1-36, 1915.

Crum, F. S., "The Marriage Rate in Massachusetts," *J. Am. Stat. Assn.*, IV (Dec., 1895), 332-39.

Dempsey, Mary V., *Infant Mortality in Brockton, Mass.* Bureau Pub. No. 37, Children's Bureau, U. S. Dept. of Labor.

Dublin, L. J., "Infant Mortality in Fall River, Mass.," *J. Am. Stat. Assn.*, XIV (1915) 505-20.

Duke, Emma, *Infant Mortality, Results of a Field Study in Johnstown, Pa., Based on Births in one Calendar Year*. U. S. Dept. of Labor Infant Mortality Series, Bureau Pub. No. 9, 1915.

Eighth Census of U. S., Vol. IV.

Eleventh Census of U. S., Compendium, Part III.

Falk, I. S., *The Principles of Vital Statistics*, Philadelphia and London, W. B. Saunders Company, 1923.

Farr, W., *Vital Statistics*, Part III, London, 1885.

Fourteenth Census of U. S., Vols. II and VIII.

Frenay, A. D., *The Suicide Problem in the United States*, Boston, R. Badger. 1927.

Garis, Roy L., *Immigration Restriction*, New York, The Macmillan Company, 1927.

Groves, Ernest R. and Ogburn, William F., *American Marriage and Family Relationships*, New York, Henry Holt & Company, 1928.

Haley, Theresa S., *Infant Mortality. Results of a Field Study in Akron, Ohio, Based on Births in One Year*, U. S. Children's Bureau, Infant Mortality Series No. 11, Bureau Pub. No. 72, 1920.

Hart, H., *Selective Migration as a Factor in Child Welfare in the U. S.* U. of Iowa Studies in Child Welfare, Vol. 1, No. 7, pp. 55-56.

————, *Differential Fecundity in Iowa, A Study in Partial Correlation*. U. of Iowa Studies in Child Welfare, Vol. II, No. 2.

Hill, J. A., "Comparative Fecundity of Women of Native and Foreign Parentage in the U. S.," *J. Am. Stat. Assn.*, XIII (1913), 583-604.

Hoffman, Frederick L., *Suicide Problems*, Newark, New Jersey, Prudential Press, 1928.
Holmes, S. J., "Size of College Families," *Jour. Heredity*, Oct., 1924, pp. 406-15.
Hunter, Estelle B., *Infant Mortality*, U. S. Dept. of Labor, Children's Bureau Publication No. 29.
Kiser, A. N., "Attempt at a Statistical Determination of the Birth-Rate in the U. S.," *J. Am. Stat. Assn.*, XVI (1919), 442-57.
Leigh, Edwin, *Illiteracy in the United States*. Annual Report of the Commissioner of Education, 1870, pp. 467-502.
Leven, Maurice, *Income in the Various States, Its Sources and Distribution, 1919, 1920, and 1921*, New York, National Bureau of Economic Research, Inc., 1925.
Methorst, H. W., "Survey of Birth-Rates of the World," *Eng. R.*, XIX (1927), 116-27.
Miner, J. R., "Suicide and Its Relation to Climatic and Other Factors," *Am. Jour. of Hyg.*, Baltimore, 1922, No. 2 of the Monographic Series of the *Am. Jour. of Hyg.*
Morselli, Henry, *Suicide, An Essay on Comparative Moral Statistics*, New York, D. Appleton & Company, 1882.
Mortality Statistics, U. S. Bureau of the Census, Dept. of Commerce, 1919, Table 8; 1920, Table 8; 1921, Table 8.
Newsholme A., and Stevenson, T. H. C., "The Decline of Human Fertility in the United Kingdom and Other Countries as Shown by Corrected Birth-Rates," *Jour. Roy. Stat. Society*, LXIX (1906), 34-87.
──────, "An Improved Method of Calculating Birth-Rates," *Jour. of Hyg.* V (April and July, 1905).
Ninth Census of U. S., Vol. I.
Ninth Census of U. S., Population and Social Statistics, XXX.
Ogburn and Groves, American Marriage and Family Relationships, Part II.
Park, Robert E., "The City: Suggestions for the Investigation of Human Behavior in the City Environment," *Am. Jour. of Sociology*, XX (1915), 577-612.

Parkinson, W. D., "Literacy and the Immigrant," *J. Educ.* XXX (1914), 567-70.
Pearl, Raymond, and Ilsley, Morrill L., "Preliminary Discussion of the Correlation Between Illiteracy and Mortality in American Cities," *Am. Jour. of Hyg.* II (1922), 587-600.
Redford, Arthur, *Labor Migration in England, 1800-1850*, New York, Longmans, Green & Co., Ltd.
Rochester, Anna, *Infant Mortality, Results of a Field Study in Baltimore, Md., Based on Births in One Year*, U. S. Dept. of Labor, Children's Bureau Pub. No. 119, pp. 1-400, 1923.
Ross & Baber, See Baber, Ray E., and Ross, Edward A.
Seventh Census of U. S., p. lxi.
Seventh Census of U. S.: Compendium, Part III.
Sixth Census of the United States: Illiteracy.
Smith, Mary R., "Statistics of College and Non-College Women," *Jour. Am. Stat. Assn.* VII (1900). pp. 1-26.
Sorokin, Pitirim, *Contemporary Sociological Theories*, New York and London, Harper & Brothers, 1928.
―――, *Social Mobility*, New York and London, Harper & Brothers, 1927.
Stearns, A. W., "Suicide in Massachusetts," *Mental Hyg.*, V (1921), 752-77.
Steele, Glenn, *Infant Mortality in Pittsburgh*, Series No. 12, U. S. Children's Bureau, Pub. No. 86, pp. 1-24, 1921.
Stevenson and Newsholme, "The Decline of Human Fertility in the United Kingdom and Other Countries as Shown by Corrected Birth-Rates," *Jour. Stat. Society*, LXIX (1906), 34-87.
―――, "An Improved Method of Calculating Birth-Rates," *Jour. of Hyg.* V (April and July, 1905).
Talbot, W., *Adult Illiteracy*, U. S. Bureau of Ed. Bul. No. 35, 1916.
Texas, University of, *A Report on Illiteracy in Texas*, Bulletin, 1923.
Thirteenth Census of U. S., Vol. I.
U. S. Bureau of the Census: *Illiteracy in Foreign Countries*, Dept. of Commerce, pp. 1-4.
U. S. Bureau of the Census: *Marriage and Divorce*, 1922.

U. S. Bureau of the Census: *Patients in Hospitals for Mental Disease*, 1923.
U. S. Bureau of the Census: *Prisoners*, 1923.
U. S. Bureau of Education: *Illiteracy in the U. S. and an Experiment for its Elimination*, Bul. No. 20, 1913.
Warren, C., *Illiteracy in the U. S. in 1870 and 1880*, U. S. Bureau of Ed. Cir. of Inform. No. 3, 1884.
Whipple, George C., *Vital Statistics, An Introduction to the Science of Demography*, 2nd ed., New York, John Wiley & Sons, Inc., 1923.
Wiggins and Chapman, "Relation of Family Size to Intelligence of Offspring and Socio-Economic Status of Family," *Pedagog. Sem.* XXXII (1925), 414-21.
Willcox, W. F., *Illiteracy in the United States, 1905*, Bureau of the Census Bulletin, No. 26.
Woodbury, Robert M., "Infant Mortality Studies of the Children's Bureau," *Pub. Am. Stat. Assn.*, XIX (1918), 30-53.
Young, A. A., "The Birth-Rate in New Hampshire," *Jour. Am. Stat. Assn.*, XIX (1905), 263-81.
Young, A. A., "The Census Age Question," *Pub. Am. Stat. Assn.*, XII (1910-11), 362.
Yule, G. Udny, "On the Changes in the Marriage and Birth-Rates in England and Wales During the Past Half-Century," *Jour. Roy. Stat. Society*, LXIX (1906), 88-132.

II. STATISTICAL

Chaddock, Robert Emmet, *Principles and Methods of Statistics*, New York, Boston, Houghton Mifflin Company, 1925.
Crum, William L., and Patton, Alson C., *An Introduction to the Methods of Economic Statistics*, Chicago and New York, A. W. Shaw Company, 1925.
Day, Edmund E., *Statistical Analysis*, New York, The Macmillan Company, 1925.
Dittmer, Clarence G., *Introduction to Social Statistics*, Chicago and New York, A. W. Shaw Company, 1926.
Groves, Ernest R., and Ogburn, William F., *American Marriage And Family Relationships*, Chapter XXIX, "A

Study in Correlation," New York, Henry Holt & Company, 1928.

Jerome, Harry, *Statistical Method*. Chapter XV, New York and London, Harper & Brothers, 1924.

Kelly, Truman L., *Tables to Facilitate the Calculation of Partial Coefficients of Correlation and Regression*, U. of Texas Bul. No. 27, 1916.

Mills, Frederick Cecil, *Statistical Methods*, New York, Henry Holt & Company, 1924.

Miner, John Rice, $\sqrt{1-r^2}$ and $1-r^2$ *for use in Partial Correlation and in Trigonometry*, Baltimore, The Johns Hopkins Press, 1922.

Neifeld, M. R., "A Study of Spurious Correlation," *Jour. Am. Stat. Assn.*, XXII, 331-38.

Peàrson, Karl, *The Grammar of Science*, Part I, 3rd ed., New York, The Macmillan Company, 1911.

Ross, Frank A., *School Attendance in 1920*, U. S. Bureau of the Census Monograph V, 1924.

Social Science Research Council Publications: *Research Method and Procedure in Agricultural Economics*, II, 272-73, 1921.

Thomas, Dorothy Swaine, "Statistics in Social Research," *Am. Jour. of Sociology*, XXXV (July, 1929), 1-17.

Thurstone, L. L., *The Fundamentals of Statistics*, New York, The Macmillan Company. 1925.

Tolley, H. R., and Ezekiel, M. J. B., "A Method of Handling Multiple Correlation Problems," *Jour. Am. Stat. Assn.*, XVIII, 993-1003.

Whipple, George C., *Vital Statistics, An Introduction to the Science of Demography*, 2nd ed., New York, John Wiley & Sons, Inc., 1923.

Yule, G. Udny, *An Introduction to the Theory of Statistics*, 8th ed., rev., London, Charles Griffin & Company, 1927.

―――――, "On the Interpretation of Correlations between Indices or Ratios," *Jour Roy. Stat. Society*, LXXIII (1910), 644-47.

THE UNIVERSITY OF NORTH CAROLINA SOCIAL STUDY SERIES

UNDER THE GENERAL EDITORSHIP OF HOWARD W. ODUM. BOOKS MARKED WITH * PUBLISHED IN COÖPERATION WITH THE INSTITUTE FOR RESEARCH IN SOCIAL SCIENCE.

BECKWITH: *Black Roadways: A Study of Folk Life in Jamaica* $3.00
BRANSON: *Farm Life Abroad* 2.00
*BREARLEY: *Homicide in South Carolina* .... *In preparation*
*BROWN: *Public Poor Relief in North Carolina* 2.00
*BROWN: *State Highway System of North Carolina* .... *In preparation*
*BROWN: *State Movement in Railroad Development* 5.00
CARTER: *Social Theories of L. T. Hobhouse* 1.50
CROOK: *General Strike, The* 6.50
FLEMING: *Freedmen's Savings Bank, The* 2.00
GEE (ED.): *Country Life of the Nation, The* 2.50
*GREEN: *Constitutional Development in the South Atlantic States, 1776-1860* 4.00
GREEN: *Negro in Contemporary American Literature, The* 1.00
*GRISSOM: *Negro Sings a New Heaven, The* 3.00
HAR: *Social Laws* 4.00
*HEER: *Income and Wages in the South* 1.00
*HERRING: *History of the Textile Industry in the South* ...... *In preparation*
*HERRING: *Welfare Work in Mill Villages* 5.00
HOBBS: *North Carolina: Economic and Social* 3.50
*JOHNSON: *Folk Culture on Saint Helena Island* 3.00
*JOHNSON: *John Henry: Tracking Down a Negro Legend* 2.00
*JOHNSON: *Social History of the Sea Islands* 3.00
JORDAN: *Children's Interest in Reading* 1.50
KNIGHT: *Among the Danes* 2.50
LOU: *Juvenile Courts in the United States* 3.00
*METFESSEL: *Phonophotography in Folk Music* 3.00
MILLER: *Town and Country* 2.00
*MITCHELL: *William Gregg: Factory Master of the Old South* 3.00
*MURCHISON: *King Cotton is Sick* 2.00
NORTH: *Social Differentiation* 2.50
ODUM: *Approach to Public Welfare and Social Work, An* 1.50
*ODUM (Ed.): *Southern Pioneers* 2.00
*ODUM and WILLARD: *Systems of Public Welfare* 2.00
*ODUM and JOHNSON: *Negro and His Songs, The* 3.00
*ODUM and JOHNSON: *Negro Workaday Songs* 3.00
POUND: *Law and Morals* 2.00
*PUCKETT: *Folk Beliefs of the Southern Negro* 5.00
*RHYNE: *Some Southern Cotton Mill Workers and Their Villages* . 2.50
ROSS: *Roads to Social Peace* 1.50
SALE: *Tree Named John, The* 2.00
SCHWENNING (Ed.): *Management of Problems* 2.00
SHERRILL: *Criminal Procedure in North Carolina* 3.00
*STEINER and BROWN: *North Carolina Chain Gang, The* 2.00
*VANCE: *Human Factors in Cotton Culture* 3.00
*WAGER: *County Government and Administration in North Carolina* .. 5.00
WALKER: *Social Work and the Training of Social Workers* 2.00
WHITE: *Some Cycles of Cathay* 1.50
WILLEY: *Country Newspaper, The* 1.50
WINSTON: *Illiteracy in the United States* 3.50

The University of North Carolina Press, Chapel Hill, N. C.; The Baker and Taylor Co., New York; Oxford University Press, London; The Maruzen Company, Tokyo; Edward Evans & Sons, Ltd., Shanghai.

www.ingramcontent.com/pod-product-compliance
Lightning Source LLC
Chambersburg PA
CBHW030113010526
44116CB00005B/231

I

STRATEGIES OF REASON

To accord to poetry the role of reason is not to deprive this art of mystery but to attend to mystery where it properly resides. Poetry, art of making, in a universe of contingencies is made out of something and by certain means. Whatever transformations, legitimate or travestied, the attitudes of history impose upon this sort of discourse[1]—reading it as ornament, invention, document, emotive fantasy, or not reading it at all, which also defines an attitude —the facts of its composition are clear. Poems are made of words. The very grammar by which they are articulated proves words to be more than simple counters. It proves as well that any activity mediated by language is intelligent, since by degrees of abstraction language as abstract mediates between the actual and the imaginable real. Prodigious combinative possibilities range between perception and concept, so that even these two poles are strained to comprehend the work to which language is set in metaphor, in the simplest poetic statement.

The artist lies
for the improvement of truth. Believe him.[2]

Doubtless the lyric poem is of all linguistic exercises the most highly organized, by its exclusions forming a new thing (not merely modifying an old) and thereby dissociating from its usual task, or transcending altogether in its concision, the discursive.

Poetry, as well as the novel after it, has been a fairly sensitive if not invariably critical register of the philosophical preoccupations concurrent with its creations. Poetry is a very

1. See Pierre Jean Jouve, *En Miroir* (Paris, 1954).
2. Charles Tomlinson, "A Meditation on John Constable," *Seeing Is Believing* (Oxford, 1960).

ancient and the novel a distinctly modern art. The latter of course must be acknowledged to have inherited its impetus from the now largely relinquished narrative form of the epic. It treats pre-eminently of the conduct of life and therefore in our time is bound to reflect from one vantage point or another the Hegelian world in which moral choices presently take place. In what way does the lyric poem approach the experience of life? Not certainly by a simple reproduction of its choices. It offers to the reader a very different sequence of "choices"—ultimately, we may say, no choice at all; it exacts from us complex inferences on the basis of the most unobtrusively organized signs, resolving these inferences in music if at all. The "newness" of a poem is precisely that which is cognitive about it. If the moral attaches itself with persistent relevance to the story, it has by no means consistently done so to poetry. The question of poetic morality is no longer debated in the simplistic terms familiar to Plato, Horace, or Sidney. (Although Brecht may be thought in some form to have transferred them to his anti-Aristotelian theater.) It is not in fact poetry which is accused now of feeding and watering the passions, but the novel, the cinema and, in short, the visually behavioral arts, not excluding advertising. Yvor Winters tells us: "The artistic process is one of moral evaluation of human experience, by means of a technique which renders possible an evaluation more precise than any other. The poet tries to understand his experience in rational terms, to state his understanding, and simultaneously to state, by means of the feelings which we attach to the words, the kind and degree of emotion that should properly be motivated by this understanding."[3] One of the factors which makes poetry a moral event is that it *is*

3. *In Defense of Reason* (Denver, 1947), p. 464.

expression. The degree of consciousness by which it reaches expression and the explicitness of its achievement emphasize the moral responsibility and the rational order in which the poem originates.

Philosophy has on the whole very few questions to ask. Regarding the philosophy of literary forms, it appears significantly clear from its earliest considerations that the questions raised are of lesser interest than the extent of self-consciousness in the matter of craft which those questions reveal. Perhaps in quite legitimately deflecting to itself the attention of moral philosophy the novel thus serves aesthetics by throwing into relief those other questions rarely if ever asked of prose fiction which yet govern the fundamental process of the poem. I refer to the questions of epistemology.

It is not for nothing that the most interested askers of these questions have been, conspicuously, poets. Plato himself stands among them. (Perhaps what the irresistible future requires of scholarship is a Freudian analysis of the foregoing, elucidating the self-destructive impulse at the bottom of the Platonic exclusion of the real poets from the ideal Republic.) But whereas Plato posed epistemological questions, his dialectic supplies moral answers to them, thus undermining the art of poetry in its very origins. What, he wonders, is the manner of existence of the poem? It is, he concludes, imitation, mimesis, and the poet thereby becomes a mere creator of appearances, of fictional substitutes, an illusionist. The only voice allowed to the poet in the Republic is the vocative one: "hymns to the gods and praises of famous men"; anything further would incur the entry of pleasure and pain into the governance of the state. "But that she [the muse] may not impute to us any harshness or want of politeness, let us tell her that there is an ancient quarrel between philosophy and poetry."[4] Is it churlish at so late a date to notice who started it? And who, in fact, dictated its course? The replies elicited by Plato from his Ion are quite attributable to an absence of customary disinterestedness on the part of the philosophical inquirer. The rhapsode, who is not permitted to ask any questions back, may well be forgiven for inferring an essential disingenuousness in the moral bias he confronts. The quarrel between the poet and the philosopher is necessarily enacted upon philosophical grounds, and as long as it expresses itself as a confrontation between poetry and morality, the poet finds himself placed in a false position in addition to a defensive one.

Plato's rhapsode is made to seem effectively irresponsible. But the irony of ecstatic possession has ever been that it, too, discriminates, is notoriously impermanent and, having occurred anteriorly (often indeed without issuing in works of art) is inaccessible. Such is the ineradicable difficulty at the heart of Coleridge's unsuccessful attempt to handle the problems of imagination in Kantian terms. As the topic recurs, it will have to be re-discussed. For the moment it should be sufficient to affirm that literary judgment has access to this agent reason only through its constituted effects. To the extent that Platonism continues among us it may be salient to recall with what clarity Biblical theology distinguishes the charismata of prophecy from the means of its expression. If a poet is in any sense a seer, he can only perform that role by descending to practical matters. Whatever the prophet's inspiration, he is left to his own linguistic devices. So is the poet, whose business is language and not the transmission of grace.

4. *Republic* X, 607.

Aristotle revised his tutor's bias and thereby confirmed himself in his own. The revision consisted of course in an organic interpretation of mimesis. In place of the shallow representative aspect of Plato's account, we have in Aristotle the vivifying notion of the biological analogy.[5] The poet's works resemble those in nature not as superficial facsimiles but in respect to internal organization and dynamic principle. The poem in the self-containing reciprocity of its particulars traffics seriously with the universal. It is more philosophic than history, if not more philosophic than philosophy. The Aristotelian poetic derives its authority from an empirical observation of art. What this scrutiny discloses is that words are bearers of a kind of action, serious, complete, and of a certain magnitude: the characters, passions, and experiences *(ethe, pathe, praxeis)* of men.[6]

A notable feature of subsequent romantic criticism is that it prefers to attend to the poet rather than the poem. If, as Gaston Bachelard suggests,[7] the poet is the genuine phenomenologist, it would seem to behoove the literary scholar to exert himself the more to competence as a critical realist. Such a study does no violence to poetry; rather, it is criticism which is vincible before such an object. Nor does this essay propose to discern the creative process where it is not to be isolated other than reflexively and after the fact. That way lie the uncompleted demonstrations that romantic psychology affords of the creativeness to which it must itself have recourse. For the

---

5. E.g., *Poetics* IV. Elizabeth Sewell pursues this theme in *The Orphic Voice* (London, 1961), a highly original attempt to delineate a "biology of poetry."
6. *Poetics* I-II.
7. In *La Poétique de l'Espace* (Paris, 1958).

mind discloses the possibilities of the rational imagination at the remove of words, in act. The beholder closest to the event cannot both compose his vision and avail himself at firsthand of a view of that composing as process. Such a *dédoublement* exceeds the capacities of self-consciousness, however subtle. Postlogic makes available poems, which all our curiosity will not convert for the amenities of discussion into a more transigent mode of discourse. For poems, although philosophic, are not philosophy and only rarely preserve their philosophical occasions from the shadow of the banal. The generalization of ideas is not a distinguishing property of poetry (as the universal is). Rather, when ideas enter poetry either they are transposed into the particulars of another mode or they tend, as Pope asserted, to do so as commonplaces subordinated to expression. Sensation, too, is discriminated by the same process and it is noteworthy therefore that a renowned Dionysian (he of the Apollonian output), Rimbaud, should have spoken in reference to his craft quite precisely of a systematic, a reasoned cultivation of that famous derangement of the senses. He concludes as well in the *Lettre du Voyant*: "La première étude de l'homme qui veut être poète est sa propre connaissance, entière. Il cherche son âme, il l'inspecte, il la tente, l'apprend." *In anima hominis dominatur violentia rationis,* said Bonaventure.

The Age of Reason in devising for itself an aesthetic would appear to have compromised lyric poetry, or at least the idea of it, to a degree. General accord assesses the situation as one that could have taken shape only in a social context of prevailing stability and conformity. Hence even the current practitioners of poetry did not exempt themselves from affiliation with a common point of view that actually diminished the scope and resources of their art. They were at home within those narrow limits. Thus Dryden with notorious infelicity at least twice allied himself with the contemporary devaluation of imagination. In the Epistle Dedicatory to *The Rival Ladies* of 1664 he remarks, "For imagination in a poet is a faculty so wild and lawless that like an high-ranging spaniel, it must have clogs tied to it, lest it outrun the judgment." And in the preface to *Annus Mirabilis*, 1666, he describes "wit writing" as "no other than the faculty of imagination in the writer, which, like a nimble spaniel, beats over and ranges through the field of memory."[8]

Behind such views lay the demotion of rhetoric as well. The Ramist reformation, having dissociated logic from the art of discourse, severed rhetoric from the art of thought.[9] Consequently poetry is reduced to a matter of propriety and decorum, style relegated to ornament. By these strictures art is maneuvered into the discredited and questionable category of fiction. Hobbes's nominalism is a forceful instance of that bias whereby imagination can be termed "a decaying sense, operating in the absence of its object."[10] Dorothea Krook[11] in a chapter called "Fear For Love" manages, it seems to me, the most generous interpretation of Hobbes's thought, even demonstrating quite credibly his relationship to the Aristotelian "low

8. *Dryden's Essays*, ed. W. P. Ker (Oxford, 1926), I, 8; I, 14.
9. Fully described by Walter J. Ong, *Ramus, Method and the Decay of Dialogue* (Cambridge, 1958).
10. *Leviathan* VIII. Other key passages in Chapter II and in the correspondence with Davenant which appeared first at Paris in 1650 and was prefixed to *Gondibert* in 1651.
11. *Three Traditions of Moral Thought* (Cambridge, 1959), pp. 94-131.

view" of human nature. Yet the differences are inescapably evident; they arise from wholly opposed constructions of reality and language. If universals are nothing but names, if truth is merely an attribute of language, if knowledge is purely deductive, if meaning is an "arbitrary institution," then poetry and indeed the greater portion of applied intelligence is a specious exercise. A world of "disconnected singulars" defies law and obviates art. Jacques Maritain considers nominalism a deep vice besetting the philosophers of our day, neo-Kantians, neo-positivists, idealists and others who

in different forms, and with various degrees of awareness ... all blame knowledge-through-concepts for not being a supra-sensible intuition of the existing singular.... They cannot forgive that knowledge for not opening directly upon existence as sensation does, but only onto essences, possibles. They cannot forgive it for its inability to reach actual existence except by turning back upon sense. They have a basic misunderstanding of the value of the abstract, that immateriality which is more enduring than things for all that it is untouchable and unimaginable, that immateriality which mind seeks out in the very heart of things. But why this incurable nominalism? The reason is that while having a taste for the real indeed, they nevertheless have no sense of being.[12]

Surely a poet's abstractions have value in so far as they are the fruit of sensible apprehension. Conversely, the sensible experience increases or extends its value precisely in being realized by the mind. The two modes, necessary to one another, are interanimating. I suppose that a poet cannot comfortably remain either an idealist or a materialist.

If the tidy categories of Aristotle or St. Thomas are uncon-

12. *The Degrees of Knowledge* (London, 1959), p. 1.

genial to the modern mind, the doctrinaire classifications of Hobbes are similarly so: "Time and education beget Experience; Experience begets Memory; Memory begets Judgement and Fancy: Judgement begets the strength and structure, and Fancy begets the ornaments of a Poem."[13] No one now would limit imagination to the efferent flux of fancy. The contrary objection to the difficult, usually in terms of the academic, is seemingly a quite transparent admission of the wish to *be* baffled by the poem—on one's own terms—to approach it not according to the reasoned disposition of its forms but with the license of the affective generalizations the reader's sensibility, rather than his perception, familiarly dictates. Yet even the discreditors of the academic acknowledge their discomfort in the presence of imagination *as a function of the mind.* The Aristotelian characterization of the mind as an active agent seems to me usefully to avoid the chief dangers of quasi-personification apparent in the fragmented Hobbesian schema.

The esemplastic imagination represented by Coleridge may be thought not to have escaped that awkwardnes, as mediator. Unity in multeity, the reconciliation of opposites, dazzling as these formulations perhaps are, and notwithstanding the precedent of Schelling, Schlegel, and the German transcendentalists in general, the essential ambiguity that blurs the argument of the *Biographia* does not lend itself to penetration. It is due to the fact that, however forgivably, the author simply has not distinguished whether he intended to write an essay in psy-

13. From Hobbes's correspondence with Davenant, available in J. E. Spingarn's *Critical Essays of the Seventeenth Century* (Oxford, 1908), II, 59. This matter is discussed in two recent books: Geoffrey Bullough, *Mirror of Minds* (Toronto, 1962); K. G. Hamilton, *The Two Harmonies* (Oxford, 1963).

chology or in literary criticism. Eclectic insights are no substitute for conceptual form—even in philosophy. There is no help for the fact that a speculation on the nature of poetry dissolves into a definition of the "ideal poet" in his perfection bringing "the whole soul of man into activity, with the subordination of its faculties to each other, according to their rank and dignity, [who] diffuses a tone and spirit of unity, that blends, and (as it were) fuses, each into each, by that synthetic and magical power, to which we have exclusively appropriated the name of imagination."[14] All our speculations upon the poet will not afford us entry into the poem.

The scepticism and caution with which contemporary scholars such as René Wellek, T. M. Raysor, Kathleen Coburn, and such critics and poets as F. R. Leavis, John Crowe Ransom, and Allen Tate regard Coleridge seems to be very well placed. Scholars have a legitimate source of dissatisfaction wherever the problems of art yield to the topic of Beauty. And those critics in our own time whose chief success has been in rescuing poetry from monism cannot be expected to look with complacence upon Coleridge, especially in view of the evidence that it is his "very looseness and incoherence, the wide gaps between his theory and his practice,"[15] in which his suggestiveness and primary appeal are to be discerned.

A recent sympathetic expositor of Coleridge's thought points out once again the unavoidable difficulty of the subject-object nexus: one of them is plainly not susceptible of observation in itself. Reason "is immediate in action and indemonstrable by discursive argument, since its grounds are in itself.

14. *Biographia* II, 12.
15. René Wellek, *A History of Modern Criticism* (New Haven, 1955), p. 187.

Itself the starting point of thought, nothing in the mind can explain it."[16]

My own assessment of the mind, which follows, is necessarily partial, governed by this realization that the mind in so far as it is definable is definable by what it does rather than what it metaphysically "is."

The intellect is a single faculty able to move in numerous ways. All the acts of which the mind is capable are distinguished by their immateriality, though they are made possible or mediated initially by contact with the sensible things of this world. Reason sees, apprehends, connects, infers, articulates. In prudence it is ordained toward acting; in the arts it is ordained toward making. Art is essentially intellectual, more so than prudence since it issues in formed experience (rather than behaviour whose expenditure endures in less tangible effects). Mental activity so varied in its operations does not become irrational when it is acting in a mode neither logically conceptual nor discursive. The dependence of each of the different kinds of mental operations upon the light and facilities of the others may be inferred from its very effects—especially in the arts, its most refined expression. Such operations are by reason of their spirituality simple, and we necessarily complicate by distinguishing them into parts the more immediately grasped. The very nature of reason, we see, is reflective. The whole process of knowing is one of progressive reflection, of subtilization, a movement beginning in sense and continuing in abstraction. Maritain describes this process further:

16. Richard H. Fogle, *The Idea of Coleridge's Criticism* (Berkeley, 1962), p. 6.

The intellect, for its part, knows things by forming them in a fruit which it conceives in the bosom of its immateriality. Following Aristotle, Thomists recognise in the intellect an active light (the "agent" or acting intellect) which, using sensible representations and setting free the intelligibility they contain in potency . . . specifies the intellect with the help of a *species impressa*, a "presentative form" abstracted from the sensible and "received" by it. Then the intellect is in initial or first act. Precisely as principle of action the intellect has intentionally become the object, which, through its *species*, is hidden in it as a fertilising seed and co-principle of knowing (just as the intellect, the sufficient principle of its own actions, already is, itself). In this way, the intellect itself actuated by the *species expressa* of the intelligible order, an "elaborated" or "uttered" "presentative form" in which it brings the object to the highest level of actuality and intelligible formation, becomes the object in final act. If the distinction between first and second act is thus once more encountered in knowledge, it is because knowledge . . . constitutes unto itself alone a whole metaphysical order apart, wherein meet in common both the distinction between essential form and existence in the line of being and the distinction between operative form and the operation in the line of action—now transposed on to one and the same line, the line of knowing. Is not knowing at once existence and (immanent) action?[17]

Thomistic philosophy in denominating art a habit of the practical intellect recalls us to its efficient origin. Implicit in this recognition is the awareness that the flaws, the failures of poetry, the more obtrusive because they mar a feat of style, may be attributed finally to imperfect knowledge. Histories of the arts and of criticisms alike may be summarized by their mistakes. No one ever knows enough.

While the study that begins here affirms a conviction of

17. *Degrees of Knowledge*, pp. 116-17.

poetry as a form of knowledge, it does not set out directly to elaborate that case but to construe in its kinds the performance of reason where its resources convene at varying distances from the discursive in the great persisting modes of English poetry. Not, it should be noted, in the modes of its conception or reception but in its achieved expressions.

So this essay is not theoretical. It proffers no dogmatic hypothesis about the art of poetry and hence would exclude none of the modes in which poetry is practiced. Rather, it intends an empirical scrutiny, in the poets selected, of the conduct of the mind which I take to be the primary and self-evident source of art and whose dynamic agency is deducible in its effects as well as from the nature of the medium in which its forces are deployed. The first premise of this work is then that "reason is a principal cause of poetry." As a function of the mind, imagination draws its materials from the sensible world and from the unconscious. I use the term rational imagination to distinguish the consciously directed and voluntary function of this faculty from the random, involuntary, and essentially passive experience of reverie and dreams.

Art in its intentional mode is associated with "vision"; in its achieved forms Art is associated with ideas of consciousness and selection. Moreover the most extreme advocates of automatic writing, namely the surrealists, never pretended to adhere absolutely to their own tenets. The principle of selection determining the poets treated here is the quality of self-awareness, i.e., consciousness, characterizing them. In metaphysical and neoclassic strategies I detect the presence of reason in its most self-aware expressions: in the one, reason reasoning and in the other, reason reasoned. These are the two major modes according to my observation, and it is modes not "movements" which concern me here. Symbolism, for example, if it was ever a habitual mode of the mind seems to me much less likely now to be so; instead it may recur as a technique effectively and appropriately employed by metaphysical and classical alike. The process of association, of analogy, and therefore of metaphor and symbol, is fundamental to all poetry. Do not all techniques ultimately conspire to serve analogy in poetry? What are they, we may remind ourselves, if not the emissaries of an eminently analogizing power?

To the extent that this critical exercise proceeds by deduction and analogy, it too may be considered a product of that same rational imagination. Presumably the only way of sophisticating this argument would be to present it in verse.

Mannerism enters these considerations as a significantly persistent post-Renaissance phenomenon distinguished by an emphatic concentration upon technique, manner becoming as crucial as substance, in some cases even overtaking and apparently superceding the latter. The chief sign of mannerism, then, is in the noticeable tension between conceptual and expressed form.

So peculiarly common is this tension among contemporary poets of whatever mode that one infers an influence pervasive in the poet's experience of this world, affecting his very summons to achieved form, and convincing him that technique is his only authority over his experience of the real. Or in extremes suggesting that technique *is* the reality that creates experience. Thus, as Arnold Hauser notes, "The tension-free formulae of balance propounded by classical art are no longer adequate; and yet they are still adhered to—sometimes even more faithfully, more anxiously, more desperately than would be the case in a relationship which is taken for granted."[18]

Mannerism might be construed therefore as the artistic portion of that doubt which is the ultimate optimism of the contemporary world. Whoever retains the capacity for doubting, as it were, possesses the freedom to judge. All our relations with reality occur upon shifting planes of equivocal sense and distorting abstraction. Dream alone, it would seem, the criticism of sleep, delivers us over to states of rapt certitude. The artist's waking cohabitation with truth is attended with all the strain and inconvenience of an adulterous connection, or at least an imprudent one. It is the discords of affiliation, apparently, that engender poems. And form is as intimately the interpreter of experience as sorrow is the completion of knowledge. Language is the one vital possession truly shared by the human race. And despite the debasement that it undergoes in disintegrating cultures, language may well measure its life in its very instability, its amenableness to change. The arts of language suffer wherever men of letters conceive of language as dead and themselves as the sole custodians. Language is alive, and great poetry keeps it so. Symbols perhaps acquire their viability in the same way that the things we live with acquire the status of personal effects; yet the relation is inevitably reciprocal, and form in poetry is in a unique way "possession." Without symbolism there can be no literature, no language, no understanding, in fact, no life. If we suggest that symbolism is unlikely to be *a* mode of the mind, it is merely to reinforce the apprehension that in the larger sense it is simply *the* mode of the mind.

It is probably impossible for the contemporary poet to be

18. *The Social History of Art* (New York, 1951), II, 99.

Strategies of Reason

anything but mannerist in some respect. Circumstances compel one to assume that never again can the act of poetry be so facile a task as setting ecstatic saints afloat upon marble clouds. Our deep psychological unrest cannot be assuaged by the illusion of space or by mere reference to tradition. Language and readers alike must be recreated, rather than simply reconvened, anew now with each successive work.

The poet as romantic in the present century has been forced by the exigencies inherent in his environment to take up technique as the most effective weapon against disorder—the inner and the outer. In so doing, he accepts the role of phenomenologist. Hart Crane is a tragic example of one who was destroyed in this attempt: whose impulse toward style was insufficient to forge an instrument capable of containing his public theme. Even if egoism were the sole condition for survival, Crane would perhaps not have survived, so destructive were his propensities toward the epic.

The romantic movement of the nineteenth century embraced no formal theory (though it entertained theories) and indeed in no way constituted a homogeneous program. One of the illuminating features of Bernbaum's standard guide to this movement is a tabulation of contradictory definitions drawn from participants and scholars alike. What the romantics have in common when they have anything in common is not a rationalized consensus of opinion but a similar appetitive preference. Reactionary or liberal, they value feeling over understanding—an attitude that may be judged to interfere with the full acceptance of the prudential role of *making* the poem. A naïve Platonism, expressing itself in free association and images of flight, solicits infinity. The mysticism that occurs is frequently self-induced and tends to resemble hysteria. What honest Wordsworth's "Intimations" suggests in this context is that seriousness is no substitute for intelligence.

Mysticism is in any case not a state to be induced so much as it is an experience whose limits ought clearly to be perceived. Precisely what distinguishes the natural mystics—William Blake no less than Julian of Norwich or Teresa of Avila—is the examples they afford of uncommon practicality and shrewdness. ("Fasting is fasting," said Teresa, "and partridges are partridges.") If Blake is a great poet, it is because he understood very well that the composition of poems is not an intransitive exercise. His London is real; its horrors are located (not "reproduced") by paradox. Shelley's universe is no universe at all, but the undifferentiated projection of ego. To fall upon imagined thorns is not persuasively painful. Indeed, it may be self-indulgent in the extreme. Creative innocence under such circumstances can afford to invoke disorder—confident that more of chaos than could be coped with would probably not descend. ("Dover Beach" is not such an invocation, but it is significant that, even at that juncture, the contemplation of chaos could still be premonitory. Seriousness would not for long be enough.)

The purpose of this summary is not the dismissal *en bloc* of the Romantic movement. To do so would be to ignore the remarkable fact that, for better or worse and at the instance of poets whose influence transcends the gifts from which this influence derived, modern poetry is quite clearly post-*Romantic*. For a more generous interpretation of the consequences of this phase of literary history, I call the reader's attention to Sir Herbert Read's "The True Voice of Feeling" and to the distinguished revaluation of Professor Abrams in *The Mirror and the Lamp*. Given the plurality of artistic results, it is always dangerous to quarrel with artistic "movements." I have nothing new to offer on this topic. Even my prejudice is borrowed. Indeed it derives from a critical bias familiar to our time which has lately been termed "the new romanticism." The intention of this thesis confines the selection of poets discussed to those who cultivate consciousness rather than those who solicit inspiration. Certain of the romantics, not least among them Keats and Wordsworth, would qualify in the matter of consciousness. It is that passive aspect of poetic procedure generally associated with Romanticism which I consider to have been damaging to the tradition, gravely damaging, but of course by default. Still, it is outside the purpose of my thesis to develop this theme any more fully than I have done here by suggestion.

Those wars which have changed the world without are duplicated in the worlds within. Recollection can scarcely now be a tranquil accomplishment. One does not reproach the romantics for knowing too little, but one cannot help seeing that their successes were partial and wishing that, instead of trying to write "better than they knew," they had tried harder to understand how they knew. For an incomplete understanding of their own resources, the exaltation of amateurism (with its antipathies toward theory) and a failed epistemology are what these poets have passed on by way of legacy to those who perpetuate the deeply romantic bias in England. A certain spiritual avarice inheres in all that ecstacy, and a gradual erosion effaces beyond recover the positive values of the amateur. To Donne, after all, to be amateur meant primarily not publishing for profit, it never meant not knowing what he was doing! Yet the avoidance of professionalism has come to entail an attitude whereby language is conceived as the poet's least responsibility. Nor is it so much the failure to respond fully to the examples of Pound and Eliot which is cause for regret. Rather more lamentable is the fact that established poets are able to go on writing as if certain problems had never been solved for them by John Donne, Ben Jonson, Thomas Wyatt, and Alexander Pope. What ails English poetry now has ailed it for a century and a half. For there has been no great native lyric poet in England in all this time. Gerard Hopkins, distinct in his Englishness, may well be taken as a cautionary example of the idiosyncratic constriction in which minor gifts of considerable intensity are fated here to burn themselves out. Thomas Hardy is another whose very virtues enforce a radical isolation from a community of letters.

Perhaps a melancholy consequence of living in long proximity with a richly distinguished tradition of letters is somehow to incapacitate its sharers for judging when that relationship leaves off being real and becomes a sustaining fiction.

To put the matter in another way, we may observe that some voices are to be explained by what they call upon:

> Your yën two wol slee me sodenly
> I may the beautè of hem not sustene
>
> . . . .
>
> Ich am of Irlonde,
> Ant of the holy londe
>   Of Irlonde.
> Gode sire, pray ich thee,
> For of sainte charite,
> Come ant dance wit me,
>   In Irlonde.
>
> . . . .
>
> Little Lamb, who made thee?
>
> . . . .

O Wild West Wind, thou breath of Autumn's being,
. . . .
Thou still unravished bride of quietness. . .

Contemporary critics, revaluating romanticism, tell us that what the romantic poet is actually calling upon is Science. One may, I think, safely propose that what the romantic voice is reaching for is more often emotional assurance than imaginative completeness. Other voices are to be explained by what they make. The vocative is capable of as many changes as the human sensibility is capable of responses; its strength and its limitations both arise from its essentially personal and intimate quality. One has only to recall an instance from a poet to whom the vocative mode is most natural to note the lameness resulting when he turns away from it. "Beauty is Truth, Truth Beauty" has troubled more than one reader of Keats's ode. Experience resists language and language resists experience, which the tensions of the poem modify—through meter—with a new substantive force. Just as every word implies an audience, so also it represents perhaps an exorcism of the real.

Before *Personae*, the last poets of a dissipated tradition continued their routine raids upon an absolute which their own motives discredited. T. E. Hulme, we recall, termed their venture "spilt religion." The inertia and muddle brought about, as it were, by the romantic arrogation, in imperfect knowledge, of infinity could be countered only by a poetry richly composed out of an audacious plundering of the contingent.

The madness of a poet, without the craft, never goes far toward resuscitating an art in decline. Pound's early lyrics, "Mauberley" and the rescription of "Propertius," with a salutary infusion of both, at least unsettled the professional amateurism that marked the moment of decline in which they appeared, while reaffirming the simple fact that lyric poetry of a high order may be composed out of

> . . . old gossip, oddments of all things,
> Strange spars of knowledge. . . .

—just as they might occur to a capacious, eclectic, and deeply disturbed mind. If this did not effect a poetic revival, it disclosed the necessity for one while initiating fulfillment of Hulme's prophecy of a return to classicism. This irony ought not to escape us: if the revision accelerated by the appearance of *Personae* originated at a moment when poetry was especially susceptible of not being written, it completes its performance now at a moment when poetry is inordinately susceptible of not being read.

The poet as opportunist is the artist in development. Prose delivers us at a destination—and disappears; poetry *is* a destination. So much closer to the poet's rationale then is the classic association of truth with expression: *adequatio intellectus et rei*. In Pound we are conscious first of the vigorous mimetic instinct for language as language. His originality is his opportunism. Yet it provides him not with mere tricks of style but a multifarious synthesizing instrument—the variable means of positing the poetic statement, musicalized. Nowhere in his work is it a matter of picking out evidence of Browning or Dowson or Dante, but of perceiving what his powers of synthesis have made of all the plundered contingencies, the ones we recognize and the ones we do not. Even when the instinct appears to be that of sheer play, the juxtapositions serve to ensure a sort of lyric peripety. (Not unlike Yeats on occasion, as in "Piere Vidal Old", "When I but think upon the great dead days/ And turn my mind upon that splendid madness"!) The blank verse cadences of "Portrait d'une Femme," the tonal echoes, owe as much to Tennyson as the conception perhaps does to Browning, yet the newness is certainly Pound's:

> Your mind and you are our Sargasso Sea,
> London has swept about you this score years
> And bright ships left you this or that in fee:
> Ideas, old gossip, oddments of all things,
> Strange spars of knowledge and dimmed wares of price.
> Great minds have sought you—lacking someone else.
> You have been second always.

A little dated now in its modernity, its edge of over-preparedness, this event has nevertheless made any number of others possible. "The Seafarer" too is brilliant *by means* of its excesses as improvisation. (I make this point lest my essay on behalf of reason be interpreted as an encomium on the "middle way.")

The arrival at style by omission we may take to be the early acquisition of any proper poet. Yet the larger talent may be bolder in borrowing, and the assimilative process merely less evident. What is available to the critic, what he is impelled to describe by recurring to the term mimetic is of course not imitation by the assumption of a posture, but translation. Alexander Pope understood and explained it when he said that esteem for the ancients expressed itself organically in the copying of nature. When we go on to those poems having their sources in the Provençal, the Chinese, and finally Propertius, we become further aware of the variety of applicable meanings of translation. It may strike us that we are in a manner dealing here with translations of translations of translations. Obviously the problem for Pound in confronting these poems was not to find referential equivalents, common to other forms of discourse, but to find the figural keys to the resemblances they embodied. Pope might have been describing Pound in the *Essay on Criticism* when he suggested how greatness may "boldly deviate from the track" or that "Great wits sometimes may gloriously offend/ And rise to faults true critics dare not mend."

We make too much perhaps of identifying the poet's "own voice." The good poet always has several voices, some of them appropriated from other poets, other poems, the very echoes of which are important to his context. If he is skillful he makes them work and by this law they become his own. Voice and technic are, I suppose, inseparable.

> Bewildering spring, and by the Auvezere
> Poppies and day's eyes in the green émail
> Rose over us; and we knew all that stream,
>
> . . . .
>
> ''Ἴδμεν γάρ τοι πάνθ', ὃς ἐνὶ Τροίῃ
> Caught in the unstopped ear;
> Giving the rocks small lee-way
> The chopped seas held him, therefore, that year.

No matter who the poet's Penelope is, we come to the disjunctive resonance of his idiom as to a calculated trap, as De Rougemont puts it, "for our rapt and intransitive attention."

A style is said to be more than the sum of its techniques, to express the consciousness of an age. Arnold Hauser says that "a style is a dialectic between works in progress and works that already exist."[19] The disharmonies of the modern age preclude the possibility of any uniform attitude toward the world. (Indeed, those individuals who give evidence of having arrived at certifiable certainty in this regard are normally to be found

19. Quoted by Wylie Sypher, *Rococo to Cubism in Art and Literature* (New York, 1960), p. xxi.

in our asylums for the insane.) An artist is far more likely to be in assured communication with the styles that precede him than with the world that surrounds him. Mannerism, it seems to me, is a sign of this state of affairs, for while mannerism is expressive of acute assurance in one realm—the technical—it is simultaneously expressive of insecurity and lack of assurance in another. Hence the interest, for me at least, of the ventriloquism of Pound who wrote in a "Treatise on Metrics" of a prosody attained by the listening ear and "not by an index of nomenclatures," who spoke of rhythm as "form cut into time" and whose own eclectic strategy is to play off against the absolute meter behind the poem, in the mind of the reader, a variable, like a kind of syncopation.

> The coral isle, the lion-coloured sand
> Burst in upon the porcelain revery:
> Impetuous troubling
> Of his imagery.

Conscious omissions, interruptions in the expected ratio between arsis and thesis, commit us on the whole to a music of irony. Even stanzas that appear superficially to be shaped by the usual metrical determinants reach us, I think, in this fashion:

> Not, not certainly, the obscure reveries
> Of the inward gaze;
> Better mendacities
> Than the classics in paraphrase!
> . . . .
> Firmness,
> Not the full smile,
> His art, but an art
> In profile;
> . . . .

> The sleek head emerges
> From the gold-yellow frock
> As Anadyomene in the opening
> Pages of Reinach.

So that caesural and end-line pauses where the words leave off may have a metrical weight equal to the spoken word. "To say many things is equal to having a home," says the voice of Propertius. The establishing of multiple identities mitigates perhaps the elusiveness of the one.

It is conceivable that even the very great artist may be unaware of the style to the creation of which he contributes.[20] One is reminded in this connection of Professor Tillyard's discerning remarks on the unconscious sources of style in Milton's *Paradise Lost*. Moreover, it goes without saying that what the profound psychologists of modern literature—from Tolstoy to Proust—have chiefly to tell us is how little we are capable of understanding each other. If our own modes of consciousness remain something of a mystery to us, so much the more mysterious are those of another. Yet literature bears liberal witness to the varieties of consciousness of which the mind is capable, and it is to literature rather than to life that we must look for the most attentive, patient, and sustained projections of those states. Imaginative completeness is a quality to be achieved only through the practical endeavor of the mind. Even the romantic who is content to prefer the heart as the organ of such registration allows that it must be *looked into* before the poet can write. Indeed, we classify the arts by the kinds of attention they bring to their subjects because this is the revelation of their "ends." Differences in natural endowment and differences in motive bring about mutations both of

20. *Ibid.*, p. xix.

kind and degree of self-awareness. Sometimes it seems to us that the very hubristic self-absorption of the romantic itself blunts and diverts the self-consciousness the artist is prepared to bestow upon his work.

The economy of the novel has ample room to become, in James's designation, "deep breathing." A poem may amount to no more than a "cry" though usually it is more subtly articulated. Nonetheless, being based upon recognition, even the slightest lyric is a specification of intelligence—intelligence differently oriented, intelligence differently applied, but unmistakably intelligence.

The two causes that Aristotle found for poetry reside in, and are deeply intrinsic to, human nature: the instinct for imitation and the instinct for harmony. Certain contemporary views reject such a formulation, preferring a scientific reduction of knowledge to "facts." Francis Fergusson on behalf of drama points out that

the objections of the semanticists to Aristotle's epistemology with its basis in the *nous*, or "apperceptive intelligence" are not very convincing but they represent an important and stubborn contemporary habit of mind. Aristotle is not as *inaverti* as they think; "what he has that they haven't got" is not naive credulity but a recognition that we are aware of things and people "before predication," as he puts it. The histrionic sensibility, the perception of action, is such a primitive and direct awareness . . . contemporary theories of art which omit or reject the notion of the imitation of an action are more disquieting than pseudo-scientific theories because of the insight they give us into the actual artists of our time. They remind us how difficult it is—after three hundred years of rationalism and idealism, with the traditional modes of behaviour lost or discredited —to see any action but our own.[21]

21. *The Idea of a Theater* (Princeton, 1949), p. 254.

This is to touch again upon that failure of the sense of being to which Maritain referred. In my final chapter, I try to establish the probability that even meter is fundamentally a cognitive experience, as a mode of perception, a mediator of recognitions.

"Only rapports are true," said Flaubert to a correspondent. And José Ortega y Gasset has observed that "perspective is one of the component parts of reality. Far from being a disturbance of its fabric, it is its organizing element. . . . Every life is a point of view directed upon the universe. Strictly speaking, what one life sees no other can. . . . The sole false perspective is that which claims to be the only one there is."[22]

Having asked: what is intelligence in poetry, may we not infer with the greatest speculative confidence that it lies in the quality of attention by which the poet exposes himself to these "rapports" to which Flaubert alludes? The disposition of the philosopher in respect to his sources is to generalize; that of the poet is both a practical and more immediate one: to make. In so far as we grasp a philosopher's thought, we retain by abstraction ideas. We apprehend a poet's work strictly in terms of his words. A poet's way of seeing becomes his way of saying. To imitate and to make new is the simultaneous gesture of the poem.

According to André Malraux, "Genius imposes on the ages a language constantly modified, like an echo answering each successive age with its own voice, and what the masterpiece keeps up is not a monologue, however authoritative, but a dialogue triumphant over Time."[23]

Returning to the mimetic principle underlying all art, we may notice that if what happens in the theater is translation—

22. *The Modern Theme* (New York, 1961), pp. 90-92.
23. *The Twilight of the Absolute,* Part III of *Psychology of Art,* trans. Stuart Gilbert (New York, 1949), p. 35.

that is, in every performance, the so-called primitive (meaning immediate) pre-verbal awareness is predicated as action—something similar takes place in the poem, a translation that is yet more durable than those two other temporal arts, music and drama, because of the way in which it is mediated by the word. (Tautology, it seems, is one of the few ways of getting at poetry.) Could we not describe the two major modes of poetry as "awareness predicating" and "awareness predicated"? The examples I have chosen for discussion in this book interest me because the poets in question are among those who bring to bear in their respective modes the least diffuse and the most attentive consciousness. The predication of consciousness is, after all, the poem's claim to permanence. I like to give to this term the full value it receives in the French *conscience* where its meaning is twofold: awareness and "conscience." Such a formulation reminds us that the artist's conscience is directed toward a public rather than a private end. To the same extent that it implies a prudential judgment, a poem implies an audience, and other poems.

The tragic continuity that has brought us in time from the fascination of the intelligible to infatuation with the self is reflected (with comic fidelity) in the arts. Malraux, an attentive witness to this scene, declares that "a culture based on man, the individual, seldom lasts long, and eighteenth-century rationalism culminated in that outburst of passionate hope which has left its mark on history; but the culture of that century summoned back to life whatever in the past endorsed its rationalism, whereas ours resuscitates all that sponsors our irrationalism."[24]

The prevalence of a false rationalism that fails to take ac-

24. *Ibid.*, p. 55.

count of the intentional nature of art and thought as well as that irrationalism which falsely opposes reason to life prompts me to this thesis. Reason, as I see it, is at the very heart of human existence. Whatever is intelligible, including passion, we encompass through the mediation of the mind. Indeed, the senses are humanly availing only to the extent that they are in collaboration with this faculty for reflection. A poem—whether by virtue of a happy gift or a strain of madness—owes its existence to the performance of the mind aroused, it would seem, to its most active concentration.

Our conventions—pure and impure—precede us, as it were, into the knowable present: conventions of feeling equally with conventions of intellect. The patterns themselves, of course, lend intelligibility in so far as they confer familiarity. Perhaps all the procedures of life and art are creative to the extent that formulas are found adaptable to their occasions. The future that is constantly made over to us by virtue of the condition of our temporality becomes the author of our sufficiency. Duration is evinced by nature; it is experienced by consciousness.

The heightened consciousness of the artist in the intensity and exclusiveness of its application may indeed be morbid. Kafka, who died of tuberculosis, is in a sense less repetitive, less superficially present in his works, than is Thomas Mann who was able to make of disease a subject. The tragic deprivation of an individual has more than once been the instance of an astonishing refertilization of a culture. A Christopher Smart, a Nerval, a Hölderlin testify perhaps as reliably as could be desired that insanity need not deprive a man of his most human qualities, but may moreover consist in a painful emphasis of them: of pity, of joy. Nor does madness—at least in so far as it becomes expressive in a work of art—imply mindlessness, but rather, again, in performance something far more suggestive of "singlemindedness." One has indeed the impression that the truly terrifying aspect of insanity is that, with the elision of certain barriers present to the rational consciousness, the mind is in fact released into activity of appalling (and morally issueless) velocity. A work of art in our own vexed moment of history is more often a way of questioning its context than of affirming it. Insanity itself is some persons' only way of posing their unspeakable questions of the universe. If "the true work of art is the one which says least,"[25] perhaps this is because it is the one which asks most.

Having completed his thesis on Plotinus in 1936, Camus resumed his reflections on the theme of Plotinian reason in his notebooks for the following year. He finds reason "not an unambiguous concept. Interesting to see how it behaves in history at a time when it must either adapt itself or perish. . . . It is the same reason, and it is not the same. It is because there are two kinds of reason, the one ethical and the other aesthetic."[26]

Naturally, I should not like my essay on reason to appear to become an endorsement of its deranging. Yet I put forward the notion that the most useful function of our dreams and that of the unconscious in general (which is not unreason but that aspect of reason usually unavailable to our surface attention) is to recover our contact with the invisible by supplying us with those concrete images which are its parables.

The prerequisite for reason is reason, even as the prerequisite for passion is passion. The estimative faculty is a risk-taking faculty in poetry. It calculates its risks simultaneously

25. Albert Camus, *Notebooks: 1935-1942* (New York, 1963), p. 103.
26. *Ibid.*, pp. 102-3.

while encountering them. The mind whose "cliffs of fall" are hazards for any who undertake intellectual pursuits in necessary solitude intensifies those triumphs that succeed. But the life of the mind is sustained as it were from without. The concrete images yield their parabolic fruit only on this condition. The mind is thus always in metaphysical servitude to things, and so, therefore, are poems: preferably the servitude of unimpeded wonder, hence of love. This, I take it, is the meaning of Eliot's "There is no freedom in art." Yet our coming upon its deepest expressions obviously is not as an intrusion upon the enacting of a private commitment. Ernst Cassirer[27] on this topic quotes Goethe, who was himself on occasion not immune to the "bad faith" of the baroque. Art, he says, "does not undertake to emulate nature in its breadth and depth. It sticks to the surface of natural phenomena; but it has its own depth, its own power; it crystallizes the highest moments of these superficial phenomena by recognizing in them the character of lawfulness, the perfection of harmonious proportion . . . the dignity of significance. . . ." And Cassirer adds that "it is interpretation of reality." Not, in other words, seduction of reality, or by it.

In being interpretation rather than emulation, a poem or any other work of art both manifests its profound intellectuality and declares its essentially autotelic condition. Intelligence is no more self-sufficient than sensibility; each exists in a context whereby alone its "rapports" are made possible. Whether the poem or the emotions originally attaching to it derive from incalculable subjective (or obsessive) depths or from literature, as in almost equal parts so often do those of Valéry, Eliot,

27. *An Essay on Man* (New Haven, 1944), p. 146. The quotation from Goethe is from Notes to a translation of Diderot's "Essai sur la Peinture," *Werke*, XLV, 260.

Pound, Stevens, the very crisis of the creative endeavor is the objectification by which such resources are "made new." It is in accordance with the ethics of this aesthetic transaction that Cocteau in *Le Rappel à l'Ordre* proposed that the artist must become the "guardian of his angels."

"We are not yet done with the nineteenth century, nor is it done with us: we still breathe its air. And it is not so much an inheritance as it is a continuing present which will not yet lapse into the past."[28] Such a statement in regard to the philosophy of Kierkegaard and Nietzsche takes on an even more impressive relevance in respect to the poetry of the post-Romantic period. It would appear that all the ways in which we are modern derive in some manner from romantic individualism, romantic rebellion. Comedy itself thus becomes romantic seriousness in disguise. "For too long a time," said Apollinaire, "the French loved beauty only because it supplied them with information." The English, alas, one is tempted to add, for too long a time loved poetry because it supplied them with mild mystification. The poetry that we call modern is in large part an attempt to rectify both these aberrations. It owes its techniques nevertheless to its predecessors in the major modes, both immediate and remote. Thus out of the irresolution of romantic feeling came somehow the resolution for the plunge into the unknown areas of the mind. As Marcel Raymond affirms, "the symbolists and especially the surrealists, broke the balance between the inner and the outer worlds in favor of the inner world."[29] But the inner, we find, may be construed only by means of the outer. The very bias toward "innerness" characteristic in a time of external disorder, violence, and unrest

28. Thomas Hanna, *The Lyrical Existentialists* (New York, 1962), p. 4.
29. *From Baudelaire to Surrealism* (New York, 1950), p. 354.

places an inevitable stress upon that procedure of objectification by which the poem is realized. Hence Eliot's "objective correlative" is seized upon as if it were a new gadget rather than simply a re-emphasis of the natural process of analogy that has ever been the fundamental mode of reason in poetry. Raymond continues: "Even though it is true that the sources of all poetry are in the mind, external nature is the surest path by which men who aspire to know themselves through means other than analysis, can approach poetry. Nature is the receptacle of the mind, the locus of all its visible and sensible symbols, the repertory of all the analogies, as Baudelaire believed. Our dream itself is perhaps only as valuable as our waking hours. Genuine poetry does not spring from sensation, but sensation must water the dark lands of memory."[30]

Memory is fruitful for art only to the extent that the estimative faculty of the mind is able to make use of it. Luck, for the poet, only attains actuality in the degree to which it is *realized*. Perhaps the most obvious difference between the artist and the amateur of art is that the former understands when he is lucky and takes the required advantage of it, whereas the latter often lacks this awareness. The best poetry of any era is marked by the acumen with which it responds to its possibilities, and the courage. It is in this quality of mind (a sort of heroic pragmatism) that poets otherwise diverse in practice resemble one another.

Certain of Emily Dickinson's poems are extreme examples of mind-power of awesome integrity creating its own advantages with ascetic and bristling intensity. Not uncommonly these are set down as definitions:

30. *Ibid.*

Strategies of Reason

> Revolution is the Pod
> Systems rattle from
> When the Winds of Will are stirred.
>
> . . . .
>
> But nature is a stranger yet;
> The ones that cite her most
> Have never passed her haunted house
> Nor simplified her ghost.
>
> . . . .
>
> Renunciation is a piercing virtue—
> The letting go
> A Presence. . . .

The expert tutelage of our great artists leaves us most disposed perhaps to think of memory as the sub-rational container of the essences of sensible events alone. Such it would seem are those intermittances for Swann. Emily Dickinson's work reveals the presence of what one might call speculative memory. Indeed it animates those numerous poems dense with abstractions like death, eternity, and, in her case, love.

It is my impression that speculative memory, with a platonist bias, is very much a part of the fabric of Wallace Stevens' poetry as well. I shall cite here only a single example, for this procedure is so self-evident and characteristic a manner that the reader's own recollection will doubtless provide spontaneous corroboration.

MAN AND BOTTLE

> The mind is the great poem of winter, the man,
> Who, to find what will suffice,
> Destroys romantic tenements
> Of rose and ice

> In the land of war. More than the man, it is
> A man with the fury of a race of men,
> A light at the centre of many lights,
> A man at the centre of men.
>
> It has to content the reason concerning war,
> It has to persuade that war is part of itself,
> A manner of thinking, a mode
> Of destroying, as the mind destroys,
>
> An aversion, as the world is averted
> From an old delusion, an old affair with the sun,
> An impossible aberration with the moon,
> A grossness of peace.
>
> It is not the snow that is the quill, the page.
> The poem lashes more fiercely than the wind,
> As the mind, to find what will suffice, destroys
> Romantic tenements of rose and ice.

Poetry would have no more metaphysical content than the confessions of Saturday Catholics if the mind were not there at the center to engage it. I am making here a large and obvious claim for poetry (not for myself as theorist) but only the claim that poetry repeatedly makes for itself. Recourse at this point to the fashionable criteria of the absurd may appear uncalled-for. If anything is absurd in a world whose chief spokesmen for the Apollonian are the technologists, it is poems. Yet this perfectly useless commodity of the mind tells us a great deal about man, its maker and destroyer. One is struck in reading the classic modern accounts of the absurd that absurdity is man-made, and that its most fastidious proofs devolve upon protagonists whose powers of attention and absorption are clearly less acute than their authors'. Absurdity is a factor to be apprehended only by an active principle of order, namely the mind, because it is in the first place perpetrated through the freedom of that agent. Disorder could not otherwise be tragic. The fundamental optimism with which Camus embraces life attests to this sense, otherwise his brilliant testimonial to his "affair with the sun" would be a manifest compromise.

A fair amount of the verse at our own given moment represents such a compromise—with, as it happens, superficial conventions of order. Such verse does not last, but as long as it does is a commentary on the vitiated moral consciousness that produced it.

Even those of us who are not Americans for nothing have yet to learn from the nineteenth century that seriousness itself may be a mode of self-deception. Creative innocence and creative ego are equally indispensable conditions of art. "The word I," as Buber has said, "remains the shibboleth of mankind." Yet not infrequently its utterance reveals the "desperateness of . . . self-contradiction."

This essay is not a defense of one kind of poetry against another; it is a personal report. Nor is it disinterested. If it makes sense, it may do so more effectively as metaphor than as argument.

"Aesthetics," says Wittgenstein, "is a reason-giving activity" of the order of further description. If his notion has any viable meaning, surely it is because art, and specifically poetry, is a product of reason. It was a poet (Gautier) who said: "L'inexprimable n'existe pas."

II

JOHN DONNE:
Reason's Double Agent

Two attributes common to the idea of lyric poetry—songlikeness, the personal—have always been unequally observed in English by the makers of the poems we most admire. So much so that we may assume the natural proprium of the most nearly perfect poetry is to strain its definitions. Still less reconcilable with the facts is the aesthetic election of "beauty" which, however generalized as "superior order," tends to be refuted by a history replete with poems that clearly could not be less intent upon beauty or order as commonly understood. The idiosyncratic dissonances, the colloquial shock of the metaphysical are reminders of a tradition notably unfaithful to its ostensible conventions. Yet the profoundest affront to our categories is the persistence in all our poetry of reason, of reason reasoning, and of logic in varying degrees formal.

In John Donne certainly the ratiocinative has been the fulcrum for intelligent recriminations from Dr. Johnson and Dryden to Legouis, as it has for enthusiasm as recent as Alvarez'. One proof that this collective burden of criticism yields is that survival of a cult may be as significant a feat as survival of neglect. The triumph of unspecified "tough-mindedness" on the part of the seventeenth century (like the toxic inspiration of another fashion) should not prevent our discerning the practical work of reason, even syllogistic, in both earlier and later lyric poets. For if Thomas Nashe's song, "Adieu, farewell, earth's bliss," is a syllogism explicitly propounded, Dunbar's "Lament for the Makaris" and Marvell's "To His Coy Mistress" are similarly propositional in structure (as J. V. Cunningham has shown[1]). Nor are these poets the first, last, or only such practitioners. The truth is that reasoning

1. In *Tradition and Poetic Structure* (Denver, 1960).

indeed is the characteristic operation of the mind, its way of laying hold of its perceptions. However intuited to begin with, from the moment they are set to language, these perceptions tend to appear in their relations and calling upon logic.

Philosophers have been understandably reluctant to delegate the authority of reason to other disciplines. (Schoolmasters have not, and in the eighth century dialectic as well as grammar and rhetoric were taken to be the poet's proper concern.²) The rationalist philosophy of St. Thomas distinguishes *cognitio per modum cognitionis* from the *cognitio per modum inclinationis* of metaphor. Yet in fact the distinction is easier to assent to than to see. For what is more evidently implicit in the *discordia concors* than the speculative relations there posited? The closer the philosopher comes to acknowledging this constant (more demonstrable, one should say, in the arts, where most deliberate) the more hesitantly it is put. Thus Madame Maritain: "Le sens logique ou rationnel n'est pas exigible en poésie pour lui-même, il semble même extrinsèque à la poésie comme telle. Et cependant, d'une manière ou d'une autre, à un degré quelconque, il accompagne toujours l'oeuvre poétique: ou bien d'une façon explicite, ou bien en faisant implicitement appel au concours de l'intelligence. Faute de quoi la poésie elle-même disparait."³

Donne's mind was nothing if not highly trained. In addition to his schooling under the Jesuits, he was subjected at Oxford and Cambridge to a regime that entailed a five-term course in logic involving frequent lectures and triweekly disputations.⁴

2. *Ibid.*, p. 41.
3. "Sens et Non Sens en Poésie," *Situation de la Poésie* (Paris, 1938), p. 13.
4. Elizabeth Wiggins, "Logic in the Poetry of John Donne," *Studies in Philology*, XLII (1945), 41.

Reason's Double Agents

Trained or untrained, however, we have not got a convertible proposition in this. Intellection is not invariably interesting. The most sage may be least illuminating to follow. Inside or outside art, so much depends upon an undesignated and unpredictable quality of the mind which elects the materials that provide the choices in the form of obstacles to be dominated.

If Donne's "Communitie" ("Good wee must love, and must hate ill") proves to be a complex disjunctive syllogism; if "The Prohibition" ("Take heed of loving mee,/ At least remember, I forbade it thee") is a dilemma; if the predicables, predication, and predicaments visibly prevail, it confirms, after all, our legitimate expectations. The claims of intellection methodized are nowhere more evidently congenial to Donne than in the instances where he takes his chief sophistical liberties. In, for example, "A Jeat Ring Sent":

> Thou art not so black, as my heart,
>   Nor halfe so brittle, as her heart, thou art;
> What would'st thou say? shall both our properties by thee
>   bee spoke,
>   Nothing more endlesse, nothing sooner broke?

Hyperbolic compliment such as that ingeniously reduplicated in the verse letters is posed in the formulae of logic (in the same relation Elizabeth Sewell elsewhere establishes in respect to nonsense[5]). So Donne, the amateur, enlivens the concept of poetry as a *jeu d'esprit* as Valéry, the professional, cannot. "To the Countesse of Bedford":

> Reason is our Soules left hand, Faith her right,
> By these we reach divinity, that's you;
> Their loves, who have the blessings of your light,
> Grew from their reason, mine from faire faith grew.

5. In *The Field of Nonsense* (London, 1954).

> But as, although a squint lefthandednesse
> Be'ungracious, yet we cannot want that hand,
> So would I, not to encrease but to expresse
> My faith, as I beleeve, so understand.
>
> Therefore I study you. . . .

By this, one is not allowed, it seems, to forget that the game is possible because the rules are observed with finesse. Whatever is trivialized must have the dimensions from which to be reduced and, like blasphemy, the act must be perpetrated by a qualified believer. A mind as conscious of its own maneuvers as of the experience recovered thereby introduces this experience into the variables of the poem. One is aware of this mental quotient in Donne's poems both as a quality and as an efficient cause. Merely by juxtaposing its achieved results with the work of a mind similarly self-occupied but lacking a conviction in the efficacy of its means to attain ends other than artificial, one is astonished by the influence of that assent. If a thought to Donne was in any way "experience" it must have been so because, like other men, he thought with words,[6] and because—as poet—he so clearly employed words as intelligible signs, words as objects, language as a means of locating and verifying truth. In the notation of the sceptical "Third Satyre":

> Though truth and falsehood bee
> Neare twins, yet truth a little elder is;
> Be busie to seeke her, beleeve mee this,
> Hee's not of none, nor worst, that seekes the best.
> To adore, or scorne an image, or protest,
> May all be bad; doubt wisely; in strange way
> To stand inquiring right, is not to stray;

---

6. Maritain, perhaps tautologically, remarks, "le poète ne peut sans cesser d'être poète aller au-delà de la parole." *Situation de la Poésie*, p. 70.

> To sleepe, or runne wrong, is. On a huge hill,
> Cragged and steep, truth stands, and hee that will
> Reach her, about must, and about must goe;
> And what the hills suddennes resists, winne so. . . .

A typical concomitant of this notion of truth as difficult but accessible is the pleasure so evidently taken in the rigors of its approaches.

Mallarmé, by contrast, is tragically impotent, unable to achieve a great projected work annulled by the very theory at its conception. For, although he spoke of poetry as "l'expression, par le langage humain ramené à son rhythme essentiel, du sens mystérieux des aspects de l'existence,"[7] he in fact engages to construct a Hegelian absolute[8] from awkward assumptions of language as magic. Since he could lay claim neither to philosophy nor magicianship, his fastidious pursuit of obscurity yields chiefly syntax, a figuration of the inimitable French drama of the unspoken.

No one remains satisfied any longer with facile glosses on Donne's "felt thought."[9] The premise is more applicable as inverted by Robert Ellrodt ("Il eut été plus exact de dire qu'une expérience se changeait en pensée dans son esprit"[10]) who perceived what Joan Bennett came near to formulating, that "il est plus fréquent que le poète se borne à tirer parti d'une idée qu'il subtilise."[11] The familiar "Extasie" is one

7. Letter to Leo d'Orfer, *Propos* (Monaco, 1953), p. 134.
8. Cf. Robert Gibson, *Modern French Poets on Poetry* (Cambridge, 1961), p. 86.
9. A dissatisfaction fully expressed by Frank Kermode, "Dissociation of Sensibility," *Kenyon Review*, 19 (1957), 169-94.
10. Robert Ellrodt, *Les Poètes Métaphysiques Anglais* (Paris, 1960), I, 95.
11. *Ibid.*, p. 96.

John Donne: Reason's Double Agent

example. Nor is so evident a habit of composition merely superficial. A glance at the practice of another almost mathematically intellectual poet reinforces our estimate of the thoroughness and method by which this tendency to refine is applied. Paul Valéry, partial as he is to images and to the abstract, at all odds prefers the crudest of all possible vehicles for their union: personification. This is the method of virtually every important poem from "Aurore" to "La Jeune Parque." If it is not Donne's way to relinquish to impersonated abstraction the whole conduct of the poem, is there a single poem of his in which a heuristic passion has not placed the poet himself, however relatively effaced, at the center of the action as supposed narrator? Such choices are not simply the accidents of ego and do not participate haphazardly in the making of poems. Just as in all valid art a measure of obscurity subsists alongside its measure of intelligibility, so each poem is in a way individuated by the character of its obscurity, the character of its intelligibility. One is left, ludicrously, contrasting the results to find in certain attempts (like the Mallarméan) purity cancelling itself out; in others, Donne's eminently, "difficulty" mediating quite transparently wit. The last part of "The Dampe" goes:

> But these I neyther looke for, nor professe;
>   Kill me as Woman, let mee die
>   As a meere man; doe you but try
> Your passive valor, and you shall finde than,
> In that you'have odds enough of any man.

The difficulties in Donne are never mysterious; they do not arise from what has been excluded from a poem. Dryden would never have objected had he preferred to baffle young ladies in that fashion. That surely has always been the accepted mode. What bothered Dryden was the unlikely gesture of providing the young ladies with data exacting thought. For the explication of the difficulties of the metaphysical poem is the poem. All is above board, nothing withheld. If ever something is missing, it is apt to be the one member of a proposition suppressed because understood: in other words, the enthymeme. Such lines require to be strong, but are not arcane. On women:

> If they were good it would be seene,
> Good is as visible as greene,
>   And to all eyes it selfe betrayes:
> If they were bad, they could not last,
> Bad doth itselfe and others wast,
>   So, they deserve nor blame nor praise.

Complexities govern the process of many of Donne's poems, but as they are complexities precisely realized, with the clarity that reason alone facilitates, there is even less excuse than is commonly allowed for the cabals and fads, the pests of art (which have, however, more noticeably followed the abstract in its non-verbal expressions).

The extended metaphor, typical as it is of the metaphysical method, actually works to reduce that aura or vibration of unequivalence from which derives the pleasant obscurity of metaphor in other poetics. All metaphor, let it be said, since it joins concepts, is intellectual. So for that matter are adjectives attributed to nouns. But metaphor, by taking a notion univocal in itself, by applying that notion analogically to another subject, changes our apprehension of that subject. This addition and this dislocation of metaphorical analogy prevent our attaining "the thing analogically known *in accordance with what is properly signified by the concept.*"[12] So metaphor is an analogy of "improper proportionality." The "improperness" is not taken up or discussed, for instance, by the romantics (who go in, as T. E. Hulme noted, for "flight") although it accounts as often as not for those "beauties" for which admirers comb the stacks. Donne indeed exhausts the patience of some readers because his wit simply cannot desist from the explicit justification of those areas of "improperness" inherent in metaphor. Such are the compasses of the "Valediction."

The presence of the poet's voice, less as a rhetorical device than as a consciousness (an intelligence in the Jamesian sense) interpreting from the center of things, disposes them dramatically. Jarring meters and the inflections of spoken speech (disjunctive, unmusical) support this effect:

> Shee, shee is gone; she is gone; when thou knowest this,
> What fragmentary rubbidge this world is
> Thou knowest and that it is not worth a thought. . . .
>
> ("Second Anniversary," 81-83)

The psychological immediacy that these techniques together arouse and simulate is at once as vividly personal as it is finely objective. "The Expiration":

> So, so breake off this last lamenting kisse,
> Which sucks two soules, and vapors both away,
> Turne thou ghost that way, and let mee turne this,
> And let ourselves benight our happiest day,
> We ask'd none leave to love; nor will we owe
> Any, so cheape a death, as saying, Goe;

---

12. Jacques Maritain, *The Degrees of Knowledge* (London, 1959), p. 419.

Reason's Double Agents

> Goe; and if that word have not quite kill'd thee,
> Ease mee with death, by bidding mee goe too.
> Or, if it have, let my word worke on mee,
> And a just office on a murderer doe.
> Except it be too late, to kill me so,
> Being double dead, going, and bidding, goe.

There is in this consciousness an address no recollected tranquility could donate. Even so brief a poem may be taken as a prospectus of the kinds of presence[13] to be adduced from Donne's metaphysics. Here is the presence of time contracted to urgent instantaneity, presence as space, presence as duration, as tactile, as discontinuous, as of two persons confronting.

To regard Donne's stance in the world, as opposed to the philosophic distance from which a Milton or Drummond surveys his ideal Plotinian universe, is to remark how Donne "thinks the world under the form of 'world-around-himself'" (as Robert Ellrodt, one of his most acute French readers, notes). Aesthetic distance is not at all the same as philosophic distance. A diffuse philosophic consciousness tends, perhaps to advantage, to lose itself beyond, but that *présence au monde* which for Donne is *présence à soi* entails a relation comprehensible only as drama. Not that what is seen at close hand is necessarily dramatic, for it may simply have been looked at with myopic eyes, but that the self as the object of its own expanded awareness, in the very impersonation of ego, secures a kind of theater:

> I am a little world made cunningly....
> This is my playes last scene, here heavens appoint....

---

13. Ellrodt gives two chapters to the discussion of presence in his excellent book, *Les Poètes Métaphysiques Anglais*.

John Donne: Reason's Double Agent

Whether the occasion is religious or secular, this detachment nevertheless ministers the act of self-awareness.

Was there ever such a thing as a unified sensibility? And, if so, should it excite special admiration? Ellrodt, at any rate, thinks it is not to be discovered accounting for Donne's complexity of accent and that analysis of certain poems (those on death, such as "The Relique") reveals the psychological origin rather "dans une conscience de soi qui est une 'dualité réfléchie.'"[14] This apartness and ensuing duality may be inferred in the verse letters as frequently as in the more familiar lyrics. "To the Countesse of Bedford on New-yeares Day" opens:

> This twilight of two yeares, not past nor next,
> Some embleme is of mee, or I of this,
> Who Meteor-like, of stuffe and forme perplext,
> Whose *what* and *where*, in disputation is,
> If I should call mee *any thing*, should misse.

From the precarious stability of these tensions—the occasion realized and the mind realizing it, the reasons reasoned and the mind reasoning—flows a dialogue of other pairs. It may be that these somewhat abstract entities come into focus more clearly in those poems where the otherness of the second person appears in the foreground. So it does in "A Lecture upon the Shadow":

> Stand still; and I will read to thee
> A lecture, love, in love's philosophy.
> These three houres that we have spent,
> Walking here, two shadows went
> Along with us, which we our selves produc'd;
> But, now the Sunne is just above our head,
> We doe those shadowes tread;

14. *Ibid.*, p. 174.

> And to brave clearnesse all things are reduc'd.
> So, whilst our infant loves did grow,
> Disguises did, and shadowes, flow,
> From us, and our cares; but, now 'tis not so.

On the side of conscience there are certitude and doubt. Certitude, the assent to accessible truth, and confidence in language have already been touched upon. Doubt also is a necessary adjunct of reason. Psychology tells us how decisive a proof it is of rational man's waking state. For in dreams or in madness we do not question the probability of what seems to be happening, but are convinced of the reality of our hallucinations. It follows that poetry proceeding from a mind as lively as Donne's should have its complement of doubt. The notion itself of doubt has, since the Renaissance, been debased by fashionable transformations. Often doubt becomes simply an attitude, the pose especially of writers lacking real subjects. In the form of melancholy, the pose was all too modish in Donne's time, and his poems reveal that he was as caught up in this atmosphere as anyone. Yet, as a poet, even in celebrating the subject matter of doubt, I believe he always made a clear distinction between the attitude of melancholy and the intellectual fact of doubt. The question has been amply aired already. One thinks of Kathleen Raine's essay on "John Donne and the Baroque Doubt."[15] It receives classic expression surely in that passage from "The First Anniversary":

> And new Philosophy calls all in doubt,
> The Element of fire is quite put out;

15. *Horizon*, 11 (1945), 371-95. It is marred by a tendency to ascribe metaphysical characteristics to baroque, a confusion corrected by Odette de Mourgue's *Metaphysical, Baroque and Précieux Poetry* (Oxford, 1953), pp. 67-102.

John Donne: Reason's Double Agent

> The Sun is lost, and th'earth, and no man's wit
> Can well direct him where to looke for it. . . .
> 'Tis all in peeces, all coherrence gone;
> All just supply, and all Relation. . . .

Contained within a meditation on the effects of Original Sin, as Louis Martz has shown,[16] the whole, moreover, is framed in terms of logical analysis: the predicament, relation, succeeded by the genus, kind.[17] Doubt is never with Donne the abdication of reason, but the incitement to reason. Quite other is the attention accorded it as an end in itself by poets immersed in a Cartesian atmosphere. Nor can it be fortuitous that out of such a milieu emerge new schools writing of and emulating dream states, since in this process, with the invocation of the unconscious, the executive will is discarded. Surrealism and automatic writing represent the extreme. Thus André Breton's surrealist manifesto has it: "Automatisme psychique pur par lequel on se propose d'exprimer, soit verbalement, soit par écrit, soit de toute autre manière, le fonctionnement réel de la pensée. Dictée de la pensée, en l'absence de tout contrôle exercé par la raison, en dehors de toute préoccupation esthétique ou morale."[18]

Donne is not unaware of the nightmare possibilities resident in the mind (and accorded so disproportionate a share in our present arts). The psychological acuity of his poems' rendering of human experience is the very stuff of his divergence from conventional Petrarchism, and a quality most congenial to comment since his recovery began a generation

---

16. *The Poetry of Meditation* (New Haven, 1954), p. 222.
17. Wiggins, "Logic in the Poetry of John Donne," *SP*, p. 53.
18. "Premier Manifeste du Surréalisme," *La Révolution Surréaliste*, 12 (Paris, 1929), 24.

ago. This kind of insight (rather than historical prognostication) informs his letter "To Sir Edward Herbert, at Julyers."

> Man is a lumpe, where all beasts kneaded bee,
>   Wisdome makes him an Arke where all agree;
> The foole, in whom these beasts do live at jarre,
>   Is sport to others, and a Theater,
> Nor scapes hee so, but is himselfe their prey;
>   All which was man in him, is eate away,
> And now his beasts on one another feed,
>   Yet couple in anger, and new monsters breed.
> How happy'is hee, which hath due place assign'd
>   To'his beasts, and disaforested his minde!

Donne may well attract, and assuredly survive, Freudian analysis. But one thing must be rather clear: Donne is not used by his dreams; he appropriates them. Only thus, dream or the idea of dream enters into the economy of several of his finer lyrics. Never more himself than in the tenth elegy, here nevertheless he comes close again to the music of an earlier predilection. "The Dreame":

> When you are gone, and *Reason* gone with you,
>   Then *Fantasie* is Queene and Soule, and all;
> She can present joyes meaner than you do;
>   Convenient, and more proportionall.
> So, if I dreame I have you, I have you,
>   For, all our joyes are but fantasticall.

If exercised in doubt, it is not, then, Donne's habit to consent to it unequivocally as to a neutralizing *weltschmerz*. Indeed, as a symptom, doubt receives expression indirectly in the poems through their shaping techniques—in the staccato asynchronous meters, dislocated perspectives and proportions, the collision of rhetorical authority and energetic speech, the permutations of tone. "To read Dryden, Pope &c," said Coleridge, "you need only count syllables; but to read Donne you must measure *Time* and discover the *Time* of each word by the sense of passion." For, as it has been noted of mannerist architecture, "the logic of the structure does not coincide with the structural elements."[19]

Contrariety is, of course, one form of relation. Alongside affinity, it furnishes another of the doubles whose tensions consort in Donne's poems. Not unexpectedly, this sense of disparity predominates; it explains the harsh accents and the strain of accommodation in certain metaphors. It is like the bad conscience of us all.

A curious rehabilitation occurs when we arrive at the calculated antitheses of Pope. In which one, we might ask, have we the truly Renaissance addiction to detail and symmetrical composition? Yet a more pertinent question to pose, because it points to the conceptual center of these two approaches to the contraries, is: how are these resources summoned? What kind of knowledge does each yield? If in Pope we discern the results of reason reasoned, we experience in Donne the process of reason reasoning: in the former as a distillation, in the latter an appetitive force; in one a version of the mind made up, and in the other a state of mind.

If "Donne's words bring with them a memory of abstract ideas,"[20] is it not the effect of his inductive method causing form to intervene in the character of speculative memory? According to Maritain, "it is the privilege, in a unique way, of creative knowledge for the idea to be at once a means *in quo* and an object *quod.*" So that, reduced to a kind of axiom, "to

---

19. Wylie Sypher, *Four Stages of Renaissance Style: Art and Literature* (New York, 1955), p. 124.
20. Joan Bennett, *Four Metaphysical Poets* (Cambridge, 1934), p. 41.

know is to the sense and intellect—taken as cognitive functions —as *to exist* is to the essence ... to the quidditative function. It is a kind of existence that defines knowledge."[21]

The practical intellect from which poems issue is a predator. For a poem to exist, both language and reality must be violated with formal intention. In Donne's poetry logic serves the very ends of metaphor. The doubleness of metaphor reflects its agent.

21. *Degrees of Knowledge,* pp. 112-13.

BEN JONSON:
The Conduct of Reason

In conjunction with a tradition specifically musical emerge the poems of Ben Jonson, as public as they are prosodic, and essentially rational. The spareness that qualifies them is like a reverse image of the prose relations from which we are told they were transposed. In fact it is because of, rather than despite, this unelaborated economy that the poems retain marks that have always characterized the discursive mode at its most apt. "Seek the consonancy and concatenation of truth," wrote Jonson in his *Discoveries*. How he goes about it in the poems is an instruction not only in the efficacy of moral judgment, or the proximate resources of craft, but in certain pre-Hegelian certitudes regarding language.

Any meaningful poetry should be governed by a conviction in the denotative capacity of the medium. But this conviction is with us often converted into an equivocal truce—for the duration of a poem—in which the trust is transferred to the ego and the poet as rival creator conceived as coercing meaning temporarily into his words. Indeed, it may be the novelty of encountering a sophisticated mind in which consciousness is not yet divided from craft by the tensions of this sort of doubt that draws us to the study of Jonson. Nostalgia for that irrecoverable faith may account as well for the neoclassic inclinations of poetry in our own century. Meanwhile, existential "freedom" has replaced medieval "Love" as the fulcrum of causality. (Even as, in philosophy, the articulation of wonder—*thaumazein*—contemplation has given way to expository questioning.)

Looking ahead to the present moment, we observe what becomes of this freedom. That which Sartre connects with the act of judging is not fundamentally creative. Autonomous thought turning upon itself in the Cartesian scheme is severely

Ben Jonson: The Conduct of Reason

limited in its freedom by the terms of its object. But judgment unconfined to interior act and concerned with the production of such a thing as a poem declares in its very performance a deference to the "thingyness" of the poem. It is a deference pronounced in the maker's overriding concern with the details that give shape and *mesure* to this "thing." For, by intriguing contraries, reference to objective accidents, a work of art achieves its irreducible distinctiveness.

The classicism of Jonson is highly idiomatic, as F. R. Leavis asserts.[1] Its most conspicuous given is formalist: structure taking precedence over metaphor. That Jonson should by such means have become "the first master stylist of the plain tradition"[2] almost ensures its impracticableness for imitators. Quite the reverse of those introspective modes anchored in free-floating consciousness, here—as opposed for example to the emotive interiority vaguely designated by the romantics—the exteriority of style has a substantive function. Yvor Winters convincingly demonstrates this strength of Jonson's while detecting figural weaknesses, style as ornament, in Shakespeare and Donne.[3]

It was Goethe who said: "Simple imitation flourishes under tranquil and satisfying conditions of existence, and whereas mannerism calls for a light touch and a fresh individuality, that which I call *style* rests on the deepest foundations of cognition, on the inner essence of things, in so far as this is given to us to comprehend in visible and tangible forms."[4] One might guess from this hint at the fundamental problem of creation the

1. *Revaluation* (London, 1953), p. 18.
2. Yvor Winters, "Poetic Styles, Old and New," in *Four Poets on Poetry*, ed. Don C. Allen (Baltimore, 1949), p. 223.
3. *Ibid.*, pp. 44-60.
4. Cited by Ludwig Curtius in *Goethe: Wisdom and Experience* (London, 1949), p. 223.

wisdom of contradicting D. H. Lawrence's famous intimations of the lifelessness and destructiveness of the rational. Is it not one of the terrible qualities of reason that it *does* have a life of its own, just as the things with which it deals have existences in accordance with their essences? Respect for these integrities, for their otherness, even when they may have only notional existence, seems a most accurate sign of the classicist tactic. Nor can there be any doubt when so detached a view is taken of the poetic materials that the executive will is thereby called upon to govern the more decisively their allocation. (How blurred by comparison this executive act becomes in poetics whose chief excuse is "self-expression.") "But style is also a question of will, of the intention, of faith in the meaning of what is expressed. So finally one cannot separate expression from content, manner from meaning. They interpenetrate dialectically, *complexio oppositorum*. But 'what is expressed'—that is never, in a significant work of art, a subjective fantasy. It is an archetypal image or myth, and fundamentally impersonal or objective."[5]

This remark adds an important note to our ordinarily minimal assumptions about style. For, if we are to know the poems, surely we must look beyond the plainness and the urbanity, which make these poems the kind of poems they are, for that subtle correspondence of means and content which effectively constitutes them as what they are.

"To the World" follows the poem "To Penshurst" in *The Forrest*. It is somewhat briefer—68 lines instead of 106—and considerably more complex, but it has never received the public attention the latter has whose richness, being descriptive, is the more easily grasped. It begins:

5. Herbert E. Read, *Forms of Things Unknown* (London, 1960), pp. 199-200.

Ben Jonson: The Conduct of Reason

>False world, good-night: since thou hast brought
>>That houre upon my morne of age,
>
>Hence-forth I quit thee from my thought,
>>My part is ended on thy stage.
>
>Doe not once hope, that thou canst tempt
>>A spirit so resolv'd to tread
>
>Upon thy throate, and live exempt
>>From all the nets that thou canst spread.
>
>I know thy formes are studied arts,
>>Thy subtle wayes, be narrow straits;
>
>Thy curtesie but sodaine starts,
>>And what thou call'st thy gifts are baits.
>
>I know too, though thou strut, and paint,
>>Yet art thou both shrunke up, and old,
>
>That onely fooles make thee a saint,
>>And all thy good is to be sold.

There is a curious pausing music about the opening passage even as it enters upon the expository business of the poem. In fact it duplicates at the outset Wyatt's cadences in:

>My lute, awake, perfourm the last
>Labour that thou and I shall wast.

One thinks of tetrameter, I suppose, as being proximate to the condition of music as longer measures are not. Because meter as meter is an abstraction, any proximity in its regard must be theoretical. Nevertheless, in the poems of a master, the meters' subjacent presence is heard and sensed as a property of language itself rather than a function imposed upon it. Shadings of stress are *in* the spoken words; the poet supplies the caesura. And between the two considerable variety is inducible even within the bounds of the four-stress line. This after all is the measure of Dunbar's "Lament for the Makaris," of Shakespeare's "Who is Sylvia?," of King's "Exequy," and the mordant clockwork of Dr. Swift's "Verses on his own Death."

Jonson did not in this instance employ his favorite couplets. Though not printed as such, the poem is in effect composed in a series of quatrains, each closed, but so linked conceptually as to be indivisible from the following. Nothing that may be called a figure here is other than commonplace to the subject: the world as a stage, its temptations as nets, its gifts as baits, and so on. Very little requires visualization. The semi-abstract play (l. 16) on good as ideal and "goods"—merchandise—is typical of the low key in which Jonson operates. Nor are rhymes either subtle or ingenious; paint—saint is the norm. If the poem is something better than versified platitude, it becomes so, like many a religious painting, by triumphing over its own contents. The poem is a great one, and a part of its triumph can be attributed to its refusal to be brilliant. It is a feat of style and a feat of judgment. The two are consubstantial. Working reason is their active principle.

Allen Tate has said, "Poetry . . . tests with experience the illusions that the human predicament tempts us in our weakness to believe."[6] This poem performs the test in a catalogue of illusions the bare statement of which is analytical. Its clarity and trenchancy obviate secondary elaboration. It is a summary of moral theology. To have noted that its terms are abstract is not the same as to have found them general. The absence of emotional coloration, the equanimity of the narrative "I" (who is addressing this argument by way of farewell to a "gentle-woman, noble and virtuous") secure it in the presence and specificity of the rational voice. The conviction

6. *The Man of Letters in the Modern World* (New York, 1955), p. 256.

that it carries, the inclusiveness of which it is capable could never have been exploited by naked intuition or verbal agility unassisted.

One cannot judiciously count on the connotative possibilities of the word unless one is certain about its denotative function. Yet a familiar practice in what may be generally classed intuitive-romantic poetics is the rush to marshal these allusive forces without having established the denotative grounds for them. Jonson solicits our wonder by pursuing the opposite extreme. He all but excludes the connotative in his resolute precising of the literal. A superficial reading perhaps even suggests that the discursive norm of prose replaces the poetic center of gravity, but this is an illusion quickly dissipated. The structural resources of prose are called upon, none of the props which make it easy, development by accretion, secondary elaboration, even figurative, being foregone. What we do not perceive at first glance is how much of the poem is sustained by its caesura, by the omissions that its concision makes articulate. This must be the most difficult of all possible ways to write a poem.

Jonson, it seems, did not even have to learn it, for—despite certain flaws, certain errors in taste—no faltering exploratory progress indicates the usual search for a congenial mode or the amateur's groping toward possession of a discipline. He taxes his readers from the start where they do not expect to be taxed, with craft, with the identification of technic with meaning. This is far from equivalent to distracting them with virtuosity. Yvor Winters'[7] attentive reading of "An Elegy" ("Though beauty be the mark of praise") and "To Heaven" ("Good and great God, can I not think of Thee") supports this contention

7. "Poetic Styles, Old and New," in *Four Poets on Poetry*, pp. 62-69.

more thoroughly than my own remarks so far. But Eliot errs, I believe, in calling Jonson's a "poetry of the surface." Given Jonson's ethical proclivity, if his poems were "of the surface" surely they would legislate. Rather, their centripetal movement is toward internal organization the exercise of which, on the poet's part a practical virtue, like prudence, is reflective. The originality that the nineteenth century disparaged him for not possessing lies in fact, as Ralph S. Walker indicated many years ago in *The Criterion*,[8] in "absorption and comprehension."

If the intellectual virtues inform and determine the lyrics, they do not crowd out the music. However, they make of that music something more abstractly ideational—a mathematic. For it does not depend as in other lyrics we remember upon eccentric stress, upon the exaggerated reverberance of rich language. Jonson's development as a poet, we have inferred, never conformed to the familiar pattern of a "search for an idiom." He was from the beginning abstemious with words because their ordination signified for him an ideal absolute. We see and hear it, I think, most perfectly achieved in the metrical composition of "An Ode. To himselfe": a dialectic of threes irregularly recapitulated by doubling in the hexameters of each sixth line closing the six stanzas. The first and last:

>   Where do'st thou carelesse lie
>   Buried in ease and sloth?
>   Knowledge, that sleepes, doth die;
>   And this Securitie,
>   It is the common Moath,
>   That eats on wits, and Arts, and oft destroyes
>   them both.
>   .   .   .   .

8. "Ben Jonson's Lyric Poetry," *The Criterion*, 13 (1934), p. 443.

> And since our Daintie age
>   Cannot endure reproofe,
>   Make not thy selfe a Page,
>   To that strumpet the Stage,
>   But sing high and aloofe,
> Safe from the wolves black jaw, and the dull
>   Asses hoofe.

Despite this extraordinarily conscious disposition of structure, these elements support and reinforce the intelligible sense; they cannot be said to detract from the unitary effect in the fashion all our experience of mannerist art prepares us to expect.

The entelechy of the poem is what absorbs Jonson. The workmanship of which we are never unaware may be all but invisible, as in the epitaphs—

> . . . .
> This grave partakes the fleshly birth.
> Which cover lightly, gentle earth.

But it is never rigidly harmonious, never the expression of inflexible conservatism. Forms that are the proof of workmanship, however transparently, carry more than a compulsive symmetry. Perhaps as short a poem as "The Houre-glasse" is most revealing of Jonson's full powers:

> Doe but consider this small dust,
>   Here running in the Glasse,
>   By Atomes mov'd;
>   Could you beleeve, that this,
>   The body was
>   Of one that lov'd?
> And in his Mistresse flame, playing like a flye,
>   Turn'd to cinders by her eye?

> Yes; and in death, as life unblest,
> To have't exprest,
> Even ashes of lovers find no rest.

A critical perception and a technical experiment. If together *(complexio oppositorum)* these constitute imitation, they do so by reproducing the inequalities that compose the perfection of all created forms. Whatever else it is, the poem is an analogue itself of the poetic process. The body of the poem, ideally a waking knowledge, moves in the glass of form. Behind it is the free poise of an independent mind. Jonson's found expression for unerring certainties at all times rare, not forced, but subtilized by craft.

IV

ALEXANDER POPE:
Requisitions of Verity

Reason's Double Agents

> *What requisitions of a verity*
> *Prompted the wit and rage between his teeth*
> *One cannot say. Around a crooked tree*
> *A moral climbs whose name should be a wreath.*
>   ALLEN TATE

Perhaps because the Augustans themselves used the word so often, it does not occur to us to question the evidence of reason in the poetry of Pope. A quality we tend to associate with prose, it attaches also to those elements of contemporary theory militating against the lyric. Music is suppressed in Pope even as meter is cultivated, and the impression of discursiveness prevails as well in those passages most technically condensed. The reason we think we see, or which we generalize to avoid thought, is the reason of *sententiae*. There is, of course, far more to be seen—a good portion of it reified through dramatic action. On the whole, however, what we discern in Pope is "reason reasoned" rather than reasoning: the reason of the mind made up, perfected, and uncommonly concentrated by methods unavailable to the sort of discourse from which we expect such results.

Hannah Arendt restates the awareness in which our reading begins: "The immediate source of the art work is the human capacity for thought. . . . Works of art are thought things, but this does not prevent their being things. . . . What actually makes the thought a reality and fabricates things of thought is the same workmanship which, through the primordial instrument of human hands, builds the other durable things of the human artifice."[1] Alfred N. Whitehead among others has remarked the kinship of poetry and philosophy. He has further observed that "Language halts behind intuition. The difficulty

1. *The Human Condition* (Chicago, 1958), p. 168.

of philosophy is the expression of what is self-evident. Our understanding outruns the ordinary uses of words."[2] How close such a conception of the work of philosophy is to Pope's own expressed conception of the nature of the poetic discipline in its relation to common sense.

Poetry is allied to philosophy not alone by its universality but through its dealing with the obvious and the commonplace. Both rely, for their excursions into infinity, upon the same particulars. For, if "the sense of reality can never be adequately sustained amidst mere *sensa*, either of sound or sight," and if indeed "the connexity of existence is of the essence of understanding"[3] neither can this understanding arise other than from that data. Simply as interpreters, each in his own fashion, of the ramifications of facts, the poet and the philosopher must be equally worldly. The deep worldliness entailed by rational activity is an aspect unexamined but widely deducible, especially from its manifestations in contemporary thought and art: but nowhere is it more so than in the strict terms of Augustan satire in the hands of Pope. Dante's "As a thing is related to existence, so is it related to truth"[4] confirms the responsibility of poet and philosopher alike to the connections of this world.

Pope is not, according to the platitude, a "thinker," not a metaphysician, yet he is as the planner and maker of *The Dunciad* an ontologist of the most impressive sort. A philosopher could say, "Logic must take care of itself";[5] another add that "The laws of logic can be discovered like other laws of nature because they are ultimately rooted in the structure of the human brain, and they possess . . . the same force of com-

2. *Modes of Thought* (Cambridge, 1938), p. 68.
3. *Ibid.*, pp. 45-46.
4. Epistle X.
5. Ludwig Wittgenstein, *Notebooks: 1914-1916* (Oxford, 1951), p. 2.

pulsion as the driving necessity which regulates the other functions of our bodies."[6] So we discover logic "taking care of itself" in the performance of Pope, its driving force unimpeded by the poet's commitment to an austere stylistic regime.

The Dunciad in particular, and in their separate respects The Rape of the Lock and the Moral Essays, record the incursions of decay upon civilized society. Disintegration is represented in the former as a migration of literary evils under the sponsorship of Dulness from the City, where it originates at the center of business, to Westminster, the focal point of government and society. One of the qualities of this presentation—despite the writer's engagement to neoclassic canons evoking the large and the general—allies itself remarkably to recent existential practice. Reiterating an exaggerated awareness of objects, contingencies, things as things, the nausea of Sartre's first novel stems precisely from the horror these factual sensations arouse.[7] This same specificity animates the moral criticism of Pope (as indeed it does quite pathologically certain passages of Swift).

We are disturbed by instances of disgust in Gulliver, as we inevitably are whenever emotion manifestly exceeds its occasion.[8] Nevertheless we accept, not imprudently, Swift's own estimate of the redemptive impersonality of his satire:

> Perhaps I may allow, the Dean
> Had too much Satyr in his Vein;
> And seem'd determin'd not to starve it,
> Because no Age could more deserve it.

6. Arendt, Human Condition, p. 171.
7. A topic elucidated by Iris Murdoch in Sartre (London, 1953).
8. Sir Kenneth Clark in The Nude (London, 1956) says: "The exploitation by the intellect of a theme usually governed by the emotions must always be disturbing to a normal sensibility." The opposite, I think, is also true.

> Yet, Malice never was his Aim;
> He lash'd the Vice, but spar'd the Name.
> No Individual could resent,
> Where Thousands equally were meant:
> His Satyr points at no Defect,
> But what all Mortals may correct. . . .[9]

Extraliterary grounds, the personal enmities of real people, have credibly interfered with the judgment of Pope's *Dunciad* as a poem. Yet, as Aubrey Williams suggests in his excellent study,[10] those individuals are, as magnified, imaginatively transformed, thus acquiring a symbolic reference at once larger than "life" and self-contained within its own mode, and therefore entitled to consideration upon those terms. Anger which, in addition to the "sin of wit," Pope has in common with Swift was pointed out by Aristotle to be the emotion closest to reason. Insofar as such a comparison is relevant, the case may be put that, respecting the apparent predispositions of their methods, Pope's does issue in the greater balance of the two.

Reason was Swift's subject; he argued it without scanting a shrewd estimate of its inadequacies. Reason informs *The Dunciad*; in its essential nature as order it is a principle of the poem's organization. It is furthermore here forcibly opposed—with all the explicit vigor of moral outrage—to the amorphous, dissociating effects of unreason and of reason malpracticed in duplicity. " 'Order' for Pope is no mere word, but a rich concept imaginatively realised."[11] Although there is no strict contrast here, one may propose that it was Swift who in fact portrayed "the vices of men," whereas Pope, taking a longer

9. From "Lines on his own Death."
10. *Pope's Dunciad* (London, 1955), pp. 1-8.
11. F. R. Leavis, *Common Pursuit* (London, 1962), p. 92.

view of the consequences of the new philosophies, exposed the denaturing of man in the scientism that concerned them both.

Pope's respect, as classicist, for the uses of reason necessarily entails an awareness of the bounds within which it is capable of acting and its actions applicable. What reason can and cannot do, what it must not be prevented from doing, is the protestation underlying the poem, a protestation no less effectively devastating as inversely put by being made the utterance of "with all the cant of wit,/ Without the soul, the Muse's hypocrite" and the powers of Dulness in whose negative kingdom solipsism spells in detail the end of sense.

The Dunciad is about that distinguishingly human feature, language. It is further concerned with the breakdown that occurs when words and matter are falsely set at variance, and indeed was written at the moment when the latter alone was becoming empirically acceptable. The consequences of the revolution Bacon assisted with such uncritical relish—casting doubt on the validity of language as a medium for truth even while insisting upon the didactic role of poetry—Pope lucidly foresaw. Book IV opens with the mindless goddess, "the seed of Chaos, and of Night" whose aim is "To blot out order and extinguish light," as she oversees Science in chains, "rebellious Logic, gagged and bound," where "stripped, fair Rhet'ric languished on the ground." Her subjects (in a state of hopelessly totalitarian stupefaction) buzz about her as about a queen bee. "The gathering number as it moves along,/ Involves a vast involuntary throng." Among these "There marched the bard and blockhead, side by side,/ Who rhymed for hire, and patronised for pride," and the literary critics who are seen to "Admire new light through holes [themselves] have made." The pedants are discovered in futile

Alexander Pope: Requisitions of Verity

> Disputes of *me* or *te*, of *aut* or *at*,
> To sound or sink in *cano*, O or A,
> Or give up Cicero to C or K.
>   (IV, 220-22)

lest we should suppose that "more true dulness lies/ In folly's cap, than wisdom's grave disguise." For these are the scholars who "explain a thing till all men doubt it,/ And write about it, goddess, and about it." The student returning broadened from his travels appears to have profited only to the extent of having

> Dropped the dull lumber of the Latin store,
> Spoiled his own language, and acquired no more;
> All classic learning lost on classic ground;
> And last turned air, the echo of a sound.
>   (IV, 319-22)

In a final travesty, those who have taken the "High Priori Road" "reason downward" till they doubt of God. Thus the systematic reduction of its own heroic terms is conducted within the poem under the approving yawn of the "divinity without a νοῦς" as "Art after art goes out, and all is night."

If the revulsions of Sartre's Roquentin seem to us artificial or at least arbitrary, we have only to reflect that his condition was accurately forecast as inevitable by Pope. The same reading may suggest to us as well the source and the relation of his predicament to the more purely linguistic one of the logical positivists. It is not exclusively the traditional humanist alliance of knowledge with virtue which animates the progress of the poem (in which Book IV may be seen to be a concise and more perfectly realized version of the preceding three books) but also the clearly experiential insight into the destruction that accompanies the deprivation of the word's authority to testify to real relations. The uncreating inertia in which the busy-ness of the hack writers culminates under the obscure dispensation of Mother Dulness and her son is a parable of the eclipse, the anarchy of mind contingent upon the trivialization of the word. Rhetoric reduced to decorum is so enervated as to be useless to convey ideas. Williams has so precisely elucidated the causes at work behind the altered perspective of rhetoric that this task need not be done again. He attributes to the Ramist reformation of logic a measure of blame for restricting rhetoric to an ornamental function.[12]

Manic though the situations and their attendant atmosphere may be in the world of the poem, it seems important to notice that their content is never irrational. Such moments are in the first place based upon classic literary precedent—for example the epic counsel such as that of Milton's Pandemonium, or the Aeneid-like visitation of the underworld. Furthermore the treatment, often by way of pointedly unequal parallels, is measured in tones of comic irony. A horror that is wholly rational is adumbrated in pictorially amusing detail, e.g.:

> Prompt at the call, around the goddess roll
> Broad hats, and hoods, and caps a sable shoal;
> Thick and more thick the black blockade extends,
> A hundred head of Aristotle's friends.
>
> (IV, 189-92)

A world not lunatic in its derangement but purposefully, even casuistically, stupid emerges *in the control* of the goddess who "bade Britannia sleep." "Laborious, heavy, busy, bold, and blind,/She ruled...." The viciousness of course lies in the voluntary and deliberate quality of this government in whose service venality is the very condition of the uses to which

12. *Pope's Dunciad*, p. 115.

language is put. Flattery, sheer foolishness, defamatory skills, a whole collocation of verbal perversions

> ... the cloud-compelling queen
> Beholds through fogs, that magnify the scene.
> She, tinsell'd o'er in robes of varying hues,
> With self-applause her wild creation views;
> Sees momentary monsters rise and fall,
> And with her own fool's colours gilds them all.
> (I, 79-84)

"Ductile Dulness," a deity without a thought, similar to the stock image of the typical administrator, can command Time to stand still, but is always capable of "new meanders." She observes with undifferentiated satisfaction

> How hints, like spawn, scarce quick in embryo lie,
> How new-born nonsense first is taught to cry,
> Maggots half-formed in rhyme exactly meet,
> And learn to crawl upon poetic feet.
> (I, 59-62)

This poem is not limited to a harsh monody for the obliteration of a civilized ideal. More drastically, *The Dunciad* re-enacts the fully logical course of the human quotient disestablished. The tactical skills by which this fraudulent disorder is achieved are, as we have just seen, a primary object of the deity's tyrannous admiration. Thus our attention too is focused upon techniques that condemn themselves. We are not to suppose that this chaos in its minutest details is haphazardly arrived at, or lacking in method. The monstrous proportions her monarchizing assumes represent the tautology of genuine Art.

The obfuscation of the human capacity for thought, the "deep intent" of the regime of Dulness, erupts in a campaign pragmatically concentrated upon the center where that economy is realized and sustained: the verbal. Moreover, the systematic offensive, being conducted upon reason's own grounds, employs the same weapons. The finesse of Pope's irony in the management of these materials is therefore far from one-dimensional. Because of the nature of its referents, the equation—formulated in terms of a Messianic advent—cannot be less than complex. Nor is the universality of the problem along with its fore-ordained conclusion diminished by the historicity of a number of its participants, for these are figurally employed.

Those subjects who in Book IV call upon the "Mother of arrogance, and source of Pride" to do away with the Creator, to "Make Nature still encroach upon His plan," to "Thrust some mechanic cause into His place" and "Make God man's image, man the final cause," confess that, seeing all in self, they are

> Of nought so certain as our reason still,
> Of nought so doubtful as of soul and will.
> (IV, 481-82)

They experience no uncertainty as to the capacity of words while invoking the uncreating (rather than the uncreated) Logos, and neither should we. Indeed the multiplicity of misuses to which their conduct proves words adaptable illustrates not an innate debility of the medium (posited in our time by semantics) so much as its astonishingly extensive powers. Even the doubt of Descartes expresses, it has been recently shown,[13] an optimistic epistemology.

The rational anger of Pope may be read as one form of dogma anathematizing others. Yet the rightness of his premises

13. Karl R. Popper, "The Sources of Knowledge and Ignorance," *Encounter*, 19 (1962), 42-57.

appears self-evident, even discounting the necessarily rigged nature of the contest in which Pope had to invent both the opposition and the defense and in doing so arranged for the opposition's own disclosures to be self-condemning. Nevertheless the persistent relevance of the tensions so brought into play perhaps attests as much to the life of the positions thus opposed as to the art of the poet. For those systems, like the Cartesian, which Pope finds pernicious have determined the direction of modern thought, and with a variety of results to persuade the most convinced opponents that durable ideas may come from faulty premises.

If Pope's absolutism seems naive or outdated to some today, none could reject the justice of his judgment of the besetting evils attendant upon modern intellectual fashions. In respect to the sources of knowledge, Pope was quite aware "What thin partitions sense from thought divide" (*Essay on Man*, I, 226). The transcendence of the ego could in Pope's view only imperil the truth of art and politics alike. Annihilating subjectivity is the prevailing note in the kingdom of Dulness. As such it furnishes an interesting point of departure for the scansion of the altering role of the subjective in post-Renaissance aesthetics. The self-centered aesthetic repudiated in *The Dunciad* could quite recently reappear without bias in an essay on "Poetry and the Behaviour of Speech."

The modern poet fears that Language by its very nature is forcing him to express not the pure Self but such gritty matter as ideas, perhaps even convictions. If words could be held apart, one could easily control them, but they have a bourgeois hankering to rush together in closed formulations and statements. Common syntax is like a spring; if you disapprove of its direction you must use force to change it. Valéry is a typical poet of his time in resenting the syntactical ghost which undermines the writer's freedom.[14]

No more effective contrast to Pope's traditionalism could occur, or more predictably under the circumstances than this.

Self-expression as an end of Art is quite taken for granted these days, preposterous as it would have seemed to Pope. And the writer's struggle to keep ideas *out* of his work attracts a sympathy that another age may again find comic. A shift in the conception of how language is equipped to handle thought —and what freedom on these occasions is—accompanies the subjective into currency. Language becomes notoriously frail or elusively fluid under the impact of creative ego. It eludes the ecstatic, but responds to the solicitation of reason. The question in any case rests whether ideas occur in verbalism as such or in the spaces between the words.

When Colley Cibber descended to the cave of Poetry what he heard was the music of emptiness.

14. Denis Donoghue, *Hudson Review*, 14 (1961-62), 537.

V

ALLEN TATE:
The Heroism of the Rational

Reason's Double Agents

The contemporary poet is a man whom our sophisticated awareness of extramental and preconscious conditions of existence causes us to credit with having even more to withstand from these quarters than he is likely to maintain in the way of technical resources with which to organize his response. If we apprehend one note common to the poems of our contemporaries, an extraordinary if diversely distributed weight incumbent upon their makers, it is freedom. For our traditions inform us cumulatively of nothing more patent than that the great modes have achieved their maturest expressions, that the most strident rebellion must follow established paths, but that where much is disponible little is apt for possession in so eclectic a time.

The poet's freedom is coextensive with the repertory of choices, formal and interior, at his command. Yet the antinomies implicit in this condition can only have been intensified by the exaggerated self-watchfulness inherited from the Renaissance. Since all language is metaphor, all the arts of language are, in a sense, arts of translation. But translation must always be as well a way of talking to oneself: at its best a truly impersonal dialogue justified equally by its content and by the forms it may be urged, perhaps gratuitously, in newness to assume. This particular conjunction of the two forces, creative ego and imperative form, seems to account for the note of *hubris* characteristic, I think without exception, of the work of every poet of superior accomplishment in the present century. One can have little doubt in reading Pound's work, for example, that it is tragic in scope, without his mediating choice, because—in the tradition of all Renaissance poetics—his is an invocation of Ego. It is, in effect, this noumenal and histrionic presence of the ego within the semblances of action which gives his version of Propertius its dramatic congruity. This surely is the identity, not of a single shadow, but of the "one tangle of shadows"

> Moving naked over Acheron
> Upon the one raft, victor and conquered together.

Operatio sequitur esse is a motto viable as ever, but laden now with ironic overtones effectively reinforced if we juxtapose merely two passages describing differently the mind. Bacon the empiricist's description is poetic but incorporates only the passive role of intelligence (in what scholastics distinguish as reason in "first act"). His postulation of the mind as "a clear and equal glass, wherein the beams of things should reflect according to their true incidence"[1] sorts instructively with another of St. Thomas', a trenchantly abstract statement treating the mind primarily as an active agent: "Reason is the first principle of all human work."[2]

Insofar as it is a thing at all, a poem is conceived as a work to be done. It is a work that reason is uniquely competent to undertake. But by affirming the intellectuality fundamental to the condition of poetry and permeating its simplest constituents, one does not disallow the accessory richness that remains undiscussed under those terms. On the contrary, certain predicates invite others and suggest at the same time something respecting their relatedness. By acknowledging the roundness of oranges one does not exclude the possibility of their being juicy as well.

The poet of these circumstances is called upon to equili-

---

1. Francis Bacon, *Novum Organum*.
2. St. Thomas, *Sum. Theol.*, i-ii, q. 58, a. 2.

brate in practice both metaphysics and science since he attends transitively to Being and Becoming at once. The science of making was by Aristotle set above both practical insight and political science *(dianoia* and *episteme praktike)* because it conduces directly to the contemplation of truth. "Contemplation and fabrication *(theoria* and *poiesis)* have an inner affinity and do not stand in the same unequivocal opposition to each other as contemplation and action."[3] The poet's mind is the copula joining these two and the poem is the expression of that intensive act.

The poetry of Allen Tate discloses a powerful intelligence in a state of urgency, a facultative concentration through which that knowledge is sought which can be effectually achieved only in "making." The strategic continuity in his poetic practice has been sympathetically reviewed by Vivienne Koch.[4] The relatively compact body of the selected poems makes that variety the more impressive whereby he subjects to the rigorous discipline of craft those motives for desperation which have inclined his lesser contemporaries with increasing pusillanimity toward the *précieux*.

Perhaps the most obvious inference to be drawn from those poems in which the formal elements common to the classic are dominant is the jurisdiction of reason. The more presentative form evinces these qualities of rhetoric, phrasing, meter, and tone, the inclusiveness, the restraint ceremonial to such a mode, the more conscious we are, in reading, of the shadow of the mind behind the *species expressa* apportioning these resources. "The Mediterranean" is such a poem:

3. Hannah Arendt, *The Human Condition* (Chicago, 1958), p. 275.
4. "The Poetry of Allen Tate," *Kenyon Review*, 11 (Summer, 1949), 355-78.

Allen Tate: The Heroism of the Rational

Where we went in the boat was a long bay
A slingshot wide, walled in by towering stone—
Peaked margin of antiquity's delay,
And we went there out of time's monotone:

Where we went in the black hull no light moved
But a gull white-winged along the feckless wave,
The breeze, unseen but fierce as a body loved,
That boat drove onward like a willing slave:

Where we went in the small ship the seaweed
Parted and gave to us the murmuring shore,
And we made feast and in our secret need
Devoured the very plates Aeneas bore:

Where derelict you see through the low twilight
The green coast that you, thunder-tossed, would win,
Drop sail, and hastening to drink all night
Eat dish and bowl to take that sweet land in!

Where we feasted and caroused on the sandless
Pebbles, affecting our day of piracy,
What prophecy of eaten plates could landless
Wanderers fulfil by the ancient sea?

We for that time might taste the famous age
Eternal here yet hidden from our eyes
When lust of power undid its stuffless rage;
They, in a wineskin, bore earth's paradise.

Let us lie down once more by the breathing side
Of Ocean, where our live forefathers sleep
As if the Known Sea still were a month wide—
Atlantis howls but is no longer steep!

What country shall we conquer, what fair land
Unman our conquest and locate our blood?
We've cracked the hemispheres with careless hand!
Now, from the Gates of Hercules we flood

Reason's Double Agents

> Westward, westward till the barbarous brine
> Whelms us to the tired land where tasseling corn,
> Fat beans, grapes sweeter than muscadine
> Rot on the vine: in that land were we born.

Where does this simplicity receive its authority? For this is an early if nearly perfect poem and simplicity is not of itself authoritative. It becomes so here, I believe—and I can only put it tautologically—through the interanimating efficacy of its figural statements.[5] The journey that stands for a birth and a recovery, a conquest and a submission, the surfeit and loss at work in the mystery of origin, is elegiac. It is a reflection on the historical possibility of belonging in a dispersed society. The journey is a journey (not a dream) of reason. It is made knowable by association with the Aeneas myth of the reinstatement of civilization, the experience of transience being one way of understanding permanence. These memories of the possible are both allegorizing and allegorized by the acts of communion (the feast) and love so explicitly likened in the very setting out. That this action is time-bound yet ever presently implicated in "antiquity's delay" is also part of the poem's message, and by a similarly time-bound act of intellectual communion we apprehend it, according to our means. Each of these primal motives recurs thematically in successive poems, sometimes with less contemplative stress, but always in the sustention of forms—order, if you will, invoked against chaos—and in them we recognize not the minor poet who must cast about for topics and await occasions, but the intelligent obsession of the significant poet whose subject has selected him.

   5. It is no accident that this critical summary must make less discursive sense than the poem that is autotelic in its perfection.

Allen Tate: The Heroism of the Rational

No man's mind is observable except analogously through the actions that it proffers for interpretation. And probably no action to which it applies itself is more highly fashioned than the poem. Tate himself clarifies the means at all our disposals when he says: "The reach of our imaginative enlargement is perhaps no longer than the ladder of analogy, at the top of which we may see all, if we wish to *see* anything, that we have brought up with us from the bottom, where lies the sensible world. If we take nothing with us to the top but our emptied, angelic intellects, we shall see nothing when we get there."[6]

The sensible world as Tate reads it is characterized not merely by succession and change, but by a nightmare disjunctiveness. History is not synonymous with order. The "famous age" is seen in a number of poems in analogical rapport with the present, never as an undiscriminated idyll, but inevitably with tragic irony. In "Aeneas At Washington," that time "when civilization/ Run by the few fell to the many" is now and carries with it its own destructive principle. The old soldier in "To the Lacedemonians" must say, "There is no civilization without death." And in the ode the Confederate dead are addressed:

> You who have waited for the angry resolution
> Of those desires that should be yours tomorrow,
> You know the unimportant shrift of death
> And praise the vision
> And praise the arrogant circumstance
> Of those who fall
> Rank upon rank, hurried beyond decision—
> Here by the sagging gate, stopped by the wall.

6. *The Man of Letters in the Modern World* (New York, 1955), p. 131.

André Malraux, in another context and of another medium, has said: "L'artiste a besoin de ses prédécesseurs 'vivants', qui ... ne sont pas toujours leurs prédécesseurs immédiats, mais les derniers grands."[7] The poems at hand are a special and complex instance of this relationship, for at its source are to be had not simply the learnable craft, but the irreplaceable lessons of *sunt lacrimae rerum et mentem mortalia tangunt.*

The most analytic passion must be constructive in poetry. Moreover, Yvor Winters rightly reminds us that language itself is a kind of abstraction, even at its most concrete.[8] These are truths with which any good poet teaches himself to work. Many a counsel from the critical sidelines endorses his requisitioning of particulars, and has long done so, as a glance at any of the twelfth-century *Arts Poétiques*[9] proclaims. Whether the rules are uttered or not, practice observes them, so that we may very well as we are told[10] disembarrass ourselves of traditional clichés regarding certain schools such as the Troubadour, "synonyme d'emphase oratoire et volubile," whose style is, in fact, extraordinarily dense. Two lines from Gaucelme Faidit's *planh* for Richard the Lionhearted is proof enough of this:

> Mortz es lo reys e son passat mil an
> Qu'anc tan pros om no fo ni no'l vi res. . . .
>
> (Dead is the king, a thousand years have gone
> no braver ruled than I have ever seen)

7. *Voix du Silence* (Paris, 1951), p. 315.
8. *In Defense of Reason* (Denver, 1947), p. 17.
9. E.g., Edmond Faral, *Les Arts Poétiques du XIIe et du XIIIe Siècle* (Paris, 1958).
10. Henri Davenson, *Les Troubadours* (Paris, 1960), p. 68. He quotes Faidit. My translation.

Allen Tate: The Heroism of the Rational

No living poet, I believe, in English has come more closely or more expertly to grips with the problems engendered by his analytical-creative purpose and the obstinate immateriality of the medium than Allen Tate.

The perfection of the virtue of art consists in the act of judging (St. Thomas). Baudelaire and Maritain in turn refer us to the necessary coincidence of the critical with the creative faculty. All poets have got to be critics, but critics are by no means necessarily poets. Yet a good many very competent poets never venture far beyond their first judicial mastery of "concrete" detail. It is the case indeed with Tate that the more analytic the content of a poem, the more specific and pressing the density in which it is achieved. In "Shadow and Shade":

> The torrent of the reaching shade
> Broke shadow into all its parts,
> What then had been of shadow made
> Found exigence in fits and starts
>
> Where nothing properly had name
> Save that still element the air,
> Burnt sea of universal frame
> In which impounded now we were.

In "The Last Days of Alice":

> All space, that heaven is a dayless night,
> A nightless day driven by perfect lust
> For vacancy, in which her bored eyesight
> Stares at the drowsy cubes of human dust.

Thus are the abstractive and the concrete brought into formal collaboration, and in too thoroughgoing and consistent a pattern, too deeply cognitive to be summarized as "tactic." This is notably so in the sonnets, in "Death of Little Boys,"

"Idiot," "Subway," "Ancestors," and more familiarly in "Ode to the Confederate Dead." There in the graveyard behind the shut gate and the decomposing wall it is constituted as

> The gentle serpent, green in the mulberry bush,
> Riots with his tongue through the hush—
> Sentinel of the grave who counts us all

by no mere trick of style. But it is most comprehensively realized in the "Seasons of the Soul."[11]

T. E. Hulme once proposed that the masters of painting are born into the world at a time when the particular tradition from which they start is imperfect. Maritain and Tate himself agree that the luckiest moments for poetry are those when great civilization is on the verge of decline. "Then the vital force of this civilization meets with historical conditions which cease being appropriate to it, but it is still intact . . . in the sphere of spiritual creativity, and it gives its last fruit there, while the freedom of poetry avails itself of the decay of social disciplines and ethos."[12]

There is nothing like deprivation in the existential realm to propel us to celebrating its integrity in more durable forms. Such was Dante's occasion for the *Commedia* and such, with even more tangible precipitants in our late wars both hot and cold, is the occasion for "Seasons of the Soul." Here is the artist shoring up the ruins of culture until he may have nothing left to do it with other than irony, and silence (invoked finally in the fourth section of this poem).

Any one stanza of this metaphysically oriented work serves

11. This poem has lately received a lengthy and close reading, beyond the scope of this chapter to repeat. See Roger K. Meiners' essay, *Sewanee Review* 70 (Winter, 1962), pp. 34-74.
12. Jacques Maritain, *Creative Intuition in Art and Poetry* (London, 1953), p. 383.

notice on us—as would any of John Donne's—that the precarious freedom of the metaphysical, like that of a religious vow of chastity, is firmly rooted in traditional forms. Were the forms not present there would be no resistance to qualify the tensions that are the necessary matrix of this mode:

> Summer, this is our flesh,
> The body you let mature;
> If now while the body is fresh
> You take it, shall we give
> The heart, lest heart endure
> The mind's tattering
> Blow of greedy claws?
> Shall mind itself still live
> If like a hunting king
> It falls to the lion's jaws?

There are four seasonal sections, each presenting six intricately rhymed ten-line stanzas, with fugal variations of each tenth verse, with internal counterpointing recurrences of certain words, all in accentual trimeters; 149 out of 240 verses are run-on; only one of twenty-four stanzas is unclosed. Yet it would be impossible to claim that this poem postulates the primacy of style or celebrates technique in the substantive flux so evident in the mannerist practice of its contemporaries.

Jean Rousset says of the baroque spirit (which seems pervasive in contemporary poetry) that it is the enemy of all stable form, that it is "poussé par son démon à se dépasser toujours et à défaire sa forme au moment qu'il l'invente pour se porter vers une autre forme."[13] We delegate such terms to account for the kinds of poetic practices, but it is as schemata that they fall into disarray. The disturbance, the unrest that qualify what we

13. *La Littérature de l'Age Baroque, Circé et le Paon* (Paris, 1960), p. 231.

name baroque are not first structural, but signify the tension of irreconcilables with which as process the perceiving mind is in the act of coping. There are conventions which, while they do not do the whole work, sustain it in a vital way. There is the old-fashioned invocation used with incremental irony in "Winter": "You, Venus, come home/ To your salt maidenhead," and later: "Irritable Spring, infuse/ Into the burning breast/ Your combustible juice." Dantean allusion (as to the wood of suicides) is predicated in Dantean simile. The same obtains as well, both in over-all plan and specific techniques, in the recent poems in *terza rima*, "The Swimmers"[14] and "The Buried Lake." Yet to have made this point is not to say that these are poems "of surfaces." It is rather to have begun to see that these poems both reveal and are about the mind engaged in meeting the unalterable manic season of the present—and prevailing, upon the only grounds where it is possible now to prevail:

> Under the summer's blast
> The soul cannot endure
> Unless by sleight or fast
> It seize or deny its day
> To make the eye secure.
> Brothers in arms, remember
> The hot wind dries and draws
> With circular delay
> The flesh, ash from the ember,
> Into the summer's jaws.
>
> It was a gentle sun
> When, at the June solstice
> Green France was overrun
> With caterpillar feet.

14. E.g., "...I saw the Negro's body bend/ And straighten, as a fish-line cast transverse/ Yields to the current that it must subtend." *Hudson Review*, 5 (Winter, 1953), 471-73.

Allen Tate: The Heroism of the Rational

> No head knows where its rest is
> Or may lie down with reason
> When war's usurping claws
> Shall take the heart escheat—
> Green field in burning season
> To stain the weevil's jaws.

Malraux has said: "L'art est une façon de faire, et non une façon de voir ou de sentir."[15] And rightly so. Yet one cannot make what one has not in some manner seen; one cannot see what has not impinged upon the senses. What use are the weevil of summer or winter's rigid madrepore if they do not perform a service beyond the mere data of the event? Here we must admit, I think, that these along with other occasionally problematical figures are instruments of a drastic revelation. The poet is at least one step deeper in his predicament than the philosopher. If both are given to reductive analyses of the world around them, the poet must also make what he sees and impart to it in the process in transreality an order that in its own state it never possesses. If we were to lose our symbolic language, I think Tate has somewhere said, then we should no longer have the means of surviving the conditions of our own humanity. A philosopher has this to say about the working conjunction of seeing and making:

> The important philosophical task is to rescue metaphor from the manipulators of the psychological image and restore it to its relevant ontological status. In the context of metaphysical structures, metaphor can be seen not as the product of wayward associations but as the embodiment of the intentional acts of the mind which terminate not only in simple objects of perception but in complex relational structures possessing real being, or having a foundation in reality. The complexity of the

15. In *Psychologie de l'Art* (Genève, 1947), p. 156.

poet's vision, on the side of its object, involves, then, a whole philosophy of participation and analogy and cannot be regarded as if it were simple. . . .

The complexity of the poetic vision on the side of the subject is another theme. . . . It is like the philosophic vision in being, as the phenomenologists call it, an intentional act. The intentionality of human experience refers not to purposive intent but to the relational structure of all human awareness and especially to the "tending toward" or conscious and significant awareness which makes active and fully rational experience bi-polar in its very nature. It contrasts with the psycho-biological "state" which is the favorite preoccupation of the image cultists and the quivering foundation of the private-precious mythos, the only real threat to the artist there is. . . .[16]

To such a threat Tate has given no indications of capitulating. Nor has he ever compromised, in the search for the completeness of knowledge which is the poem, his views of what this office as maker demands of the poet. In the purity of his attention to the task at hand lies the heroism of the rational.

16. Robert Jordan, "Two Modes of Revelation," *Sewanee Review*, 67 (Winter, 1959), 22-23.

VI

YVOR WINTERS:
Poetics as Rectitude

Reason's Double Agents

> *Toute maîtrise jette le froid.*
> STÉPHANE MALLARMÉ

The times that deprive men of the occasions for belief are the times that impel men of letters to become moralists. Camus and presently Sartre assume this role no less than Kierkegaard, whose Either-Or became Brand's All or Nothing.[1] It was Ibsen's Both-And, for the latter's romantic anti-romanticism disclosed the egomania of "idealists" only to recommend a *hubris* that was Nietzschean in its implications. Here, between the intuitive leap and the discursive lag, is a summary of the ethical motivations and contradictions of recent literary history. It embraces Winters in a polar and implacably absolutist posture, embarrassing by reason of his theoretical reinforcement to those of his contemporaries bent upon escaping the doctrinaire associations of Arnold as well as Shelley.

My subject here is the poetry, with reference to the criticism only in so far as it explains poetic practice. A look at either may impress one as a frontal demonstration of technique as exordium, yet either reading must convince as well that Winters' conception of the morality of poetry accommodates without equivocation the first tenet of the opposing anti-moral view: "The artist is necessarily autonomous in his own sphere."[2] With the poems before us we cannot convict this poet of unaesthetic ethics; we may question instead his critics whose moral notions are unaesthetic. Winters has been objected to

---

  1. See Arnold Hauser, *The Social History of Art* (London, 1962), IV, 202-3.
  2. Quoted by William K. Wimsatt, Jr., *The Verbal Icon* (New York, 1958), p. 85.

Yvor Winters: Poetics as Rectitude

for excluding so much by those who neglect to note how much and of what he in fact includes. He does include, even of feeling, only that upon which the mind has a firm executive grasp. What is purposefully excluded is vagueness, the fugitive impressionism characteristic of adolescent art in all ages. Impressions are drawn firmly into the conceptual realm and are rendered constructive rather than peripherally evocative. He would leave nothing in a poem that does not clearly designate that which it calls upon. Thus the poet addresses "The Moralists" of whom he is himself one:

> You would extend the mind beyond the act,
> Furious, bending, suffering in thin
> And unpoetic dicta; you have been
> Forced by hypothesis to fiercer fact.
> As metal singing hard, with firmness racked,
> You formulate our passion; and behind
> In some harsh moment nowise of the mind
> Lie the old meanings your advance has packed.
>
> No man can hold existence in the head.
> I, too, have known the anguish of the right
> Amid this net of mathematic dearth,
> And the brain throbbing like a ship at night:
> Have faced with old unmitigated dread
> The hard familiar wrinkles of the earth.

Although the second part may strike us as hilariously flawed by the note of *angst* in verse 10 and the brain-as-ship image, which may call up visions of a looming Cunard liner (with stabilizers), the whole could well be taken as a definition of the poetic act. How clearly above all the act is here distinguished from its source. The problem at the center of poetry is qualitatively the same as that confronting us all in the choices that are the condition of our humanity: the procedure of rationalism. "The procedure of rationalism," says Alfred N. Whitehead, "is the discussion of analogy. The limitation of rationalism is the inescapable diversity."[3] Quite as a resolution of Ludwig Wittgenstein's notations on the propositional sign,[4] a poem of Winters' does yield what it asserts—exactly by implying what it is capable of asserting. The yield is in this sense moral. As it is expression, the act of poetry may be read as an analogue of all human election, the permanent recovery of the inwardness of experience effected in its outward rendering. This concentration upon what is expressible, upon the ethics of the expressible, results, in the poem, not in ideas but in knowledge, not in exposition but in fruition. Nor is it words that are defective symbols supporting this endeavor, but men's minds that prove, in accordance with the poet's observation, imperfect reservoirs. ("You would extend the mind beyond the act/ ... No man can hold existence in the head.")

What prudence is to behavior, style is to the making of art. When André Malraux undertakes to answer the question: what is style? he declares that "la peinture tend bien moins à voir le monde qu'à en créer un autre; le monde sert le style, qui sert l'homme et ses dieux."[5] And when he asks: what is art? the answer is "Ce par quoi les formes deviennent style." The truism and the mystery are that the visible world can be made to serve style in poetry only inasmuch as it is translated into a medium whose properties of precision and resonance—if not deeper and wider than—are different from the qualities of color, line, and depth that identify the other. The distinctness

3. *Modes of Thought* (Cambridge, 1938), p. 134.
4. *Notebooks: 1914-1916* (Oxford, 1951), p. 40.
5. *Voix du Silence* (Paris, 1951), p. 270.

Yvor Winters: Poetics as Rectitude

of each stands as an independent value that simple imitation on either side disserves. Winters' briefest early lyrics, several of them a single verse in length, are not imagist efforts. (For example, "A Song of Advent": "On the desert, between pale mountains, our cries:/ Far whispers creeping through an ancient shell.") Rather, they resemble quite abstractly essays toward a poetic to be achieved.

To recur to style is to be reminded of the irreducible dissension governing art in its causes, the difficult conciliation of psychological and formal values. Something about this antagonism holds poems, buildings, and whole states together. In this sense the most perfectly articulated works traced to their cognizable sources originate in discord, have as their point of departure dissolution. Precisely by incorporating the details of unequivalence to be overcome, the Parthenon achieves a perfected appearance of balance and symmetry. The fundamental discord, always present, is accommodated or suppressed by style. It may be all that is discernible, or scarcely discernible, or, as in the Chekhovian anacrusis, subtly emphasized by strategies of avoidance. Winters in his preference for the difficult imparts no doubts. His scruples are defined. He entertains no apprehensions on the side of execution, only a few well-placed ones regarding the audience about which he is stoic in his expectations. Here we might say is the tragedy of perfect vision, of one who sees too clearly what he is looking at, not least when he is staring the reader in the eye.

A consequence of the notion of the lyric as an achievable executive act rather than a simply vocative one is naturally the stressing of craft. (If a poem yields what it asserts, it can only do so by being *made* capable of the assertion. The burden is such that prose cannot well be caused to bear, though poets who write theses habitually attempt it.) But the assumption that such emphasis on making is merely another rehearsal of the bourgeois ideal, another illustration of middle-class morbidity in relation to work, is not documented by these poems. Even when he writes, as in "On Teaching the Young":

> A poem is what stands
> When imperceptive hands,
> Feeling, have gone astray.
> It is what one should say.
>
> Few minds will come to this.
> The poet's only bliss
> Is in cold certitude—
> Laurel, archaic, rude,

it cannot be put down as the Puritan rectitude of the quietist whose "I believe" is the justification of "I am." On the contrary, the movement toward form, borne out in the poems as a whole, is the classic solicitation of permanence, the search for *substantial* form, an undertaking as far removed from a precious indulgence in technique as it is from the predatory emotionality of the romantic.

Although the question of feeling may seem to offer the least promising point of entry into these poems, I should like to pursue it. It was romanticism, after all, that separated feeling from thought and classicism that presumes to set the two in relation. ("Donc soyez d'abord perméable," says Max Jacob, "c'est-à-dire sérieux."[6]) Among the poems that re-argue this relation by example, the following does so with undoubted distinction.

6. *Conseils à un Jeune Poète* (Paris, 1945), p. 16.

TO THE HOLY SPIRIT

from a deserted graveyard
in the Salinas Valley

Immeasurable haze:
The desert valley spreads
Up golden river beds
As if in other days.
Trees rise and thin away,
And past the trees, the hills,
Pure line and shade of dust,
Bear witness to our wills:
We see them, for we must;
Calm in deceit, they stay.

High noon returns the mind
Upon its local fact:
Dry grass and sand; we find
No vision to distract.
Low in the summer heat,
Naming old graves, are stones
Pushed here and there, the seat
Of nothing, and the bones
Beneath are similar:
Relics of lonely men,
Brutal and aimless, then,
As now, irregular.

These are thy fallen sons,
Thou whom I try to reach.
Thou whom the quick eye shuns,
Thou dost elude my speech.
Yet when I go from sense
And trace thee down in thought,
I meet thee, then, intense,
And know thee as I ought.

> But thou art mind alone,
> And I, alas, am bound
> Pure mind to flesh and bone,
> And flesh and bone to ground.
>
> These had no thought: at most
> Dark faith and blinding earth.
> Where is the trammeled ghost?
> Was there another birth?
> Only one certainty
> Beside thine unfleshed eye,
> Beside the spectral tree,
> Can I discern: these die.
> All of this stir of age,
> Though it elude my sense
> Into what heritage
> I know not, seems to fall,
> Quiet beyond recall,
> Into irrelevance.

Winters has in common with Donne his intellectuality. Like Donne he employs his intellectuality in the verification of feeling, but by quite different tactical means. Where there is tension in Donne, there is a passivity in Winters—not an inert passiveness by default, but an achieved passivity, the result of characteristic work. So we attribute to Donne a histrionic sensibility and to Winters an introspective one.[7] When it comes to comparing methods, we cannot fail to notice how consistently Winters bases his command of feeling—as in the first two stanzas quoted above—upon a precise reconstitution of visual detail. Donne's reconnaissance of his world,[8] on the other hand,

---

7. Francis Fergusson's terms, *The Idea of a Theater* (Princeton, 1949), pp. 10-11.
8. Robert Ellrodt, *Les Poètes Métaphysiques Anglais* (Paris, 1960), I, 247.

quite obviously interests him not in so far as it is perceived but according to how it is conceived. Either way, intelligence is the qualification for feeling, just as it is in the Jamesian appraisal.

"The new world," wrote Herman Melville, "is the world of the mind."[9] The new aesthetics, it might be observed, is the aesthetics of consciousness. But if existence becomes merely the content of consciousness, then must art become merely inventory? The simple technique noted here (rather like the Ignatian "composition of place") could by itself recede to those limits. Yet its presentation in the trimeters of this poem argues a greater degree of selection and a subtler order. If, however, no poem of Winters was ever fished at random from the subconscious, neither is it likely that—having eliminated that sort of richness along with that redundance—any poem of his should surrender in its purposeful simplicity to a record of an event. His poetics evidently intends the ultimate reduction of highly conscious experience to its most inclusive terms. As such it must issue in new events. He is proof against the difficulties inherent in his purposes, like James on the side of intelligence, because he makes the voice of the poem always that of the *raisonneur* rather than that of unleashed consciousness.

So it follows that emotion, instead of being declared, is accounted for in its causes. The complex emotions of the rationalist addressing the Holy Spirit upon existential, not pious, grounds are evoked precisely by understanding, for it is reason that assesses irrelevance and reason that judges what meanings remain whose predecessors in the elision of sense are "quiet beyond recall." Here is a calculable refutation of the poetics of "qualitative progression"[10] which emanate from

9. *Mardi,* Chapter 169.
10. Yvor Winters, *In Defense of Reason* (Denver, 1947), pp. 57-64.

diffuse revery and the presuppositions of the unconscious, the *huis clos* of subjectivism that nullifies and frustrates at its source the realization of valid emotion. For the validation of emotion depends on the distinction between consciousness and an otherness. ("Calm in deceit, they stay,/ .... Can I discern: these die".) The response must arise to a recognized, not necessarily conceptually differentiated, cause. Otherwise it is the expression of a general malaise: *acedia*, the sickness of self. *Sunt lacrimae rerum* is a declarative statement, not in addition to, but in the same moment that it is poetry. What the classic writer could take for granted, Winters in our time must maintain with what appears to some a strident conviction. Indeed, a certain moral vitality comes from knowing what things are worth the expenditure of emotion. At least it is not casually that he criticizes that "search for intense feeling" which fails to be a search "for a just feeling, of feeling properly motivated."[11] If the commonplace is correct that thought exists only as it is formulated in language, then the truth of feeling has an equally logical claim to location if it is to "make sense" in any durable reality.

It is his skill in placing feeling and the conviction from which this work proceeds, far more than his almost archaic strictness of form, that I think allies Winters most fundamentally to classicism. The thou's in deference to a discredited Spirit are not the asset to the articulation of the poem which its prosody is. A rather common unconscious bias of readers somehow associates technique raised to a power beyond the desultory with intemperance. In fact such an extreme is imaginable, but not in Winters whose seriousness in forging a

11. *Ibid.*, p. 439.

Yvor Winters: Poetics as Rectitude

style is directed entirely to saying "the difficult and true"[12] and precludes undertaking any display of metrical virtuosity *per se*. He himself comments that "rhythm, for reasons which I do not wholly understand, has the power of communicating emotion; and as a part of the poem it has the power of qualifying the total emotion."[13] Memory, I believe, considered as a gift of language,[14] in its deeper rhythms functions as the source of form in the shaping of these poems. Not memory vulgarized and distorted by sentiment, but that memory which Pascal said is necessary for all the operations of reason.

At this point our critical apparatus falters and gives way, for such memory is not open to discursive exposition. Yet one of Winters' loveliest poems, "The Castle of Thorns," in treating the ancient staples of folklore and romance—the Robber Knight whose castle in the wood of thorns is reached only by crossing water, "symbol of the barrier between the two worlds"[15]—is about death, but could be a metaphor of the artist's performance, the poet's crossing over:

> Through autumn evening, water whirls thin blue,
> From iron to iron pail—old, lined, and pure;
> Beneath, the iron is indistinct, secure
> In revery that cannot reach to you.
> Water it was that always lay between
> The mind of man and that harsh wall of thorn,
> Of stone impenetrable, where the horn
> Hung like the key to what it all might mean.
> . . . .
> Peace to the heart that can accept this cold!

12. From Winters' poem, "To a Military Rifle."
13. *In Defense of Reason*, p. 12.
14. Whitehead, *Modes of Thought*, p. 46: ". . . an articulated memory is the gift of language, considered as an expression from oneself in the past to oneself in the present."
15. From Winters' own notes to the poems.

The theme is one that deeply absorbs Winters and reveals itself under various aspects in a number of poems, among them "To Emily Dickinson," "The Fable," "Midas," "Apollo and Daphne," and, at some length, "Heracles" which treats specifically the artist's "semi-intuitive combat with experience."[16] How equivocal the experience of intuition can be, one may infer from "Apollo and Daphne":

> Deep in the leafy fierceness of the wood,
> Sunlight, the cellular and creeping pyre,
> Increased more slowly than aethereal fire:
> But it increased and touched her where she stood.
> The god had seized her, but the powers of good
> Struck deep into her veins; with rending flesh
> She fled all ways into the grasses' mesh
> And burned more quickly than the sunlight could.
>
> And all her heart broke stiff in leafy flame
> That neither rose nor fell, but stood aghast;
> And she, rooted in Time's slow agony,
> Stirred dully, hard-edged laurel, in the past;
> And, like a cloud of silence or a name
> The god withdrew into eternity.

And from "Heracles":

> Older than man, evil with age, is life:
> Injustice, direst perfidy, my bane
> Drove me to win my lover and my wife;
> By love and justice I at last was slain.
>
> The numbered Beings of the wheeling track
> I carried singly to the empty throne,
> And yet, when I had come exhausted back,
> Was forced to wait without the gate alone.
> . . . .

16. *Ibid.*

Yvor Winters: Poetics as Rectitude

> Perfect, and moving perfectly, I raid
> Eternal silence to eternal ends:
> And Deianira, an imperfect shade,
> Retreats in silence as my arc descends.

Few artists have the courage to endure the solitude, unique to their trade, of "the mind, lost in the word's lost certitude," subserving "a slow obscure metonymy of motion,/ Crumbling the inner barriers of the brain." It is not madness to which these poems testify, but the consultation of reality. Jacques Maritain once regretted that "men gifted with the sense of poetry load poetry with burdens against which its nature rebels, *onera importabilia*," but (on the same page) calls poetry "the heaven of the working reason."[17] Not the heaven perhaps so much as, in this instance, the purgatory.

17. *Art and Scholasticism* (London, 1954), p. 80.

JOHN BERRYMAN
AND
MISTRESS BRADSTREET:

A Relation of Reason

Reason's Double Agents

The muse is not, strictly, a poet and Mistress Bradstreet, the "Tenth Muse Lately Sprung up in America," in all strictness perhaps never was one except through the accommodation of the metonymy. Some three hundred years after her death she has become literally the muse of a poem among the few distinguished efforts of substantial length in its period, a poem whose very flaws compel interest because they are intelligent. It may be the endearing incompetence of her verse that qualifies her for this role, for her failures are the typical results of an all too adequate feminine sensibility. It is this in her person, the stamina in frailty ("Pioneering is not feeling well"), which the poet celebrates, partially by dialogue, and this which contributes to the occasionally insurmountable problems of his composition.

Hart Crane, with whose *Bridge* we first think to compare the *Homage,* to the extent that he had a theme, possessed an abstraction. His sense of myth is less remote than his sense of person, but what emerges from this collocation of fragments—portions of them very badly written indeed—is neither "America" nor "history" but a horrifying transcript of the poet's own disintegration. At the time of that writing he was simply unequal as composer to the endurance of his own insights. Yvor Winters has discussed the self-defeating quality of Crane's version of transcendentalism. He is like the surrealists, only more convincingly tragic, of whom Jacques Maritain has remarked that where they succeed in writing genuine poetry "they fall short of their own dogma, and obey despite themselves the secret music of intelligence."[1]

Tautness, density, linear tension are qualities of Crane and Berryman alike, but the incoherence to which Crane's intuitive

1. *Creative Intuition in Art and Poetry* (London, 1953), p. 81.

John Berryman and Mistress Bradstreet: A Relation of Reason

procedure disposed him does not endanger the *Homage* at any point. Berryman's control even at the grammatical level is such that a subject introduced at the close of the fifth stanza is united to its predicate after eight intervening elliptical lines with no diminution of lucidity. The stanza that bears the remarkably various strain of narrative and lyric has eight lines in accentual stresses owing much to the sprung and counterpointed rhythms of Hopkins, but avoiding outriding or slack feet. It runs: 5, 5, 3, 4, 5, 5, 3, 6. Most of the stanzas (all but eleven out of fifty-seven) are closed. Clearly linear values are subordinated to the multiple unit of the stanza. This is apparent not only from the number of lines that are run-on or, as Gerard Manley Hopkins would put it, "rove over," from the practice of capitalizing only for grammatical beginnings, but especially from the cumulative movement set up by this kind of scansion. It is natural, as Hopkins said, for lines to be run over in sprung rhythm, "for the scanning of each line immediately to take up that of the one before, so that if the first has one or more syllables at its end the other must have so many the less at its beginning; and in fact the scanning runs on without a break from the beginning, say, of a stanza to the end and all the stanza is one long strain, though written in lines asunder."[2]

The opening passage in the poet's own voice, later to meld into that of the woman, is an extraordinary and moving performance whose technical precision is entirely in the service of the motion of meaning:

1

The governor your husband lived so long
moved you not, restless, waiting for him? Still,

2. Author's Preface, *Poems* (3rd. ed.: Oxford, 1948), p. 8.

Reason's Double Agents

> you were a patient woman—
> I seem to see you pause here still:
> Sylvester, Quarles, in moments odd you pored
> before a fire at, bright eyes on the Lord,
> all the children still.
> 'Simon . . ' Simon will listen while you read a Song.
>
> 2
>
> Outside the New World winters in grand dark
> white air lashing high thro' the virgin stands
> foxes down foxholes sigh,
> surely the English heart quails, stunned.
> I doubt if Simon than this blast, that sea,
> spares from his rigour for your poetry
> more. We are on each other's hands
> who care. Both of our worlds unhanded us. Lie stark,
>
> 3
>
> thy eyes look to me mild. Out of maize & air
> your body's made, and moves. I summon, see,
> from the centuries it.
> I think you won't stay. How do we
> linger, diminished, in our lovers' air,
> implausibly visible, to whom, a year,
> years, over interims; or not;
> to a long stranger; or not; shimmer and disappear.

For fifteen more stanzas this motion continues unflawed, the poet's exordium dissolving (4.8) into the woman's narrative and becoming (from 12.5) throughout the second section (to 39.4) a colloquy in which the poet's voice when it recurs seems to do so as a product of the woman's alienated imagination. The first complicating mistakes are in the preternaturally speedy and literal parturition recounted in the space of three stanzas (19-21).

John Berryman and Mistress Bradstreet: A Relation of Reason

The truth is, as may be observed in the passage quoted, that all the desirable effects of sprung rhythm are here obtained with scarcely any recourse to the technical liberties that it permits. The two primary licenses allowed in sprung rhythm, the musical rest and outriding feet, do not so far occur. The musical rest is introduced in the seventh stanza and is used sparingly thereafter, and judiciously, in the difficult hexameter lines such as:

> dyings—at which my heart   rose, but I did submit
> (7.8)
> and that he is able to
> keep   that I have committed to his charge.
> (8.8)
> Stricken: 'Oh. Then he takes   us one by one.' My dear
> (23.8)
> You must not love me, but   I do not bid you cease.
> (26.8)
> Hover, utter, still
> a sourcing   whom my lost candle like the firefly loves.
> (57.8)

Although counterpointed or reversed feet are used, these tend to fall within the permissible limits of syllabic meters. Indeed, along with all the syntactical indications of sprung rhythm, there are in each of the first two stanzas seventy-two syllables in the usual proportions and, in the third, seventy-six with no noticeable violations of the syllabic norm. The effect might be described as that of trochaic-anapestic measures laced with iambic rather than the expectable opposite. This is due certainly in great part to the open-endedness of the lines suggesting a cumulative scansion. The strategy was by no means invented for this occasion (only expanded), but it cannot be mere happenstance that Milton in *Samson Agonistes* and Sir

Walter Ralegh (if he is the author) in "As you came from the holy land" employed it similarly for choric and dialogue purposes. So subtle are the tactical possibilities in the altering *duration* within given measures that Ralegh can achieve through it a fluid and elliptical music:

> As you came from the holy land
>   Of Walsinghame
> Mett you not with my true loue
>   By the way as you came?
> . . . .
> Such an one did I meet, good Sir,
>   Suche an Angelyke face,
> Who lyke a queen, lyke a nymphe, did appere
>   By her gate, by her grace.
> . . . .
> Butt true Loue is a durable fyre
>   In the mynde euer burnynge;
> Neuer sycke, neuer ould, neuer dead,
>   From itt selfe neuer turnynge.[3]

And Berryman the disjunctive directness of immediate thought and free speech:

Chapped souls ours, by the day Spring's strong winds swelled,
Jack's pulpits arched, more glad. The shawl I pinned
flaps like a shooting soul
might in such weather Heaven send.
Succumbing half, in spirit, to a salmon sash
I prod the nerveless novel succotash—
I must be disciplined,
in arms, against that one, and our dissidents, and myself.

(11)

   3. *Poems*, ed. Agnes Latham, Muses' Library (London, 1951), pp. 22-23.

John Berryman and Mistress Bradstreet: A Relation of Reason

> . . . I remember who
> in meeting smiled & was punisht, and I know who
> whispered & was stockt.
> We lead a thoughtful life. But Boston's cage we shun.
> (16.5-8)

Artlessness as an achieved end is almost invariably the result of single-minded and even passionate absorption with the problem of style. Berryman is like no one so much as Hemingway in this respect, for Hemingway forged a stylistic instrument of uncommon incisiveness to convey the impression of conversation and to bear transumptively in the same compass the burdens of exposition and epiphany. There was never any such talk as his characters' until he invented it. And there can have been no substitute for intelligence in the elections this incurred.

By dramatistic means Berryman has devised an idiom that "acts the effect." What would doubtless fault a stage performance as involving, for that medium, omission, becomes in the literary perspective a most viable commission. Almost telescopic contractions, inversions, verbal strategies derived, only infrequently by misappropriation, from Hopkins accomplish the effects of verisimilitude and abolish the tedium of its fact.

One aim is, properly, to imply rather than to reinstate the heroine's archaic speech pattern. Few tasks of such apparent simplicity could exact greater trials of an artist's skill, for the echoes of her speech must, while abstaining from caricature, establish Anne Bradstreet as a person and support through her credibility the gravity of the theme. In a manner similar to but rather more intensive than Ford's *Good Soldier* (and of course substituting for the latter's ironic mode the elegiac) the whole narrative responsibility rests with a speaker who, in seeing and telling all, perceives less than the reader must through her agency comprehend. She must represent a good deal more than she relates and she must elicit a sympathy larger than the sum of her virtues, her writings, or her sufferances required. She must, in short, assume the dimensions of a person in order to become an acceptable archetype. And for this it is positively preferable that she should have been, like her unfortunate models Du Bartas and Quarles, an undistinguished versifier. (In fact she is far more in the American vein by being first with the most: the first woman to write English verse in America, seven thousand lines of it.) The stature that her own art cannot confer accrues in another century through her subjection to superior praise.

Then her story, by being personal, is figurable. The difficult crossing on the *Arbella*, landfall, Henry Winthrop's drowning, all the initial hardships (". . . and I am Ruth/ away: open my mouth, my eyes wet: I would smile:/ vellum I palm, & dream. Their forest dies/ to greensward, privets, elms & towers, whence/ a nightingale is throbbing./ Women sleep sound. I was happy once. . . ."), girlhood and marriage in retrospect the catalogue of disease, theocratic intolerance, childbirth, deaths. And interspersing this the puzzling communion of the woman and the poet who receives his voice from her. Wholly vocal, the passional timbre of this exchange strikes one as misjudged. An intellectual fabrication, this, not unlike in character the relations in Sartre's *Altona*; the embrace into which those fall who have too little to say to each other instead of too much. The condition is distinctly contemporary. If it flaws the poem here, it does so having gained entrance through the poet's telltale inadvertence in a passage oddly inflationary

John Berryman and Mistress Bradstreet: A Relation of Reason

compared with the controlled sthenic energy of the remainder. There is delirium in such lines as:

> I *want* to take you for my lover.—Do.
> —I hear a madness. Harmless I to you
> am not, not I? —No.
> —I cannot but be. Sing a concord of our thought,
> (32.5-8)

and we feel it to be arbitrary. In place of the plausible concord of their thought, each in an anguished duet reflects the spiritual desolation of the other. (". . . My breath is scented, and I throw/ hostile glances towards God./ Crumpling plunge of a pestle, bray:/ sin cross & opposite, wherein I survive/ nightmares of Eden. . . .") The mental state is as accurately described as are the diseases that come into the narrative ("Father is not himself. He keeps his bed/ and threw a saffron scum . . ."), but symptoms of hysteria trespass upon the needful sovereignty of the crafting of the verse.

The temptation is to assign the poetic difficulty in such a case to a defect intrinsic to the stanza form, yet such an attribution I am convinced is as spurious as it is tidy. How should we expect from any structural component the tyranny or the overriding grace of an absolute? A poem is an informed form; and that form itself remains an abstraction until the poet, freely delegating his resources, informs that hypothetical existence by giving it a body. Is Berryman's stanza suited only to grand effects? Local evidence throughout these fifty-seven strophes amply affirms the opposite, and with the irrefutable assurance of singular art. Tone, like meter, coexists in words with meaning.

Berryman himself in a later poem of equal technical subtlety resolves this problem for me. "A Winter-piece to a

Reason's Double Agents

Friend Away," as if written from "The massive sorrow of the mental hospital," where "Friends & our good friends hide./ They came to call," lends to a similarly confessional monologue the unspoken. Aesthetic distance is here a medium for a most potent truth of feeling.

> Your letter came. —Glutted the earth & cold
> With rains long heavy, follows intense frost;
>   Snow howls and hides the world
> We workt awhile to build; all the roads are lost;
> Icy spiculae float, filling strange air;
> No voice goes far; one is alone whirling since where,
>   And when was it one crossed?
>   You have been there.
>   . . . .
> Hardly theirs, moment when the tempest gains,
> Loose heart convulses. Their hearts bend off dry,
>   Their fruit dangles and fades.
> —Solicitudes of the orchard heart, comply
>   A little with my longing, a little sing
> Our sorrow among steel and glass, our stiffening,
>   That hers may modify:
>   O trembling Spring.—
>
> Immortal risks our sort run, to a house
> Reported in a wood .. mould upon bread
>   And brain, breath giving out,
> From farms we go by, barking, and shaken head,
> The shrunk pears hang, Hölderlin's weathercock
> Rattles to a tireless wind, the fireless landscape rock,
>   Artists insane and dead
>   Strike like a clock:
>
> *If the fruit is dead, fast. Wait. Chafe your left wrist.*
> *All these too lie, whither a true form strays.*
>   *Sweet when the lost arrive.*
> Foul sleet ices the twigs, the vision frays,

John Berryman and Mistress Bradstreet: A Relation of Reason

Festoons all signs; still as I come to name
My joy to you my joy springs up again the same,—
  The thaw alone delays,—
  Your letter came!

Without the structurally vitiating and disgressive qualities, or the redundance to which the stream of consciousness device is liable, are reconstituted here the nuances of a vulnerable mind in a state of active reflection. Not simply the gist, the strain, the tone, but far more exactly the turns and hiatuses: the junctures whose economy is postlogical yet not irrational. Interior reminiscence and external perception connect prosodically as if in the irregular pulsations of the mind's motion. The achieved detachment, while consistent with certain disturbed mental states as with normal meditation, is quite indispensable to the poetic function. (So it is in the *Homage* where it gives unerring clarity, for example, to the funeral passage: "We commit our sister down./ One candle mourn by, which a lover gave,/ The use's edge and order of her grave.") Perhaps there is no lyric potency so expedient as that in the declarative statement. Conceptually disjunctive but metrically linked, their very constellation creates relations unattainable by discursive succession. Disjunction then in other words can become a lyric bond. Berryman has, I think, forged a stylistic solution viable enough for application to the larger task of handling the fusion of narrative and lyric modes undertaken in the *Homage*.

A crisis of sensibility and its resolution in the "Winter-piece," reprieved from its topical limits, is nonetheless moving by reason of an austere use of those imaginal threads alone which conduce inferentially to the universal: a view, through the transient lucidity of the mental patient, of the stark and isolating hospital of this world. Within formal bounds whose very strictness is turned into a precision instrument, altering measures, syntactical inversions are made to count for the occluded and segmented rhythms of the perceiving mind. The winter weather of the outer world, not unlike the storm in *Lear,* has a definition emphasizing the precarious isolation of the inclemency within. Whatever the discernible strategic indebtedness, the results surely are closer to Shakespeare than to Hopkins, for conceptual breadth does here exceed and sustain technical intensity.

The counting of the mad should begin in those environs where our current mania for rationality devises the means of holocaust and delegates their use. The Apollonianism of destruction, though it contributes to our mutual atmosphere, stands no closer than ironic apposition to the indissoluble connectedness of the true lyric. So richly conceived and strongly wrought are Berryman's that their miscalculations themselves bridge the gulf between unmodified reality and its relations in reason.

REASON AND METER:
A Reciprocity Re-Divined

Reason's Double Agents

"Music itself," says St. Augustine, "is *scientia*, a kind of knowledge" (*De Musica* I, iv, 9). Its abstractness makes it the most purely intellectual of the arts although, curiously enough, its effects may be the most directly sensuous. Therefore the philosopher who establishes "that the utmost abstractions are the true weapons with which to control our thought of concrete fact"[1] must be adverting to a reciprocal relation. Yet even those whose pleasure in music is intellectual, on the subject of music in poetry, incline to the unconsidered romantic assumption of its primitiveness. There are perhaps more ways of considering music than of making it. Ontologically it returns us to the notion of a mathematics and to the irreducible evidence of our and the world's finitude. Pythagoras, who saw in numbers the element of all things, to whom numbers were no mere attributes, believed them the stuff out of which all objects we see or handle are made—the rational reality.[2] The conceptions of the ancients in which we find the liveliest poetry (or indeed mistranslation) science tends uncannily to confirm.

"Everything is number. Number is in everything."[3]

As the idea of number penetrates and lends a character to virtually every corner of terrestrial experience: space, time, order, continuity, succession, change, unity, dispersion, motion, dimension, passage, duration, measure, content, it is no wonder that poetry, combining these attributes—some separately, some differently verifiable in painting and music—should do so most consciously and with an urge to perfection. But it is always a wonder how poetry accomplishes this ordination and what it

1. Alfred N. Whitehead, *Science and the Modern World* (Cambridge, 1933), p. 41.
2. H. W. Turnbull, *The Great Mathematicians* (London, 1929), p. 9.
3. Charles Baudelaire, "Fusées," *Journaux Intimes* (Paris, 1949), p. 7. My translation.

Reason and Meter: A Reciprocity Re-Divined

causes us to comprehend, which other media, or language outside of poetry, cannot occasion. According to Henri Bergson, "on définit ... le nombre une collection d'unités ou, pour parler avec plus de précision, la synthèse de l'un et du multiple. Tout nombre est un, en effet, puisqu'on se le représente par une intuition simple de l'esprit et qu'on lui donne un nom; mais cette unité est celle d'une somme; elle embrasse une multiplicité de parties qu'on peut considérer isolément."[4] There can be no question that numericalness is a basal constituent of language or that poetry makes demands on this quality, not alone in play.

Meter, strangely, is a topic about which people are apt to feel violently. Our attitude toward it is highly indicative of our whole approach to poetry: how we read the poem, what we expect it to do or not to do, and in what manner. Likewise the poet in his composing. The fact that the notion of meter can provoke extreme partisan antagonisms itself suggests its pervasive influence as an element in the poem; the prevailing fact of a metrical presence in all poems, either formally syllabic, accentual, or in cadence proves how deeply implicated it is in the poetic act. One simply cannot have poetry without meter or some compensatory adjustment, also numerical, mitigating its severest mode. ("Compensations" for the absence of rhyme, on the other hand, can be of another and subtler order altogether than rhyme, as in the internal vowelling of the Anglo-Saxon hemistichs. Greek poetry of course avoided rhyme entirely in its preference for less crude effects.)

When we are thinking about meter in itself, as opposed to thinking about it as it exists in given poems, it is clearly an abstraction: a wholly intellectual pattern whose intervals have

4. *Oeuvres* (Paris, 1959), pp. 51-52.

only an adaptive correlation with what occurs in language as such. This impression persists in respect to the quantitative meters of Latin, for here we observe a mathematical precision that is quite irrelevant to the natural inflections of the spoken words. But in a language governed as is English by vivid natural stresses, then it seems legitimate and somehow inevitable to come to perceive meter, like metaphor, as one of the resources of language itself. So interwoven are the resonances of meaning with accentual stress that we may decide the meter is *in the words,* even as meaning is, rather than something put upon them by artifice. Poetic practice in any case offers presumptive evidence supporting a double theory of meters, a synthetic and an analytic. And one of the most convincing if backhanded demonstrations of the latter's probability surely lies in the wasted efforts of those who from time to time have recommended or experimented with a "return to the source" by adopting Greek or Latin quantitative meters in English. From Harvey and Spenser to Coleridge and Robert Bridges' contemporary, William Johnson Stone, the advocates of classical scansion more often substantiate their proposals with stray verses than with whole poems. Stone in the course of his scheme for determining the quantity of English syllables[5] quotes Gray's

The breezy call of incense-breathing morn—

concerning which his avowed interest is concentrated upon the pleasure to be extracted from -"censbr"-. For those who manage, like Arthur Clough, entire poems in these measures, the results (even allowing for considerable alterations of taste in the intervening generations) are rather tepid and suggest

5. *Classical Metres in English Verse* (Oxford, 1901), p. 150.

nothing so much as that the poet has succeeded metrically only at the expense of those very qualities of language which the good poet normally seeks to control by inclusion since their vitality is unique and irreplaceable.

The most recent historian of English meter proposes quite justly that metrical patterns are constructed in imitation of the essential structure of our language and that meter's "essential function can only be to make the language also imitative—imitative of its own structure."[6] Meter "does for language what the forms of any art do for their materials. It abstracts certain elements from the experience of the senses and forms them into patterns . . . similar to those the senses experience all the time, but art characteristically makes the patterns simpler and clearer and the artist regards them as having a kind of independent existence." And he concludes, "If there is one meaning which the metrical pattern enforces on all language submitted to its influence, it is this: *Whatever else I may be talking about, I am talking also about language itself.*"[7]

"All art is a game with and a fight against chaos; it is always advancing more and more dangerously towards chaos and rescuing more and more extensive provinces of the spirit from its clutch."[8] Time, number, and space are for the arts means of securing the order which is part of its primary intention. The undulance of time is at least as intrinsic a property of poetry as space is of painting, but while it may on occasion be employed synthetically one is aware, I think invariably, in such instances that it becomes so only as a modification of a time that was already there. Indeed, the effects of synthetic

6. John Thompson, *The Founding of English Metre* (London, 1961), p. 10.
7. *Ibid.*, pp. 12-13.
8. Arnold Hauser, *The Social History of Art* (London, 1962), IV, 233.

meters derive explicitly from their being maintained in conscious apposition to a prior time, the fixed being set off against the variable. In any case, time in poetry, unlike space in painting or architecture, is not readily conceivable as an emptiness to be filled. It may take the place of spatial reference, but it tends to do more, and always from an operative position of privileged innerness, literally in and of the medium, participating in its material condition. Baudelaire says, "La musique donne l'idée de l'espace . . . le nombre est une traduction de l'espace."[9] And Ezra Pound, that "Rhythm is form cut into time, as a design is determined space"; adding sensibly that "Prosody and melody are attained by the listening ear and not by an index of nomenclatures."[10] St. Thomas in the prologue to his commentary on the Psalms states quite factually the simple truth, especially relevant to plain chant (and perhaps too frequently borrowed from this context), that "Song begins where speech breaks off, *exultatio mentis prorumpens in vocem.*"[11] But all poetry, particularly that which we take most seriously, is not song. It may have another kind of music, perhaps less easily assimilable, which we might call analytic and which we recognize as differently articulated, even more self-contained. Whereas in the cinema space and time become interchangeable, in the lyric poem (notably in the lyric poem of metaphysical intent) the nature of whose very strategies entails condensation and ellipsis, we could describe our findings about time as a sort of homeostasis of language outside the applicable relations of the Bergsonian flow or the Heraklitean flux. A poem always *is* what it is about, and its integrity

9. "Mon cour mis à nu," *Journaux Intimes,* p. 95.
10. *ABC of Reading* (London, 1961).
11. Quoted by Jacques Maritain, *Art and Scholasticism* (London, 1954), p. 47.

Reason and Meter: A Reciprocity Re-Divined

is oriented to intelligence in a ratio corresponding more to the manner of Bach than of *lieder*.

Before "La Jeune Parque," Paul Valéry wrote: "Un poème est une durée, pendant laquelle, lecteur, je respire une loi qui fut préparée."[12] And he recounts elsewhere[13] how the "Cimetière Marin" first came to him as a "figure rythmique vide" which he began to apprehend as decasyllabic in strophes of six verses. The "demon of generalization," he says, suggested that he try to carry this ten to the power of twelve. He foresaw the necessity of a line dense and "fortement rythmé" to shape an unfolding monologue whose speaker, a certain "moi," is envisaged as an "amateur d'abstractions." All this before the words came. But such an inception, with varying states of self-awareness, undoubtedly typifies the experience of many poets. It suggests a cognitive connection between meter or cadence and the language it elicits, between incipient form and concomitant articulation. The notion is one that asks for an epistemology that by reason of its grounds can only remain speculative and provisional in its conclusions, however compelling. Such are the limits of psychology and self-consciousness. (Yet meditation on relativity in this context can bring us in a circuit to questions equally suggestive: could there be any functional relativity without an absolute anchoring this plurality within its limited ambience? What is the plurality, the melodic sequence of words if not a gesture toward an absolute of expression that we assume is possible until it is fulfilled? Words call upon each other and it is out of the rapport of their intrinsic patterns that meanings arise.)

I think one could reasonably propose, on the evidence of a

12. *Oeuvres* (Paris, 1957), p. 95.
13. *Ibid.*, pp. 1496-1507.

few great poems in any language, that all meter is potentially analytic, even that whose quantitative rationale classifies it as superficially synthetic. Contemporary studies such as W. F. Jackson Knight's on *Accentual Symmetry in Vergil*[14] do fortify this contention with ample illustrations. The more we discern of the empirical processes of poem-making, the more credible it becomes to assume that meter in some fashion gives the conscious mind access to the unconscious.[15] And we must remember (if the imperfectly realized poem does not give us cause to) that the unconscious is not un-reason but merely that part of reason not immediately available to our surface attention. Indeed, meter is probably that part of poetry which causes poets to write "better than they know." Nevertheless, meter can mark, as we have been readier exclusively to believe, a relinquishing of mental activity in so far as knowing is in searching. Wherever popular taste encourages a somatic surrender to comfortable emotions, it provides and is provided for by a similar motive in romantic practice. The narcotic meters of Swinburne and of Shelley's "West Wind" argue—not that all meter is primitive—but only that these poets in this case have deliberately restricted it to this function. Some minds and interests, like some artistic possibilities and intentions, are shallower than others. But the arts have never been governed substantively in this respect by the lowest common denominators.

We must look into our own minds and into the great poems in the major modes and then into those most nearly perfect poems of our own times and within our frame of reference. Doing so, we come, I believe, as close to certitude as rational

14. (Oxford, 1939).
15. Cf. W. F. Jackson Knight, *Roman Vergil* (London, 1944), p. 281.

speculation can concerning the cognitive role of meter. No less wise a man than St. Augustine precedes us in this endeavor and he was able to distinguish six kinds of rhythm, five of them in the mind. The characteristically medieval and quasi-theological direction his treatise takes indicates a selective emphasis on that portion of experience attractive to his conscience,[16] but it does not indicate a distortion of the original details as recounted, for we may verify these in our own experience and, if we prefer, decide that they issue in relative truths (miraculously attenuated under the duress of the skills they evoke).

In addition to sonant or corporeal rhythm in the body, Augustine names in connection with the work of the mind: occursive (or heard) rhythm, progressive rhythm (in which the mind both moves the body and also moves itself in response to, *ad*, the body), recordable rhythm (or memory, preserving or retaining, *continere*, what the previous movements achieved), perceptive rhythm (which enjoys), and finally somewhat mysteriously, judicial rhythm, an estimative faculty of mind capable of discerning the correspondences given in the other rhythms, but itself more vital, *sine quibusdam uiuacioribus numeris*.[17]

Augustine arrives at the mystery of judicial numbers with disarming medieval dispatch; yet his distinction as one of the most profound psychologists of all time gives us reason enough for attending seriously to his ideas which we may in the end find no more difficult to conceive than the archetypes of Jung. He affirms what we have been holding in conjecture: a faculty of mind, mathematically ordered, for locating, for securing in

16. Cf. W. F. Jackson Knight, Foreword, *St. Augustine's De Musica, A Synopsis* (London, 1949), p. 3.
17. *Ibid.*, pp. 85-104. (*De Musica*, VI, i, 1-x, 25).

translation the whole-sight that issues in the shape of poems; it is a heuristic movement "agile with temporal intervals, and it modifies what it finds, (serving the Lord of All Things)." Thus "a craftsman, *faber*, operates rationally with rhythm in his art," in which as an incremental creation exists "a regular progression, *analogia*, which may be Latinized as 'corrationality.'" What the mind responds to judicially is the "eternal presidency of numerical rhythm, similitude, equality, and order," a presidency of mathematical structure which, Augustine says, if taken from the earth, nothing remains.[18] Common sense, and the distinctions Augustine makes leading up to the judicial, emphasizes the mind's responses to harmony as to something co-natural to its own condition. If we consent to the notion of a judicial rhythm, we must see in this juncture with the critical the source of the creative, a proof if ever we need one of the presence of an estimative, critical judgment in the very act of making.

Dante, who undoubtedly was familiar with Augustine's writings, himself talks about curial language in his *De Vulgari Eloquentia* (as he does about its transumptive power in the letter to Can Grande) and he goes on as a poet to give, in the way of a good cook, his recipe working out the practical implications of the curial respecting word values as far as the making of *canzoni* is concerned. And his discussion of what he calls combed-out, glossy, shaggy, and rumpled words is in fact pragmatic rather than fanciful. (Combed-out words are those "which have three, or as nearly as possible three syllables, which are without aspirate, without acute or circumflex accent, without the double letter z or x, without double liquids, or a liquid placed immediately after a mute, and which, having

18. *Ibid.*, pp. 123-24. (*De Musica*, VI, xvii, 57-58).

Reason and Meter: A Reciprocity Re-Divined

been planed (so to say), leave the speaker with a certain sweetness, like amore, donna, disio, vertute, donare. . . .")

But, to return to the judicial rhythm as the obscure source and agent (fitted perhaps by Leibnitz' denomination of music: "occult arithmetic") of the poet's knowledge-for-making; we may think we discern a tragic illustration of this quality in a poet like Baudelaire. Neurotically absorbed for the whole of his creative life in essentially hysteric states of consciousness, he himself has annotated (in a characteristically uncompleted statement) his sensation of this gulf and its "vertige": "non seulement du gouffre du sommeil, mais du gouffre de l'action, du rêve, du souvenir, du désir, du regret, du remords, du beau, *du nombre*. . . ."[19] Given the personal chaos in which the comment is realized, the writer's failure to distinguish here between sensational and intellectual phenomena is understandable. But to what then, if not to some undisturbed and deeply judicial habit of mind, are we to attribute the balance, equality, similitude, harmony, and order subsisting in the poems?

> La nature est un temple où de vivants piliers
> Laissent parfois sortir de confuses paroles;
> L'homme y passe à travers des forêts de symboles. . . .
>
> *(Correspondances)*

The "transports of the mind" *are* intellectual even while mediated by sense, and the organization of the perceptions thus donated to the poem is by no means confused.

One is tempted to generalize that in the most accomplished poets, the more deeply engaged they are with the pressure of serious matter, the more their expression tends to be achieved

19. *Journaux Intimes*, p. 38 (my italics).

Reason's Double Agents

through a precision, even a complexity, of technical means, as if technic were somehow expressive of the mind's hold upon the particulars of the difficult and true.

Tate's "Seasons of the Soul," surely one of the finest poems of this century, is a marvel of such intricate (analytic) simplicity:

> When was it that the summer
> (Daylong a liquid light)
> And the child, a new-comer,
> Bathed in the same green spray,
> Could neither guess the night?
> The summer had no reason;
> Then like a primal cause
> It had its timeless day
> Before it kept the season
> Of time's engaging jaws.
>
> Two men of our summer world
> Descended winding hell
> And when their shadows curled
> They fearfully confounded
> The vast concluding shell. . . .

The practitioner of synthetic meters works as it were at the opposite end of the mannerist spectrum. And he uses his measures, often with considerable virtuosity, as a complement to simply descriptive feats. Richard Wilbur's "A Baroque Wall-Fountain in the Villa Sciarra" sustains this sort of performance with uncommon grace for fifteen stanzas:

> Under the bronze crown
> Too big for the head of the stone cherub whose feet
> A serpent has begun to eat,
> Sweet water brims a cockle and braids down

Reason and Meter: A Reciprocity Re-Divined

> Past spattered mosses, breaks
> On the tipped edge of a second shell, and fills
> The massive third below. It spills
> In threads then from the scalloped rim, and makes
>
> A scrim or summery tent. . . .
> (from *Poems 1943-1956*)

From this we may return with renewed interest to the earliest shapers of the English pentameter line. Wyatt's meters may remain a scholarly puzzle; the odd music of his poems has a continual fascination, and since his apparent "mistakes" are not improved by Tottel's ministrations and are moreover in the direction of density (rather than the metronomic looseness and indecision that usually accompanies amateur practice) we are probably right in assuming that the meters we have in his poems are there on purpose. I think it need not be only other poets, with their eyes fixed on the tools of the trade, who respond to the ingenious richness of a pentameter line, like the last one of "They fle from me," which supports such various readings that every single syllable is capable of receiving, one way or another, a primary stress:

> I would fain knowe what she hath deserued.

(If the scholar deserves what he finds, the poet prior to him earns his luck as well, and surely must do so by an attentive apprenticeship to judicial resources within his own intelligence.)

When we have got the poems, it is unnecessary to speculate about which came first, the meter or the words, yet their inescapable intimacy provides the rational imagination with something very like a key to the very sources of creative originality.

INDEX OF NAMES

Index

A
Abrams, M. H. 18
Alvarez, A. 40
Apollinaire 33
Aquinas, Thomas 10, 41, 79, 85, 122
Arendt, H. 66, 68, 80
Aristotle 6, 9, 13, 27, 80
Arnold, M. 92
Augustine 118, 125, 126
Avila, Teresa of 18

B
Bachelard, G. 6
Bacon, Francis 70, 79
Baudelaire, C. 34, 85, 118, 122, 127
Bennett, Joan 44, 53
Bergson, H. 119, 122
Berryman, J. 105-16
Blake, W. 18
Bonaventure 7
Brecht, B. 3
Breton, A. 51
Bridges, R. 60
Browning, R. 22, 23
Buber, M. 37

C
Camus, A. 31, 37, 92
Cassirer, E. 32
Chekhov, A. 95
Cibber, C. 76
Clark, K. 68
Clough, A. 120
Coburn, K. 11
Coleridge, S. T. 5, 10-11, 120
Crane, Hart 17, 106

Cunningham, J. V. 40

D
Dante 22, 67, 86, 88, 126
Descartes, R. 74
Dickinson, E. 34-35, 102
Donne, J. 19-20, 39-54, 87, 98
Donoghue, Denis 75-76
Dryden, J. 8, 40, 45-46, 53
Dunbar, W. 40, 59

E
Eliot, T. S. 20, 32, 34, 62
Ellrodt, R. 44, 48, 49

F
Fergusson, F. 27, 98
Flaubert, G. 28
Fogle, R. 12
Ford, F. M. 111

G
Gautier, T. 37

H
Hanna, T. 33
Hardy, T. 20
Hauser, Arnold 15, 24, 92, 121
Hemingway, E. 111
Hobbes, T. 20
Hölderlin, F. 30
Hopkins, G. M. 20, 107, 111
Hulme, T. E. 21, 22, 47, 86

I
Ibsen, H. 92

J
Jacob, Max 96

133

Index

James, Henry 27, 99
Jonson, Ben 20, 55-64
Jordan, Robert 89-90
Jouve, Pierre Jean 2

K
Kafka, Franz 30
Keats, J. 18-19, 21
Kermode, F. 44
Kierkegaard, S. A. 33, 92
Knight, W. F. J. 124, 125
Koch, V. 80
Krook, D. 8-9

L
Lawrence, D. H. 58
Leavis, F. D. 11, 57, 69
Leibnitz, G. W. 127

M
Mallarmé, S. 44-45, 92
Malraux, André 28-29, 84, 89, 94
Mann, T. 30
Maritain, Jacques 9, 12-13, 28, 43, 47, 53-54, 85-86, 103, 106
Maritain, Raissa 41
Martz, L. 51
Marvell, Andrew 40
Melville, H. 99
Milton, J. 26, 48, 72, 109
Murdoch, Iris 68

N
Nash, T. 40
Nerval, G. 30
Nietzsche, F. W. 33, 92
Norwich, Julian of 18

O
Ortega y Gasset, J. 28

P
Plato 3-6, 17
Plotinus 31
Pope, A. 7, 20, 23-24, 53, 65-76
Pound, E. 20-26, 33, 78, 122
Proust, M. 26
Pythagoras 118

R
Raine, K. 50
Ralegh, Sir W. 110
Ramus, P. 8, 72
Ransom, J. C. 11
Raymond, M. 33-34
Read, Sir H. 18, 58
Rimbaud, A. 7
Rougemont, Denis de 24
Rousset, Jean 87

S
Sartre, J. P. 56, 71, 92, 112
Schelling, F. W. J. von 10
Schlegel, F. von 10
Sewell, E. 6, 42
Shakespeare, W. 57, 60
Shelley, Percy 18, 92, 124
Sidney, Sir Philip 3
Smart, C. 30
Stevens, Wallace 33, 35-36
Swift, J. 60, 68-69

T
Tate, Allen 11, 60, 66, 77-90, 128
Thompson, John 121

Index

Tolstoy, L. 26
Tomlinson, Charles 2

V
Valéry, Paul 32, 42, 45, 75, 123

W
Wellek, René 11
Whitehead, A. N. 66-67, 94, 101, 118
Wilbur, R. 127-28
Williams, Aubrey 69, 72
Winters, Y. 3, 57, 61, 84, 91-103, 106
Wittgenstein, L. 37, 67, 94
Wordsworth, W. 18-19

Y
Yeats, W. B. 22

www.ingramcontent.com/pod-product-compliance
Lightning Source LLC
Chambersburg PA
CBHW030115010526
44116CB00005B/264